THE HISTORY (
19TH DIVISIO

MILITARY HISTORIES
BY THE SAME AUTHOR

The History of the
2nd DIVISION, 1914-1918

The
WEST YORKSHIRE REGIMENT
IN THE WAR
1914-1918

The History of the
SOMERSET LIGHT INFANTRY
1914-1918

The History of the
MIDDLESEX REGIMENT
1914-1919

The History of the
EAST YORKSHIRE REGIMENT
1914-1918

The History of the
62nd (WEST RIDING) DIVISION
1914-1919

The
17th ROYAL FUSILIERS
1914-1919

The
LINCOLNSHIRE REGIMENT
1914-1919

The History of the
DUKE OF CORNWALL'S LIGHT INFANTRY
1914-1919

The History of the
GLOUCESTERSHIRE REGIMENT
1914-1919

The
50th DIVISION, 1914-1919

The
KING'S REGIMENT
1914-1919

THE BRITISH BARRAGE AT THE BATTLE OF MESSINES, 7TH JUNE, 1917

In the original of this unique oblique aeroplane photograph
the troops may be seen going forward

Frontispiece

THE
NINETEENTH
DIVISION
1914 – 1918

By
EVERARD WYRALL

WITH 7 PHOTOGRAPHIC ILLUSTRATIONS
AND 8 BATTLE PLANS

PUBLISHED BY
THE NAVAL & MILITARY PRESS

Made and Printed in Great Britain

CONTENTS

LIST OF ILLUSTRATIONS

LIST OF MAPS

vii

CHAPTER I

THE CALL TO ARMS

O N the morning of the 7th of August, 1914 (after the declaration of War between Great Britain and Germany on the 4th of August), the emotions of the British public were still further stirred by the following announcement which appeared in the newspapers and on hoardings throughout the United Kingdom:

"YOUR KING AND COUNTRY NEED YOU. A CALL TO ARMS.

"An addition of 100,000 men to His Majesty's Regular Army is immediately necessary in the present grave National Emergency.

"Lord Kitchener is confident that this appeal will be at once responded to by all who have the safety of our Empire at heart."

Two days previously (on the 5th) the House of Commons had authorised an increase in the establishment of the Regular Army by 500,000 men. On the 6th Lord Kitchener became Secretary of State for War and at once set to work to provide reinforcements, which he foresaw would be necessary in large numbers. With a prescience few possessed, he predicted a long war.

The first 100,000 of these new troops was obtained within a few days: they eventually formed Kitchener's First Army ("K.I"), consisting of six divisions, i.e., 9th, 10th, 11th, 12th, 13th and 14th. On the 11th of September the formation of a Second Army ("K.II"), of a similar number of divisions, was authorised and the 15th, 16th, 17th, 18th, 19th and 20th Divisions came into being.

Such, briefly, was the sequence of events which led up to the formation of the 19th (Western) Division in September, 1914, with Major-General C. G. M. Fasken in command: the three Infantry Brigades were the 56th, 57th and 58th.

By the middle of September the 500,000 men authorised by Parliament had been recruited: but to recruit the men was far more easy than to provide officers and N.C.O.s to train them.

Even with the re-enlistment of ex-non-commissioned officers of the Regular Army (authorised on the 17th of August), regular officers at depôts, British and Indian Army officers on leave in England from India who were detained under Lord Kitchener's orders, reserve officers, retired officers, officers invalided home and convalescent—the number was still woefully small wherewith to staff the great influx of recruits who had to be formed into various units of the Army.

Thus it came about that, although a number of the senior officers of the newly-formed 19th Division had seen service with the Regular Army, scarce one of the junior officers had had any previous experience of soldiering. The number of experienced N.C.O.s was also extremely small.

Apart from the difficulties of officering the New Armies and providing them with N.C.O.s, the problem of housing, clothing and feeding the men became so great that when, in the middle of September, the 500,000 recruits had been obtained, the standard of physique was raised, which retarded recruiting.

The various units forming the 19th Division arrived on Salisbury Plain in civilian clothes, with no rifles or equipment. Though met by almost every kind of discomfort (their camp was on swampy ground), their keenness triumphantly brought them through the first stages of a soldier's life. Rations were good and when, a little later, a few "D.P." rifles arrived and were issued, all ranks were enthusiastic in learning small-arms drill.

Until early December the Division remained on Salisbury Plain: a move was then made to comfortable billets in Weston and Clevedon.

March 1915 found the Division clothed in khaki, and hard training in close-order drill soon produced smartness. Several officers of the Division were also sent to the Staff College, Camberley, for a course, among whom was Lieut. Garvin, son of the well-known journalist. Before the month was out the Division returned to Tidworth, where manœuvres and the equipping of all units proceeded rapidly. New rifles and machine-guns were issued to the infantry and transport was formed. In June H.M. the King inspected the whole Division on Salisbury Plain and, as this usually preceded embarkation for an overseas theatre of the War, all ranks were greatly excited. But it was not until about the middle of July that the 19th Division left England, embarkation taking place between the 16th and 18th of July.[1]

The Order of Battle of the Division on leaving England was:

G.O.C. and 19th Divisional Headquarters.

C.R.A. and Headquarters 19th Divisional Artillery: 86th, 87th, 88th and 89th Brigades, R.F.A.

C.R.E. and Headquarters 19th Divisional Royal Engineers: 81st, 82nd and 94th Field Companies, R.E.

19th Divisional Signal Company.

"C" Squadron, Yorkshire Dragoons.

19th Divisional Cyclist Company.

56th Infantry Brigade:
  7th King's Own Royal Lancaster Regiment.
  7th East Lancashire Regiment.
  7th South Lancashire Regiment.
  7th Loyal North Lancashire Regiment.

57th Infantry Brigade:
  10th Royal Warwickshire Regiment.
  8th Gloucestershire Regiment.
  10th Worcestershire Regiment.
  8th North Staffordshire Regiment.

58th Infantry Brigade:
  9th Cheshire Regiment.
  9th Royal Welch Fusiliers.
  9th Welch Regiment.
  6th Wiltshire Regiment.

5th South Wales Borderers (Pioneers).

57th, 58th and 59th Field Ambulances.

154th, 155th, 156th and 157th Companies, A.S.C.

31st Mobile Veterinary Section.

19th Divisional Supply Column.

---

[1]Several changes took place in the division before it left England. In April, Lieut.-Colonel P. M. Davies, A.S.C., was appointed A.A. and Q.M.G., *vice* Lieut.-Colonel Drake Brockman, who was forced to relinquish his appointment by sickness. In June, Brig.-General D. Mackenzie Stuart succeeded Brig.-General Becker as G.O.C., 58th Infantry Brigade. In the same month also, Brig.-General Stuart, R.A., who had been C.R.A. since November, 1914, was succeeded by Brig.-General C. E. Lawrie.

CHAPTER II
ARRIVAL OF THE DIVISION IN FRANCE AND
INTRODUCTION TO TRENCH WARFARE

IT is unnecessary to go into all the tedious details of the embarkation in England and disembarkation at Havre and Boulogne, but very briefly and yet adequately, the General Staff Diary sums up the arrival and concentration of the 19th Division in the following terms:

"Tilcques, 21st (July). Whole division concentrated near St. Omer; 23rd. Moved to area between Hazebrouck and St. Omer; 24th. Division moved to area Aires–St. Venant–Busnes–St. Hilaire, and came under Indian Corps, First Army, Headquarters at Norrent Fontes; 25th. Headquarters moved to Busnes Château by orders from Indian Corps."[1]

And the next entry describes the work which lay before the Division for the next few weeks:

"27th (July). Orders received to move between 29th and 31st to a new billeting area round Merville, in Corps Reserve. While there each brigade will go into the trenches with the Meerut or Lahore Divisions to get experience of the conditions, and to learn the geography of the front line which they will eventually have to take over. Classes of instruction in hand grenades and trench-mortar work will be held, and Staff and Administrative Officers will be attached to similar branches in the Meerut or Lahore Divisions."

By the end of July the 56th Infantry Brigade was located, between Merville and Lestrem and north of Merville with Brigade Headquarters at Les Lauriers; the 57th Brigade was north-east of Merville with headquarters at Epinette; the 58th Brigade had moved to a billeting area between Le Sart and Haverskerque, headquarters in the Château.

On the 1st of August the Indian Corps was holding the line from Port Arthur on the La Bassée road, inclusive, to the Fauquissart road, exclusive, Lahore Division on the right and Meerut Division on the left, a sunken road being the dividing line between the two divisions.

[1]Strength: 552 officers, 133 sabres, 13,379 rifles, 2,783 artillery personnel, 64 guns, 39 machine guns.

A month was to pass before the 19th Division held a sector of the front line on its own; it was the 31st of August when General Fasken assumed command. That month was a milestone in the history of the Division, for the business of learning how to make war within rifle shot of the enemy was vastly different from the training (excellent though it was) on Salisbury Plain.

On the 3rd of August the A.A. and Quarter-Master General records that:—

"In order that the various battalions should have preliminary instruction in trench work previous to taking it up permanently, arrangements have been made to attach two battalions to the Lahore and Meerut Divisions for a period of a week, and it is considered that all the battalions and the field companies will complete their training by the end of a month and be more qualified to take their place in the defensive line. The first battalions to be so attached are the 7th King's Own Royal Lancasters, the 7th Loyal North Lancashires, the 10th Royal Warwickshire and the 10th Worcestershire."

The two former battalions belonged to the 56th Brigade, and the two latter to the 57th Brigade. These battalions began their instructional tours in the front line on the 4th of August, platoons or companies each going into the trenches for forty-eight hours. Battalions spent a week thus, when they were relieved by other battalions. Battalions of the 58th Brigade began their trench instruction about the middle of August.

This method of gaining an insight into the life in the forward trenches occupied the three infantry brigades for about a month. Instruction in the line consisted of practical instruction in the use of trench-mortars, sniping, and the detection of the enemy's many wiles to conceal his snipers, the construction and maintenance of trench defences, wiring, bomb-throwing, and the many details of trench life, such as sanitation and trench discipline. Out of the line, practice in bomb-throwing, trench-mortaring, machine-gun firing, the use of gas helmets and bayonet fighting, occupied all ranks from morning to night, with intervals for games and rest. There were also special courses for officers and instructional schools were attended by senior officers.

Tactical exercises, liaison work between infantry in the front line and the guns (which at that period were just being introduced with excellent results) and instruction in artillery duties, registration of targets, etc., occupied the 86th, 87th, 88th and 89th Brigades, R.F.A., of the 19th Division before the latter definitely took over a portion of the line.

The three Field Companies of Royal Engineers—81st, 82nd and 94th—spent their early days in such duties as fitting up wire entanglements, revetting and improving trenches and communication trenches, the repair of defensive posts, and in receiving instruction from the sappers of the Indian Corps. Carpenters were engaged in making frames for the trenches; other companies were busy on the roads.

The medical units of the Division—57th, 58th and 59th Field Ambulances—had plenty of work, for not only were the wounded attended to, and in many cases evacuated, but the sick had also to be cared for. The medical officers, moreover, had to go through a certain amount of training, and the following are some of the items which engaged the attentions of the doctors of the Division: "All available officers of the ambulance attended during the morning a demonstration by expert entomologists of the breeding places of flies, their life history and the best methods for their destruction." That may seem a small matter, but flies are typhoid carriers and can spread disease in an alarming manner. One of the marvels of the war was that there were no epidemics in France and Flanders such as we had in the South African War of 1899–1902; enteric fever and dysentery were proportionately far less between 1914 and 1918 than in South Africa—a fine tribute to the medical authorities and those who were responsible for the health of the troops.

Medical officers also had to receive gas training: "All officers passed through a trench full of gas wearing smoke helmets. There was no appreciable effect of the gas felt. Regimental aid posts, advanced dressing stations, and casualty clearing stations were also visited by the medical officers of the Division, and studied."

The Pioneers (5th South Wales Borderers) received their instruction in pioneer work of a division from both the Lahore, and Meerut Divisions. They dug trenches, constructed hurdles, and carried out their own training in bomb-throwing, machine-gun firing—a mixture of infantry and pioneer work.

Divisional and brigade staff officers were attached to similar staffs of the Indian Corps and learned not only the duties of staff officers in the field, but were instructed how to extract the hundred-and-one "returns" and "reports" from worried C.O.s in the front line—to the eternal disgust of the latter!

A month was thus passed by all units of the 19th Division in gaining an insight into trench warfare. Like every other division that knowledge was not gained without loss, for casualties both in officers and men were suffered.

On the 22nd of August it was known that the Division before the end of the month was to relieve troops of the 2nd and 7th Divisions in the front line. The front selected was from Grenadier road communication trench, just north of Givenchy, to Farm Corner, near Festubert. The line was to be divided into two sections; the 58th Brigade was to take over the right and the 57th the left; the 56th Brigade to be in Army Reserve in the Les Lobes–Lawe Canal–Lez Choquaux–La Tombe Willot area. Three battalions of each front-line brigade were to hold the front line with one in support, the dividing line between brigades being a point where the Orchard Support trench ran into the fire trench on the southern side of the Orchard Apex.

On the 24th of August all Royal Artillery Brigade and Battery Staffs moved into the line with the Royal Artillery of the 7th Division.

The Division began to take over the line on the 28th, the 57th Brigade relieving the 22nd Brigade of the 7th Division at night. The 10th Warwicks took over the right in the orchard, the 10th Worcesters the centre, and the 8th Gloucesters the left, the North Staffords being in reserve. The 82nd Field Company Royal Engineers and the 59th Field Ambulance also took over their allotted places in the 57th Brigade area.

The following day all Field Companies of the Royal Engineers took up permanent billets about Le Touret, and the 58th Brigade and 58th Field Ambulance began to move up towards the line. The brigade began the relief of troops of the 7th Division at nightfall on the 30th, the 9th Cheshires taking over the right, the 9th Royal Welch Fusiliers the centre, and the 6th Wiltshires the left sub-sectors of the brigade front; the 9th Welch were in reserve.

It should be mentioned here that on going into the line the machine-gun and grenadier sections were detached from their battalions and were placed under the direct command of the Brigade Commander. Two batteries of trench-mortars—one of $1\frac{1}{2}$ in. mortars and the other of 4 in. mortars—had been allotted to the left and right sectors respectively; they were transferred from the Lahore Division.

But an instance of the way in which the Division was handicapped when it first went into the line is given in the General Staff Diary on the 29th of August, after the 57th Brigade had taken over a sub-sector of the line. The report says: "The night passed quietly, but in the morning about 6 a.m., a number of large shells were fired at the orchard, blowing in a considerable length of trench and causing several casualties. At present the 57th Brigade has only one West bomb thrower to retaliate. Instructions have been given to the O.C., Grenadier Company, to get down another and also several catapults, so that we can retaliate more effectively. Our bombs are not satisfactory yet as no good fusee lighter has yet been supplied. The one for the Pitcher bomb is very dangerous as it is apt to set off the detonators by itself, causing a premature explosion. The Nobel is not much better as there is no means of knowing whether it has lighted the fuse or not. Consequently, with the exceptions of Nos. 1 and 2 (percussion grenades), the grenadiers have to light each bomb with a fusee or match. This is no very serious drawback in bombing a trench, but in an attack across the open it would hardly be possible to light grenades in this way." And in wet weather it was often impossible to light them at all.

Some idea of the dangerous nature of hand grenades at this period is reflected in the Diary of the Pioneer Battalion (5th South Wales Borderers) on the 28th: " 'A' Company bombing party had paraded for instruction under Capt. T. E. Lewis at 9.30 a.m. The morning went well until at about 12.15 p.m. a bomb burst and Capt. Lewis was killed, and Lieut. B. O. Jones and Private Dart injured, the latter dying that night."

At 10 a.m. on the 31st of August General Fasken assumed command of the first front-line sector held by the Division in France and Flanders. Divisional Headquarters were at Locon.

The sector taken over by the 19th Division was, at this period, comparatively quiet. The trenches were not really trenches, but breastwork defences built up on soft ground of sandbags and earth. In summer time the low-lying country between the La Bassée Canal and Armentières was practically free from floods unless torrential rain fell as sometimes happened, then the defences would quickly become waterlogged; in winter the water and mud were terrible. As yet, however, the 19th Division had not experienced those conditions and the marsh countryside was practically dry.

For the first three weeks of September there is little to record but trench warfare, which, after a year of war, was still somewhat in its infancy. The Germans were, however, much better provided with trench-mortars, grenades, bombs, etc., than we were; they had foreseen a state of static warfare—we and the French had not. There were, therefore, in our lines, all sorts of odd contrivances—ancient mortars used in wars long forgotten, quaint patterns of "throwers" for projecting bombs into the German trenches, often more dangerous to our men than to the enemy. Up and down the line there travelled numbers of "experts," all of whom seemed to have some new invention for destroying the enemy's defences and making life generally uncomfortable for the Boche; these invariably resulted in life being made particularly uncomfortable for us, for no sooner had these "experts" let off their infernal machines than the Germans retaliated with every kind of bomb, grenade and objectionable thing they possessed. The visits of these "experts" were, therefore, far from welcome. Nevertheless, to give these enthusiasts their due, they were brave fellows, and in the end mostly succeeded in evolving adequate means of dealing with the enemy.

Once settled in the line the infantry brigades of the Division set up a system of reliefs, so that battalions had some measure of rest and opportunity for continuing their training when out of the line. The gunners quickly got to work in registering the German trenches and targets; the sappers were soon hard at work on roads, communications and the multifarious duties which no one but the "R.E." seemed able to accomplish. The Field Ambulances opened "aid posts," dressing stations and casualty clearing stations; the Army Service Corps instituted systems of issuing rations and supplies.

CHAPTER III

THE BATTLE OF LOOS

ON the 21st of September, Divisional Headquarters received information concerning forthcoming operations.

The Tenth French Army, on the right of the First British Army, was to attack the enemy from west of Lens to the Vimy Ridge. The First British Army (IV, I, Indian and III Corps) was to attack from south-west of Loos to just north of Givenchy (the main attack), with subsidiary attacks from opposite Pietre and Fromelles, while the Second British Army, on the left of the First, was to attack east of Ypres at Bellewaarde.

The 19th Division was to co-operate with the 2nd Division (I Corps) by attacking the Rue d'Ouvert as soon as the attack of the 5th Brigade, 2nd Division, developed successfully. The 58th Brigade was to carry out the attack of the 19th Division, the front of the brigade being contracted to the portion of the line between Grenadier road and Barnton road; the 56th Brigade was in line on the left of the 58th and was to extend its front to take over the line up to Barnton road, exclusive. The 57th Brigade was to be in Army Reserve. The attack was to be preceded by a four days' artillery bombardment; gas[1] and smoke candles (subject to the wind being favourable) were to be used on the morning of the assault, fixed for the 25th of September.

At 8 a.m. on the 21st the Divisional Artillery opened fire on the enemy's trenches and continued firing for twenty-four hours. The enemy's reply was feeble, though considerable damage was done to his parapets, wire entanglements and machine-gun emplacements. The bombardment was carried out on the 22nd, 23rd and 24th, the German artillery making little response. Machine-gun and rifle fire was opened on the hostile trenches in between the artillery bombardments in order to prevent the enemy's working parties repairing the damage done by our guns.

---

[1]Asphyxiating gas was used for the first time by the British at Loos; it was not a success on that occasion, for the wind was not favourable and blew the fumes back into our own trenches putting numbers of officers and men out of action.

The attack of the 58th Brigade was to be made in the following manner: as soon as the 5th Brigade, on the right of the 58th Brigade, had gained its first objective (which included the crater salient on the right of the 58th) a right flanking party (consisting of 100 men of the 9th Royal Welch Fusiliers, one platoon of the Brigade Grenadier Company, and four machine-guns, all under the command of Capt. K. I. Nicholl), was to advance under cover of the left of the 5th Brigade in an easterly direction and take up a covered position which would enable it to enfilade the enemy's left flank. Then, as soon as the leading battalions of the 58th Brigade had captured the enemy's front trench, the right and flank party were to take up positions where they could enfilade the German support trench.

The assaulting battalions of the 58th Brigade were to be the 9th Welch Regiment (Lieut.-Colonel C. H. Young) on the right, and 9th Royal Welch Fusiliers (Lieut.-Colonel H. J. Madocks) on the left, supported by the 9th Cheshires (Lieut.-Colonel W. B. Dauntesey) and 6th Wilts. (Lieut.-Colonel A. G. Jeffreys) respectively. Each attacking battalion had a frontage of about 350 yards.

As may be conjectured, everyone was in a state of suppressed excitement during the night of 24th/25th, for the operations in the morning were the first on a large scale in which the 19th Division was to take part.

At 9.30 p.m. on the 24th, Battalion Headquarters of the 9th Wiltshires moved up to the front line, and at about 4 a.m. on the 25th, "C" and "D" Companies began moving up No. 6 and No. 4 communication trenches in readiness to support "A" and "B" as soon as the signal (a sheaf of rockets sent up from Brigade Headquarters) was given to "go over the top." The C.O. of the 9th Royal Welch Fusiliers similarly moved up to the firing line, making his headquarters in "A" Company's mess. Of the 9th Cheshires, who were to support the Welch, "A" Company was in occupation of the front-line parapet, "C" Company was on the right and "B" on the left, disposed so as to lend immediate assistance to the Welch; "D" Company in support of "C" and "B." The 6th Wiltshires were, apparently, in the intermediate lines, formed up with the Welch Fusiliers whom they were to support. The right flanking detachment of Royal Welch Fusiliers, under Capt. Nicholl, found the seven right bays of the front line which the party was to take over and from which it was to advance, already full when it arrived at 3 a.m. on the 25th. Capt. Nicholl had, therefore, to put all the grenadiers into the inspection trench and a few men in the passage leading between the fire and communication trenches; the company and machine-gun detachment had to stay in the communication trench for they were unable to move.

The gas was to be released and smoke candles lighted at 5.50 a.m. At that hour also the guns were to open fire on the enemy's trenches; the infantry assault was timed for 6.30 a.m.

Dawn on the 25th broke on a thoroughly miserable morning; a thin rain was falling and what wind there was was obviously unfavourable, for it was, at the best, only a breeze which changed direction continually. Smoke helmets were put on by all ranks.

The gas was discharged and hung in a thin cloud, first over our trenches in an exasperating manner, and then began to drift slowly—very slowly—towards the enemy's trenches. The smoke candles had been lighted and created a pall of dense smoke in front of our trenches, thereby doing more harm than good.

No sooner were the gas and smoke clouds visible above our trenches than the enemy's guns opened with a terrific roar and placed a very heavy bombardment on the front and support lines of the divisional area. His machine-guns and rifles also swept No Man's Land and the parapets from behind which the troops were waiting to advance, with a storm of bullets.

The 58th Brigade Diary records that at 6.25 a.m. a message was received from the 5th Brigade reporting the capture of the enemy's front line, unopposed. Simultaneously the artillery forward observing officers reported that the enemy's second line had also been captured by the 5th Brigade. At 6.30 a.m. word was given to order the assaulting troops to advance, and a sheaf of rockets burst in the sky. Lieut.-Colonel Young, commanding the 9th Welch, thereupon gave the order to advance. He states of his officers and men "that nothing could have exceeded the gallantry of the whole battalion." They went forward splendidly, though already having suffered a heavy gruelling from the enemy's guns in the congested and narrow trenches before the assault began.

Furious machine-gun and rifle fire met that advance, and

within fifteen minutes 12 officers, 4 company sergeant-majors and approximately 300 other ranks had been killed or wounded. No Man's Land had become a dreadful place—full of dead and dying. Under that terrific hail of bullets no one of the battalion succeeded in getting more than about eighty yards forward, excepting a small party collected by Second-Lieut. A. J. Williams, who, being near an old German communication trench, managed to crawl to within eighty yards of the enemy's line opposite a point about 100 yards north of House 19. "A gallant feat," records his Colonel, "in the face of such a fire."

Seeing the utter hoplessness of attempting any further advance, Colonel Young shouted and passed the word to survivors to crawl back through the saps. It had not been possible to observe the direction from which came the great volume of machine-gun fire; the presence of a large number of machine-gun emplacements in the Crater Salient had been reported, but could not be reduced by the artillery.

The Cheshires, who were to support the Welch, when their turn came to go over the parapet, saw not a man standing in No Man's Land. Capt. T. S. Jackson, who commanded "B" Company, said: "I saw none but dead and wounded men, no one was standing up. I saw a whole line of dead on my left kneeling with their heads drooped." The advance of the Cheshires was thus hopeless and they were ordered not to go forward.

The left of the attack (the 9th Royal Welch Fusiliers) had great difficulty in deploying for the attack. Their trenches were not only narrow, but were muddy and slippery, defeating all attempts to get over quickly. Moreover, the trenches contained numbers of casualties which further impeded progress. But eventually "A" and "B" Companies were all out and part of "D" Company. Lieut.-Colonel Madocks was in a bay, almost mid-way along the line, observing, but it was difficult to see clearly owing to the cloud of smoke over No Man's Land. At about 7.15 a.m., the Colonel, who was looking over the parapet, was shot through the head and fell dead, the command of the battalion then devolving on Major C. Burrard.

Reports reached the Major that the saps were choked with dead and wounded, and in his narrative of the operations he says that these messages "brought home the fact that the advance was not the 'walk over' that had been expected, but I had not yet realised that the whole ground was raked with machine-gun fire." Capt. and Adjutant L. S. Hogg then went out to confer with Capt. C. A. Acton, but did not return; both had been killed. At 7.30 a.m. Major Burrard sent word to all the sap heads that no further advance was to be made and that the men out in the open were to crawl back as best they could. Only a few gallant souls reached the German wire, but they could not penetrate it and were too small in numbers to be effective.

Of the Wiltshires, supporting the Welch Fusiliers, only one company advanced, but even so had forty other ranks killed and seventy-five wounded; the remainder of the battalion was ordered not to advance.

The reasons for the failure of this attack were several. The gas and smoke were of no assistance to the attack, the former was too weak even if it reached the German lines, which is doubtful; the enemy's wire entanglements had not been sufficiently cut; the method of deployment was wrong, although it should be remembered that we had yet to learn that the best method was to creep forward behind the barrage. This knowledge did not come until the Somme Battles of 1916. The muddy nature of the ground, which was thick in mud, not only in No Man's Land, but also in the communication trenches, clogging the rifles and equipment, was another factor which assisted to nullify the very gallant efforts of the troops to achieve success.

The 5th Brigade, on the right of the 58th Brigade, *had* gained the enemy's front-line trenches, all but the extreme left of the attack, the left battalion of the brigade having to retrace its steps and advance again *south of the mine craters* (and presumably the Crater Salient), from which the enemy poured a destructive enfilade fire on to the left of the 5th Brigade and right of the 58th Brigade. And by 9.45 a.m. the whole of the former brigade was back in its trenches.

During the morning reports reached 58th Brigade Headquarters of impending counter-attacks, none of which, however, materialised, "owing, I believe," the Brigadier adds, "to the excellent way in which Colonel Wilson, commanding my artillery, handled his guns."

At 12.30 p.m. orders were issued for the 9th Welch and 9th Welch Fusiliers to withdraw to the old British line, while the 9th Cheshires and 6th Wiltshires remained in possession of the Brigade front line.

Brig.-General Mackenzie Stuart (commanding 58th Brigade) concludes his report with the following words: "It is gratifying to be able to report that the behaviour of all ranks under very trying circumstances, and in their first action, was excellent. The two leading battalions came under very heavy enfilade fire from machine-guns on either flank from the start of the attack, and were also subjected to fire from high-explosive shells, but all ranks displayed the greatest courage and coolness under fire, junior officers and N.C.Os. assuming command as their seniors became casualties.

The brigade has, indeed, acted like seasoned soldiers."

The casualties suffered by the 58th Brigade were heavy indeed. The 9th Welch had lost 4 officers and 57 other ranks killed, 9 officers and 140 other ranks wounded; 24 other ranks missing. The 9th Royal Welch Fusiliers, besides their C.O. (Lieut.-Colonel H. J. Madocks) had lost 6 officers and 24 other ranks killed; 3 officers and 137 other ranks wounded, and 79 other ranks missing.

Of the two supporting battalions the Wiltshires had the heaviest losses; 3 officers and 22 other ranks were killed; 2 officers and 65 other ranks were wounded; 20 other ranks missing.

The Cheshires lost 1 officer and 9 other ranks killed and 2 officers and 45 other ranks wounded.[1]

It is abundantly clear from the records that while the attacking battalions went forward most gallantly, those units of the Division in support and reserve, as well as all those in the Divisional area who had to endure the heavy shell-fire of the enemy, acquitted themselves bravely in this, their first battle. One company commander who lay wounded, cried out "Forward the Welch and Cheshires; three cheers for the Welch!" The stretcher bearers behaved with great devotion and some of the men of a company of a battalion occupied during the forenoon of the 25th in bringing in wounded, went out nearly 100 yards, though fired on by the enemy. Another brave fellow—Lance-Sergeant J. Williams—of the 9th Royal Welch Fusiliers, although badly wounded, one hand hanging by two threads only, spent his time in bandaging men near

[1] Summarised, the losses of the 58th Brigade were as follows: Officers killed, 15; wounded, 18; other ranks killed, 107; wounded, 409; missing, 123. Total casualties in the division numbered roughly 2,000.

him and in encouraging the wounded. Unfortunately he died of his wounds.

The 56th Brigade, on the left of the 58th, came in for the heavy bombardment put down by the enemy; "Hell let loose," the Diary of the 7th King's Own calls it. The battalion had one other rank killed and twenty wounded during the day. The 7th East Lancashires lost Second-Lieut. W. R. Morris and one man killed, and Capt. Hampson, Second-Lieut. Spicer and fifteen other ranks wounded. The 7th Loyal North Lancashires had only one man wounded, but the 7th South Lancashires do not record any casualties.

Barring a move to the eastern end of Tuning Fork Road at 8 a.m., the 57th Brigade did not come into action, and shortly after 6 p.m. marched to billets in the neighbourhood of Le Touret—Le Hamel.

The field ambulances of the Division did fine work and the O.C. of one of them records that: "The spirit of the men of the field ambulance is splendid." Evacuation of the wounded was carried out rapidly.

The South Wales Borderers (Pioneers) had the unusual experience of one of their companies taking the place of infantry in the line during the battle. "B" Company was behind the Wiltshires, who were supporting the Welch Fusiliers, when a company of the second-named battalion was cut up. The Pioneers were, therefore, ordered to take their place in the firing line, which they did. This company was heavily bombed by trench-mortars, but fortunately escaped with only one casualty. A trench-mortar battery belonging to the Pioneers did good work in bombarding the Pope's Nose.

The C.R.E. thus sums up the battle from the sappers' point of view: "The course of operations on the front of this Division gave no opportunities for R.E. action."

Although it seemed possible that the enemy might attempt to counter-attack the Division on the 26th, no such action took place. The guns were all ready to repel any such attempt, but the enemy's shell-fire on the day following the beginning of the battle, i.e., on the front of the 19th Division, was negligible. Sniping was less active and less accurate also on the night of the 25th/26th; possibly the enemy's nerves were not too good.

The 26th and 27th were occupied in bringing in the wounded, burying the dead, and generally cleaning up the trenches. Rifles and equipment were salved and the communication

Sailly

Pont de la Trompe

D.A.C.

D.A.C.2

Cité Ouvrée

D.A.C 1

D.A.C.

D.A.C.3

la Gorgue

Estaires

R. LYS

R. LYS

Le Lawe

Rouge de Bout

Laventie

Lestrem

Pont Rochon

Pont Riqueul

Petit Marais

C.83 W.L.

Riez Bailleul

London

la Flinque

Wangerie

Rue Masselot

Fauquissart

Pont du Hem

Rouge Croix

Fme Verbecke

Mauquissart

Bt de Pietre

FRONT LINE

26 Hy.

H.Q.

Hurry

B.H.Q.

Croix Barbee

St. Vaast

Pont Logy

Neuve Chapelle

FRONT

Zelobes

Vielle Chapelle

Richebourg St. Vaast

J.B.H.A

Parc Arthur

BRITISH

GERMAN

Les Lobes

La Tombe Willot

LAWE CANAL

Le Touret

Locon
Div H.Q.

Richebourg l'Avoué

Rue du Bois

La Tourelle

56th Bde.

Largies

B.H.Q.

Le Hamel

Laisne

Indian Village

Fme de Bouteille

THUNE

Rue du Bois

& Wilts.

Rue du Marais

57th Bde.

Festubert

58th Bde.

Marais

le Plantin

R.B.W.F.

Wilts.

Cheshires & Welch

Le Quesnoy

Le Coeur de Fer

LA BASSÉE CANAL

5th Bde.

Givenchy

REFERENCE.

Front of attack by 19th Div on 25th September, 1915.

Artillery positions, billets, & wagon-lines
on first arrival in the area.

Scale of Yards.

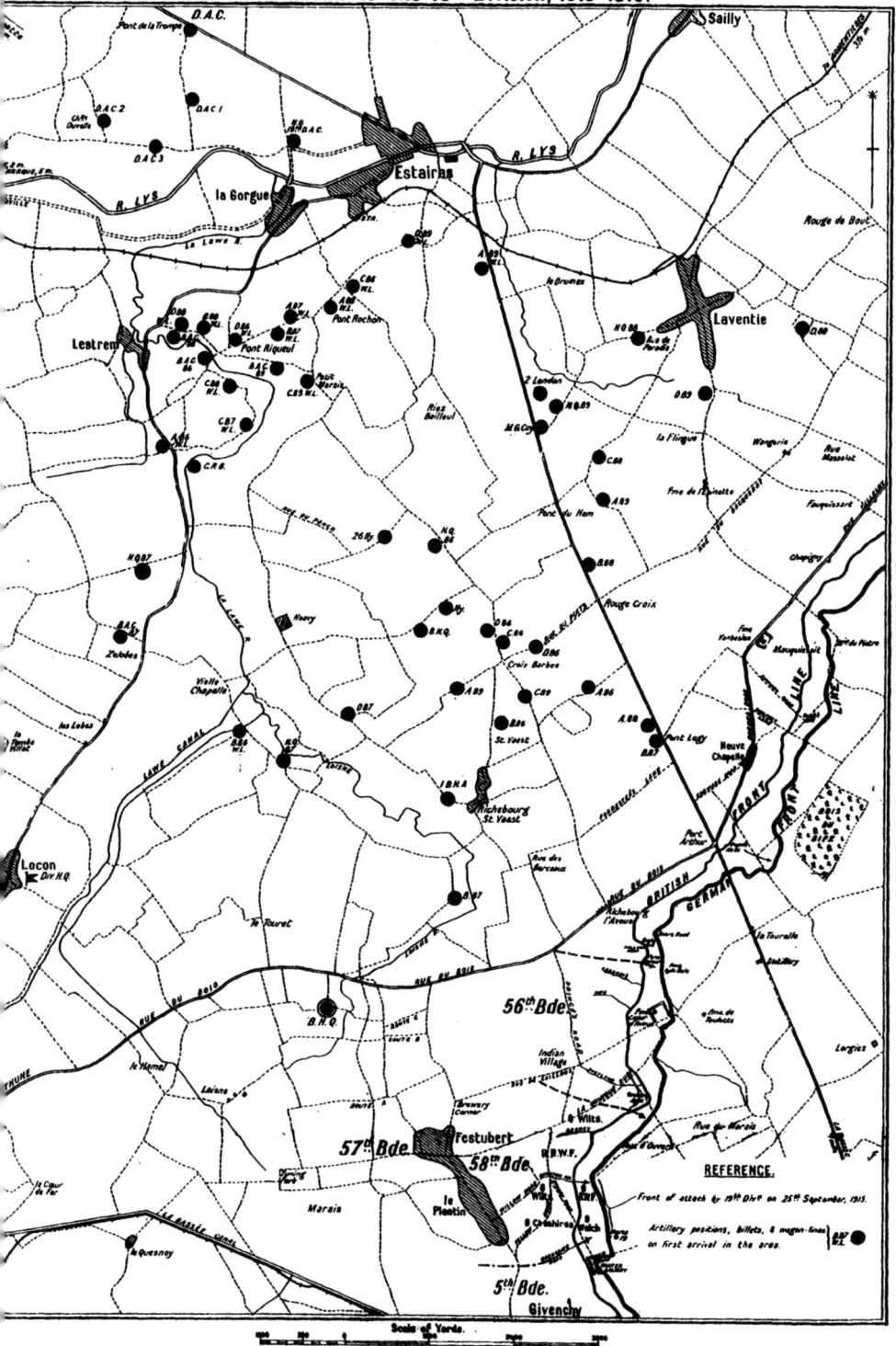

THE FIRST SECTION OF THE LINE KNOWN TO THE 19TH DIVISION; AND THE TRENCHES DURING THE BATTLE OF LOOS.

16.

trenches, littered with all sorts of stores, were tidied up. On the night of the latter date bursts of rifle and machine-gun fire were directed on the enemy's trenches by the troops holding both of the sub-sectors; this was to prevent the enemy mending his wire. During the afternoon the enemy had put several shells into Festubert and Le Plantin, and the last fired into the latter village wounded six men of the South Wales Borderers.

On the night of the 29th/30th, the 57th Brigade began the relief of the 58th Brigade, the 9th Royal Welch Fusiliers and 6th Wiltshires moving back to billets at Locon, and the 9th Welch and 9th Cheshires to Le Touret. All ranks were looking forward to a decent rest after their first heavy fight, but it was not to be, for at about 12 noon Brigade Headquarters received orders to march at 3.30 p.m. and take over trenches south of the La Bassée Canal, in the Cambrin sector, from troops of the 2nd Division.

Wet weather, congestion on the roads and the fatigue of the men, delayed the brigade, and it was 1 a.m. on the 1st of October before the relief was completed, the 9th Cheshires and 6th Wiltshires taking over the front line and the 9th Royal Welch Fusiliers and 9th Welch support points.

There is the following note at the end of the Diary of the 58th Brigade for September: "The brigade has now been occupying trenches since 31st of August without a break. Men very tired but cheerful. Latterly weather has been very bad and the trenches in a horrible state."

So far as the 19th Division was concerned the Battle of Loos was over.

c

CHAPTER IV

THE WINTER OF 1915–1916

BEFORE the Battle of Loos was over the winter of 1915–1916 had begun to settle down over the battle-fields of France and Flanders. First the rain, with its destructive effects on the front-line and communication trenches, turning them in many sectors into water channels, deep in mud and filth from which, if a man fell in, it was often difficult to drag him out. Then snow and frost, producing alternately slush and ice-bound trenches in which men were not infrequently frozen to death. Then came a thaw and once again the line would be an almost impassable mass of mud with sand-bag breastworks and emplacements slipping to the ground, to the despair of those who bravely strove to keep the defences intact.[1]

And yet the 19th Division was not as badly off as were those fine old divisions of the British Expeditionary Force, which had passed through all the horrors of the first winter of 1914–1915 in the front line, before anything, or little, had been done to cope with the terrible conditions, because they had not been foreseen. Probably at this period the worst part of the line was in the Lys Valley, where the low-lying ground made the digging of trenches impossible and sand-bag breast-works alone were possible.

It is advisable to write "at this period," because towards the end of 1916 the conditions of trenches on the Somme, and in 1917, those in the Ypres Salient, defy description.

---

[1]General Jeffreys adds the following note: "At this time such *trenches* as existed were all flooded and impossible to use, consequently they had been replaced by *breastworks*, built up and revetted with sandbags. Some of these breast-works had been constructed in the previous winter, and where they had been kept in repair they were not impossibly bad. In other places, *e.g.*, where the line had been advanced as a result of the battle of Festubert, the flooded trenches had merely been evacuated and in a good many places no breastworks had been built to take their place. It required very hard work and no little skill to build up these breastworks, which had to be constructed entirely by night. The 58th Infantry Brigade built a long stretch of breastwork in the sector opposite Ferme Cour L'Avoué across a space several hundreds of yards long where no defences existed. This was a very fine performance and the brigade bridged the gap and completed the work before being relieved in this sector."

Comparatively, therefore, the 19th Division began its first winter in the trenches, certainly under poor conditions, but not as bad as the Division was to experience subsequently.

Between the close of the Battle of Loos and the Somme Battles of 1916, *i.e.*, from the 13th of October, 1915, to the 1st of July, 1916, few operations (and these only of a local character) took place along the British front in France and Flanders. There was, therefore, a long period (the only one throughout the war) of nearly nine months during which our troops in the front line carried out trench warfare of a more or less vigorous nature.

Trench warfare was not the dull and uninteresting method of waging war which some would have us think. Indeed, there were phases of it which not only provided the greatest excitement, but which tested to the highest possible degree the bravery and nerve of the troops taking part in it. It was at times perhaps a greater strain upon the individual courage of officers and men than that needed in a great battle. To have to remain in a trench, or even sheltered in a dug-out, for hours during a terrific bombardment of the line, in which the enemy was using trench-mortars of every calibre, field guns and howitzers of every size, including his huge siege guns, spreading death and destruction on every side, required as much courage as to go forward across No Man's Land amidst a storm of machine-gun and rifle bullets.

The 58th Brigade, detached from the Division and sent to the Cambrin sector just south of the La Bassée Canal, spent the 1st of October in settling into the new trenches. There was a little shelling by the enemy, but nothing serious. Colonel Jeffreys (commanding 6th Wiltshires) was badly hurt owing to an accident on this day and had to be evacuated to the field ambulance: Major Hartley assumed command.

On the 7th the 9th Welch and 9th Royal Welch Fusiliers supplied large working parties to carry up gas cylinders to the front line. At 8 p.m. the enemy exploded a mine near Cockshy Lane, but made no attack, blowing down nearly 120 yards of parapet, burying four or five men of the Wiltshires and four miners. Both edges of the crater were at once occupied by us and an extra platoon of grenadiers and a machine-gun were sent up as reinforcements. Working parties soon got to work and communication was soon restored between the right and left companies of the Wiltshires.

The relief of the 58th Brigade began on the 7th and by the 8th all four battalions were back in billets in the L'Epinette, Eglise, Paradise area.[1] Two officers were wounded during the tour of the 58th Brigade south of the canal, *i.e.*, Lieut. W. Arnold of the 9th Welch, and Capt. V. N. Smith, 6th Wiltshires, on the 3rd of October.

Early in October the front of the Indian Corps was readjusted and the 19th Division held the sector from Orkney Road to Vine Street, *i.e.*, roughly from east of Festubert to east of Richebourg Avoue. The line was sub-divided into two sections.

From the diaries of all three infantry brigades it is evident that the Division was now settling down to trench warfare, though under difficulties to which the Diary of the General Staff refers thus: "We are still extraordinarily deficient of ammunition for either No. 4 Trench Battery (4 in.) or No. 18 Trench Battery ($1\frac{1}{2}$ in.). We also can obtain no rifle grenades. Consequently all along the line and especially at points like the Orchard Salient, where we are close to the enemy and are continually being bombarded with grenades and *minenwerfer* bombs, all units are at a grave disadvantage."

The diaries of all four battalions of the 56th Brigade show considerable activity in the front line. The 7th Loyal North Lancashires began the month with active patrolling, and on the 2nd of October Second-Lieut. J. E. Lord was wounded in the knee. The following extracts from the Diary of this battalion give some idea of the constant strain in the front line: "One of the enemy's *minenwerfer* bombs fell on our trench-mortar and destroyed it; we replied satisfactorily with bombs." But the loss of a trench-mortar in those days was a serious matter. "The enemy were very lively at 5 p.m., sending over a number of 'whizzbangs,' which knocked down the parados in three places and sent off a box of Very lights, much to the amusement of the Huns." There are daily accounts of hard work on the defences, not only in but out of the line. The 7th South Lancashires refer to the condition of the trenches on the 3rd of October during a relief: "One man literally unable to move out of the mud and had to be dug and carried out." The 7th East Lancashires suffered a great deal from the enemy's rifle grenades, one of which killed Lieut.-Colonel M. V. Hilton,

---

[1]There is an entry in the Diary of the 6th Wilts. dated 4th, 5th and 6th (October) which states that the casualties of the battalion to date were 5 officers killed, 3 wounded, 38 other ranks killed, 101 wounded, 16 missing.

the C.O., on the 20th of October. Two nights later Second-
Lieut. Wilson was wounded.

On the 13th, the day that attacks were taking place at the
Hohenzollern Redoubt, south of the La Bassée Canal, a feint
attack—smoke and rapid fire—was ordered along the front
of the 19th Division. The 7th King's Own report that the only
result was that ten of their men were badly burned. One
officer and three men were also "gassed" by the smoke bombs.

Of the 57th Brigade the 8th North Staffords also refer to the
rapidly-growing-worse condition of the front line. The
battalion was relieved on the 1st of November: "Got plenty of
rain this tour," records the Diary, "the trenches getting in
very bad state: dug-outs, parapets and traverses falling in, the
liquid mud being up to one's knees." On the 9th of October
Second-Lieut. R. P. Pinsent, of the 10th Royal Warwicks, was
killed—shot in the head. The 8th Gloucesters reported the
activities of a German *minenwerfer* opposite Vine and Bond
Streets, which enfiladed the line in the neighbourhood of
Boar's Head. On the 14th this mortar for two hours fired a
large bomb every three minutes; "the holes made by the shells
were of an immense size and a large amount of damage was
done to the parapet which was broached in several places
and communication stopped between 'A' and 'B' Companies; two other ranks were killed and seventeen wounded as
the result of this bombardment." The 10th Worcesters report
the loss of two officers during October: Lieut. R. Hartley was
killed on the 26th, and Lieut. A. G. Bishop wounded on the
30th.

The work of the gunners during October consisted largely in
retaliation shoots and in opening fire on selected points at the
request of the infantry in the line. It is possible also to observe
from the diaries of the artillery brigades and batteries how the
enemy's shell-fire gradually lost volume, until by the end of the
month he was firing shells in twos and threes only, where
previously he fired dozens. He was *getting* short of artillery
ammunition; we had never been anything else but short.
C/89 Battery records its first casualty—one of the telephonists
being wounded on the 6th of October whilst returning from
the O.P. On the 3rd of October the 88th Brigade, R.F.A.,
lost two officers and four gunners in the following manner:
a hostile howitzer battery began at about 3 p.m. to shell
B/88 Battery, first with high-explosive and then with gas

shells. In all eight shells were fired. The last but one, unfortunately, struck a dug-out in which Capt. A. F. Chance (the Battery Commander), Second-Lieut. A. R. Hebblethwaite and four N.C.O.s had taken refuge. The shell passed clean through the roof and burst inside, instantly killing all the occupants. This shell contained gas, and four men who were digging the bodies out were overcome, one being sent to hospital.

It is probable that in no previous war in which Great Britain had been engaged was sanitation so largely studied as in the Great War, and, therefore, it is of interest to note the work of the 19th Divisional Sanitary Section (Lieut. O. H. Peters, commanding). Their work consisted in the inspection of camps, billets and trenches, the testing of water supplies, the provision of baths, collecting clothes for delivery to the laundry, disinfection of men's clothing, etc., and the redistribution of clean underclothing.

In the Diary of the 19th A.D. Veterinary Section, the issue of smoke helmets for horses is recorded.

The 19th Divisional Cyclist Company (Capt. C. H. Smith, commanding) was used principally for duty as orderlies, guards on prisoners' cages, and under the A.P.M. as stragglers' posts during operations.

It was at Locon on the 25th of October that the following general arrangements were made concerning the Divisional Mounted Troops, *i.e.*, "C" Squadron, Yorkshire Dragoons (Major J. L. Ingham, commanding): The Divisional Squadron, Divisional Cyclists, assisted by the Salvage Corps, to perform all duties in connection with (*i*) disposal of prisoners; (*ii*) burial of dead; and (*iii*) collection and disposal of war material. The following optimistic remark follows the enumeration of the above duties which they were to perform "until they are required for duty as *mounted troops for the advance!*" Months and years were to pass before mounted troops took part once more in an advance and carried out their normal functions as cavalry.

It is interesting to note from the Diary of D.A.D.O.S. (Capt. W. Smith, commanding) that on the 17th of October, 1915, 100 steel helmets were received. Steel helmets were then in the experimental stage and were found of such protective value that all troops were subsequently equipped with them. Their use, however, did not become general until 1916.

From the end of October to the close of the year 1915, there is little of interest to record. All units were largely concerned in fighting the elements with as much vigour as fighting the enemy. Indeed the opposing forces were similarly engaged in combating the ravages caused first by rain and then by frost and snow.

Before the end of the year certain changes took place in the Divisional Staff. On Christmas Day Major-General G. T. M. Bridges, whose exploits in the cavalry during the operations of 1914 are well known, assumed command of the Division. In December also, Brig.-General C. C. van Straubenzee succeeded Brig.-General G. B. Lewis in command of the 56th Brigade. Brig.-General R. Fitzmaurice, on the 26th of December, succeeded Brig.-General Lawrie as B.G., R.A.

On the 13th of December the Divisional Troupe—"The Follies"—newly formed, gave their first performance at Lestrem.

The 4th (Special Reserve) Battalion of the King's Regiment (Liverpool), commanded by Lieut.-Colonel J. W. Allen, joined the 19th Division on the 3rd of December and was attached to the 56th Brigade. This Battalion had been serving for several months with the Indian Corps, but on the latter leaving France in November, had been transferred first to the 46th Division and then to the 19th Division. On December the 19th the King's were posted to the 58th Brigade.

On the 19th of December Sir John French handed over command of the British Army in France and Flanders to Sir Douglas Haig, and returned to England.

*   *   *   *   *

Between the 1st of January, 1916, and the beginning of the Somme Battles of 1916, the life of the Division may be divided into two periods; first from the New Year to the middle of April, when the Division was engaged in trench warfare, and from the middle of April to the 30th of June, when all units were out of the line in hard training for the great offensive to to be launched on the 1st of July.

The Division began the New Year still holding the Lestrem area, with the 56th and 58th Brigades in the line and the 57th Brigade in reserve. Trench warfare of a strenuous nature kept all units in the line continually on the alert, and there was much "small fighting" between the battalions in the line and the Germans. The guns were very active on both sides, and bombardments were heavy. But towards the end of the month the Division was relieved by the 38th (Welsh) Division and moved back for a well-deserved rest; all excepting the artillery which covered the old divisional front for some days after the infantry brigades had been relieved. Poor gunners! they were often first into a new sector and invariably the last to leave it—theirs was a hard life indeed.

By the end of the month the 56th Brigade was located in the Calonne area, the 57th Brigade at Robecq and the 58th Brigade at Les Lauriers; Divisional Headquarters were at St. Venant. These moves were completed by the 24th of January. Battalions were billeted in farms and villages in their respective brigade areas.

During the month, Lieut.-Col. R. M. Johnson was appointed G.S.O.I., vice Lieut.-Col. Buckle.

The first thing on coming out of the line was usually a good "clean up." Then equipment and arms had to be overhauled and replacements issued. There was also great activity at the baths and in the laundries. These things accomplished, hard training began and hard playing also, for sports were invariably included in the day's programme. At night, concerts, cinema shows and performances by "The Follies" relieved for the time being the strain upon the nerves, for many an officer and man came out of the trenches more or less quivering from the agony of the front line. In official language the 19th Division was now "at rest."

On the night of the 16th of February, however, the Division began to relieve the 38th and Guards Divisions in the front line, taking over from Plum Street (inclusive) to Sign Post Lane (exclusive) from the 38th, and from Sign Post Lane (inclusive) to Erith Post from the Guards. The 56th Brigade relieved the left brigade of the 38th Division, and the 58th the right brigade of the Guards Division on the night of 16th/17th of February, the 57th Brigade being in Divisional Reserve; Divisional Headquarters were at La Gorgue.

There now began another period of strenuous trench warfare, which was not to end until the third week of April. It is not possible to give all the details of an existence full of excitement, lived always in the presence of death, and yet written down in all reports as "quiet." The word "quiet" is used only in a comparative sense. But the following excellent summary of trench warfare at the period, given in Sir Douglas Haig's first despatch, after he had taken over command of the British forces in France and Flanders at the end of 1915, gives a very true picture of life in the front line when the situation is described as "quiet."

"The maintenance and repair of the defences alone, especially in winter, entails constant heavy work. Bad weather and the enemy combine to flood and destroy trenches, dug-outs and communications; all such damage must be repaired promptly, under fire, and almost entirely by night.

"Artillery and snipers are practically never silent, patrols are out in front of the lines every night, and heavy bombardments by the artillery of one or both sides take place daily in various parts of the line. Below ground there is continual mining and counter-mining, which, by the ever-present threat of sudden explosion and the uncertainty as to when and where it will take place, causes perhaps a more constant strain than any other form of warfare. In the air there is seldom a day, however bad the weather, when aircraft are not busy reconnoitring, photographing and observing fire. All this is taking place constantly at every hour of the day or night and in every part of the line.

"In short, although there has been no great incident of historic importance to record on the British front during the period under review, *a steady and continuous fight has gone on by day and night above ground and below it*. The comparative monotony of this struggle has been relieved at short intervals by sharp local actions, some of which, although individually almost insignificant in a war on such an immense scale, would have been thought worthy of a separate dispatch under different conditions, while their cumulative effect, though difficult to appraise at the true value now, will doubtless prove hereafter to have been considerable.

"One form of minor activity deserves special mention, namely, the raids or 'cutting-out parties,' which are made at least twice or three times a week against the enemy's line. They consist of a brief attack with some special object, on a section of the opposing trenches, usually carried out at night by a small body of men. The character of these operations and the preparation of a road through our own and the enemy's wire, the crossing of the open ground, the penetration of the enemy's trenches, the hand-to-hand fighting in the darkness and the uncertainty as to the strength of the opposing force, gives special scope to the gallantry, dash and quickness of

decision of the troops engaged, and much skill and daring are
frequently displayed in these operations."

The above is a very fair summary of "trench warfare," but
it is interesting to add that the British took the initiative in
these raids and the enemy followed suit. The Boche was a
great copyist and frequently paid us the compliment of
imitating our efforts, not that he always appreciated them!

Two incidents at least, which took place along the Divisional
front between the middle of February and the third week in
April, merit description; both took place in March.

The first event, though it took place just outside the Divisional area, is nevertheless of interest, as the Pioneers of the
19th Division—the 5th South Wales Borderers—rendered
very special service.

At 6 o'clock on the morning of the 14th of March the
Germans exploded a mine beneath the Duck's Bill,[1], which
lay just astride the left sector of the 19th Division, in the Sign
Post Lane–Frith Post sector, which on the 7th of March had
been taken over from the 57th Brigade by the 106th Brigade
(35th Division).

"A" and "D" Companies of the 5th South Wales Borderers
were, at the time of the explosion, attached to the 225th
Tunnelling Company for tunnelling, "B" and "C" Companies
being at work under the C.R.E. The explosion of the mine
completely wrecked the northern half of the salient and killed
or wounded the majority of the garrison and destroyed the
greater part of the work, the remainder of which was vacated
by the survivors. The enemy's guns, which opened fire immediately the explosion occurred, levelled the communication
trench leading to the Bill. At the same time the enemy's fixed
rifles,[2] machine-guns and snipers continually fired at the
damaged portion of the salient, with the idea no doubt of
preventing repairs.

A Company of the 5th South Wales Borderers was at the
time working in the neighbourhood, and Capt. D. W. Croft,
organising a rescue party consisting of Lieut. St. G. Yorke,
18th Battalion H.L.I., Second-Lieut. C. B. Lochner, 5th
South Wales Borderers, three N.C.O.s and four privates of the

[1]There were at least two Ducks' Bills along the Western Front; the one here
referred to was about 700 yards north-east of Neuve Chapelle.

[2]This was a device first used by the enemy and consisted of a number of rifles
fixed on a stand with an appliance by which the rifles could be fired simultaneously.

5th South Wales Borderers, went across to the Duck's Bill, organised the defence of the post and held it until relieved. One N.C.O. and a private were killed on the way across No Man's Land to the Bill.

Later in the day, during a hostile bombardment, during which the enemy used gas shells, one of the latter pierced the roof of No. 15 mine shaft and exploded inside, killing an officer of the 225th Company R.E. and a private of the 5th South Wales Borderers. Notwithstanding the fact that the shaft was full of poisonous fumes from the shell, another private of the South Wales Borderers remained at his post for three-quarters of an hour and continued to pump fresh air down to the men working in the mine galleries below. This action undoubtedly saved the lives of the men working in the mine.

No attempt was made by the enemy to occupy the crater formed by the explosion under the Duck's Bill.

The second incident took place a week later—on the 21st of March, when the 8th North Staffords raided the enemy's trenches.

The object of this raid was to kill or capture Germans and to sweep that portion of the German salient which lay opposite the Birdcage. There were three parties; (*i*) a bombing party of one officer and 27 other ranks; (*ii*) a sweeping party of one officer and 40 other ranks; and (*iii*) a covering party of one officer and 30 other ranks. The whole under the command of Capt. P. B. Purves.

Five mines were to be exploded along the front of attack just before 10 p.m., and at the latter hour the bombing party was to rush across to the enemy's trenches, followed by the sweeping party,[1] At 10 p.m. also, the guns and trench mortars were to open a heavy bombardment on the enemy's lines and place a curtain of fire round the sector to be raided. Other troops were to open rifle and machine-gun fire on the flanks of the attack.

The mines "went up" and directly the debris had subsided the raiders rushed across No Man's Land, crossing the crater in their advance. The bombing party was first in and bombed down the main fire trench, driving the Germans in front of them. The sweeping party, advancing directly across the apex of the salient, entered the mine crater in which the bodies of at least twenty Germans were found. But the heat and gas in

---

[1] Called "moppers-up," or "clearing parties," later.

the crater were so overpowering that it was impossible to stay to search the dead. The covering party remained under shelter of the crater to cover the withdrawal of the raiders.

The raid as a whole was successful, though no live Germans were brought back. One man, who was captured but refused to accompany his captors, had to be killed; a similar fate befell a German under-officer who refused to surrender; his coat and documents were brought in. From ten to fifteen Germans were killed altogether.

The North Staffords lost one man killed and one officer and nine other ranks wounded, all of the latter being brought in.

On the 14th of February the 56th, 57th and 58th Brigade Machine-Gun Companies joined the 19th Division from the United Kingdom. The Division had come to France armed with four Lewis guns per battalion in place of Vickers guns. The Lewis guns had been formed into brigade companies, the personnel being drawn from battalions. On the arrival of the new brigade machine-gun companies, however, the Lewis-gun companies were disbanded and returned to their battalions.

Following the raid by the 8th North Staffords on the 21st of March, the enemy retaliated by exploding a mine in the Colvin System, thus forming a new crater about twenty-five yards from the trenches and in front of the divisional wire. The crater was about twenty-five yards in diameter. No casualties were suffered by the Division, and, as the Diary of Divisional Headquarters states: "the net result is that the enemy saved us the trouble of springing a defensive mine in that neighbourhood, as their own answered our purpose."

The remainder of March was a very active period in so far as trench warfare was concerned; both side were always on the alert for the slightest opportunity of "hitting hard." Gradually the 19th Division was becoming hardened to trench life.

The 1st of April was an "extremely quiet" day; it was un-usual, but the weather was good and the ground rapidly drying, which gave the opposing forces opportunity for work on the defences, such as building up parapets and improving the line generally.

On the 12th of April orders were received that the 19th Division was to be withdrawn from the line by the 20th, to the reserve divisional area, whence it would proceed for training purposes to the First Army area.

Between the 19th and 22nd of April the Division marched into billets in the Therouanne area, where three weeks intensive training was to be carried out. On the 14th Brig-General G. D. Jeffreys, G.O.C., 58th Brigade, who was returning from the front line with the G.O.C., Division, was wounded by shrapnel at Rue du Bois. He was carried to No. 2 Casualty Clearing Station at Merville. Lieut.-Colonel R. A. Berners, commanding 9th Royal Welch Fusiliers, assumed temporary command of the brigade until the arrival of Brig.-General A. J. W. Dowell on the 29th of April.

CHAPTER V

THE BATTLES OF THE SOMME, 1916:

I THE DIVISION IN TRAINING

ALTHOUGH the 19th Division subsequently joined the III Corps of the Fourth Army on the Somme, it began training with the First Army in the Therouanne area.

Under the heading of "Notes for Guidance during 19th Division Training," there is a document attached to the General Staff Diary of the Division, a programme of work to be carried out by all units.

It begins thus: "It should be impressed on all ranks that the period to be devoted to training is short and that it is the duty of every man to endeavour to obtain the utmost instruction out of this short course of training . . . . Training is to be progressive in order that the foundations for good work may be laid down. By this means commanders down to section and platoon commanders should get a 'grip' of their men, gauge their capabilities and foster 'esprit de corps.' "

Brigade and other commanders are enjoined to have a programme of work "just the same as everyone else." The march discipline of infantry units was to be specially watched and the good dressing, cleanness of men, horses and vehicles of the transport, were to be examined during an advance to the training ground and again when returning to billets. The infantry were to be practised in rapidity of turning out of billets. Standing on parade for long periods before marching off was rightly condemned as "a waste of energy." Regular mealtimes are recommended, dinners to be taken out in order to ensure a "really good day's work" is suggested, but the keeping of dinners "till the men get home" is to be discouraged.

The following points are laid down for the guidance of C.O.s: platoon training, physical training, running, jumping, getting out of deep trenches, climbing over walls, games (such as are included in physical training), bayonet fighting, fire discipline, rapid loading, movement in extended order, intercommunication during battle, reconnaissance before and during battle, supply of ammunition (lectures and practical) instruction in the use of gas helmets, rapid movement wearing gas helmets, steady drill, arm drill and parade movements.

Company training: steady drill movements and extended order movements; organising a company for rapidly placing a captured village or locality in a good state of defence; advancing over open country under shell-fire and distant rifle-fire; company in the attack, to include practice in reinforcing, inter-communication, supply of ammunition and water; night operations, to include marching by compass.

Battalion training; battalion drill; advancing over open country under shell-fire, etc.; attack and defence, including rapid deployment for attack and closing for an advance, *i.e.*, pursuit; during attack and defence the actions of machine-guns were to be included; supply of ammunition and water; counter-attack; reconnaissance before and during battle; inter-communication and night operations.

Brigade training was to include combined exercises for one brigade with one brigade artillery, one Field Company, R.E., and a troop of cavalry. Divisional training was to occupy two days: on the first a march forward to a position of deployment and preliminary deployment for attack; on the second an attack was to be made, in continuation of the first day's programme.

The artillery had a separate programme, and here it may be said that the gunners of the 19th Division benefited greatly during this period of training.

During platoon and company training the signallers were to work under the Brigade Signalling Officer for visual signalling only. Until battalion training began the machine-gunners were to be drilled in the "mechanism" and "action" of Lewis guns and Vickers guns. Battalion and company bombers were to train under their own officers until battalion training began, when they were to join their units and take part in operations as *bombers!*

With such a programme of work the Division set to work to train hard. Yet, in accordance with the old adage that "all work and no play," etc., all units were given sufficient time and leisure in which to enjoy themselves. The Divisional Troupe played to crowded houses: there were football matches (and as the warmer weather arrived, cricket matches), battalion, brigade and divisional "shows" of all sorts, and as this was the first occasion since arrival in France that the Division had enjoyed a "rest," all ranks saw to it that no time was wasted, either in work or play; they "lived" every minute.

And perhaps it was just as well, for down on the Somme grim preparations had already begun; the whole area behind the battle front was already as busy as a beehive. Battalions out of the front line, in so-called "rest" billets, found work so heavy that they not infrequently wished themselves back in the front line. The industrious Boche was observed always at work; nothing damped his ardour for digging.

If we had only known the surprise he was preparing for us when we were ready to attack him!

The first period of training came to an end on the 6th day of May, and on the 7th the 19th Division was transferred to the III Corps area, Fourth Army, though still in G.H.Q. Reserve.

On the 10th of May divisional training was continued in the neighbourhood of billets, the 56th Brigade area being La Chausée, the 57th area Vignacourt, and the 58th Brigade area Flesselles, where also Divisional Headquarters were established.

For another fortnight, therefore, all units, with certain exceptions, carried on with the programme of work. The exceptions were certain units of the 56th Brigade, the Divisional Field Company, R.E., Divisional Artillery and the Pioneers, who, under orders of III Corps Headquarters, moved up to the forward area to work on the defences under the 8th and 34th Divisions, which at that period held front-line trenches opposite Ovillers and Ovillers la Boisselle—names soon to become a nightmare to every officer and man in the 19th Division. All officers of the three infantry brigades were also attached to the 8th and 34th Divisions for reconnaissance work and to familiarise themselves with the local systems of trenches.

On the 29th of May the infantry brigades of the Division began to move to yet another training field; the 57th and 58th marched to the St. Riquier training area, headquarters of the former being established at Drucat and the latter at St. Riquier.

By the 1st of June the whole area behind the British front line from Maricourt to Hébuterne had assumed the appearance of a vast armed camp. In the front line the utmost activity prevailed. Patrolling at night was specially active and raids were frequent, as it was necessary to keep careful watch on the enemy's dispositions. Gas was frequently discharged and

THE DIVISION "IN GREAT HEART"

mines were blown. But the enemy appeared strangely quiescent.

Behind the front lines large parties of troops were hard at work on the communications, dug-outs, the formation of dumps and all the necessary duties connected with the staging of a great battle. Guns were everywhere, of all calibre. The preparations for the Somme Battles presented an amazing sight.

In these preparations the 19th Division took an active part as well as continuing the training of all units.

The 57th and 58th Infantry Brigades began the month of June still in the St. Riquier training area, but the 56th Brigade with the Divisional Field Company, R.E., the Divisional Artillery and Pioneers, were still in the forward area, at work on the defences under the 8th and 34th Divisions. On the 7th of the month the 56th Brigade (less the 7th Loyal North Lancs. and 7th King's Own Royal Lancs at work in the forward area) moved to Flesselles where training was carried on in the neighbourhood of billets and in the training area between Flesselles and Fremont. The two battalions of the Brigade were, however, relieved on the 14th by one battalion each from the 57th and 58th Brigades.

From the 13th to the 20th of the month four parties of officers and N.C.O.s from the 57th and 58th Brigades visited the trenches for a two-days tour, being attached to the 8th and 34th Divisions.

The 19th Division moved to a new training area on the 16th of June, situated east of Doullens–Amiens road; Divisional Headquarters were at St. Gratien, 56th Brigade at Molliens-au-Bois, 57th Brigade at Rainneville, and 58th Brigade at Frechencourt. Parties from the Division were still attached to the two divisions holding the front line.

At this period the Division was in great heart. Everyone was keen on the big offensive soon to begin, and training was enthusiastically carried out.

Early in the year General Bridges had introduced the "Butterfly" as the Divisional sign. The Division was immensely proud of the sign, which was widely known throughout both the British and French armies. In 1916, for instance, when serving in Champagne with the French army it was always known by the French as "La Division Papillon."

D

CHAPTER VI
II. THE OFFENSIVE IS LAUNCHED
THE BATTLE OF ALBERT, 1st-13th JULY
THE CAPTURE OF LA BOISSELLE

FOR two years the enemy on the Somme had, during that long period of comparative quietude and calm, turned his attentions to making his position almost impregnable. From the northern bank of the river and as far north as the Gommecourt Salient, his defences were of extraordinary strength; such indeed that they could be held by weak forces against an attacking force of much greater numbers. The existence of villages, actually in or just behind his front-line trenches—all of which he had fortified—added vastly to the strength of his defences, and to the difficulties which attacking troops would have to overcome. His front-line and support trenches, protected by formidable belts of barbed-wire entanglements, were admirably sited, mostly on rising ground from which he could overlook the British forward positions. Two villages in particular—La Boisselle and Ovillers[1]—were so situated that any attack upon them—frontal or from the flank—could be enfiladed and brought to a standstill.

It is with La Boisselle that this story principally deals, for subsequently it fell to the lot of the 19th Division to attack that place.

La Boisselle was a hamlet of some thirty-five houses, lying just south of the main Albert–Bapaume road. It was in the centre of a small but very pronounced salient in the German front line, the apex of which was little more than 100 yards from our own front-line trenches. The region had been the scene of much mining activity, and No Man's Land was a confused and tumbled mass of white chalk craters, debris and wire entanglements—a death trap to troops attempting to cross the dread space between the opposing lines. The village itself, even before the final bombardment which began on the 24th of June and lasted seven days, was little else but a

---

[1]Its proper name is Ovillers-la-Boisselle, but "Ovillers" is used to distinguish it from La Boisselle, just south.

heap of ruins, lying amidst torn, bare and broken trees, blasted almost to stumps. But the gaunt walls of the wrecked houses and cottages, shell torn though they were, had been clothed by the industrious Boche in sand-bags and formed machine-gun posts and strong points, capable of putting up a stout resistance.

To the naked eye, viewed from our trenches, La Boisselle appeared but a mass of brick and mortar, strewn here and there with the beams and rafters of tumbled roofs. Yet below ground all was different, for beneath the troubled surface, and deep in the bowels of the earth, the enemy had made himself secure. Like the mole he lived underground; he had constructed, during the two years he had held that position, vast dug-outs and shelters, often as much as thirty feet down. These were connected, one with the other, by passages, proof against the heaviest shells we could hurl against them.

To all appearances, therefore, La Boisselle was but a rubble heap, which afforded poor protection against an attacking force; actually it was a terribly strong position in which a small garrison of brave and determined men could offer a stout resistance for a considerable length of time, causing heavy casualties amongst assaulting troops. And the German troops which had been entrusted with its defence were the 110th R.I.R. of the 28th Reserve Division, which had lived in it for more than a year and knew every hole and corner of the place.

Such was La Boisselle.

South of the village was a valley which ran from Becourt (behind the British lines) in a north-easterly direction, crossing No Man's Land and continuing through the German trench system south-east of La Boiselle in the direction of Contalmaison Wood; this was known as Sausage Valley. Immediately north-west of the village another valley ran through both lines of trenches and divided La Boisselle from Ovillers; this was Mash Valley.

From La Boisselle, therefore, troops passing across No Man's Land and operating in these valleys, could be badly enfiladed. Moreover, whereas the apex of the salient was but 100 yards from our front line, No Man's Land south and north of the salient, i.e., where the two valleys crossed the space between the opposing lines of trenches, was broader than elsewhere along the whole front, varying from about 700 to nearly 1,000 yards.

The defence, therefore, had unusual advantages over the attack. On the 22nd of June Divisional Operation Orders were issued containing full details of the launching of the great offensive:

"The III Corps[1] is to attack the enemy's position on 'Z' day at 'Zero' hour, the time of which will be communicated later, between the points X.20.d.7.2 and R.31.d.9.0[2] and to seize and consolidate the line Acid Drop Copse (inclusive)—The Cutting–Pozieres—R.28.c.2.0 marked green on the plan B already issued to G.Os.C. infantry brigades. This will constitute the first phase of the operations in so far as the III Corps is concerned. The 21st Division of the XV Corps is to attack on the right of the III Corps, and the 32nd Division of the X Corps on the left; the dividing lines are shown on the plan B referred to above. The III Corps attack is to be carried out by the 34th Division on the right and the 8th Division on the left, the dividing line between the two being X.14.a.5.6–X.14.b.7.9–X.5.c.1.5. The 19th Division is to be in Corps Reserve for the first phase and the 12th Division in Army Reserve."

The Operation Orders then give details of the tasks which might be allotted to the 19th Division in certain eventualities. (i) To capture the southern half of the second objective in case the 34th Division failed to get further than the first objective; (ii) to capture the northern half of the second objective should the 8th Division fail to get beyond the first objective; (iii) capture the whole of the "Intermediate" line if both the 8th and 34th Divisions were held up; and (iv) to capture the final objective should both the 8th and 34th Divisions take the first and second objectives but fail to get beyond the latter.[3]

The first objective ran from a point just south-west of Peake Woods, thence (following west of Bailiff Wood) to the eastern

[1]The III Corps consisted of the 8th, 34th, 19th and 12th Divisions.
[2]All co-ordinates and the objectives generally are shown on the maps.
[3]General Bridges adds the following note:
"Secret orders were given to the Divisional Commander in case the general attack was successful. A cavalry division, two battalions of cyclists and several mobile batteries were to be placed under his orders, and the 19th Division was to march on Bapaume as the spear-head of the Army. Actually quite a different task fell to its lot. But in order to mystify the enemy as much as possible, the 19th Division was warned off from the front line."

outskirts of Ovillers, then north to the northern Corps boundary about 1,200 yards south-west of Mouquet Farm. The
second objective (or German "Intermediate Line") ran from
just east of Peake Woods, past the western outskirts of Contalmaison, Contalmaison Wood and Pozières to a point about
150 yards south-east of Mouquet Farm. The final objective
(the German line mentioned in the Order) ran as previously
given. The dividing line between the 34th and 8th Divisions
ran through Mash Valley, between La Boiselle and Ovillers,
so that La Boisselle and Contalmaison lay in the 34th Divisional area of attack and Ovillers and Pozières in the territory
to be captured by the 8th Division.

Interesting as the Divisional Operation Orders are it is only
possible to give the salient points, chief of which were the
orders relating to the positions all units were to be in when
"Zero" hour on the 1st arrived. The 58th Brigade and the
94th Field Company, R.E., were to be in the preliminary
assembly trenches about the railway south of Albert; the 56th
Brigade and 81st Field Company in the preliminary assembly
trenches north-west of Albert (on the eastern side of the Albert–
Bouzincourt road); the 57th Brigade with the 82nd Field
Company, R.E. and 22nd Durham Light Infantry (Pioneers[1])
concentrated about Millencourt. The Divisional Ammunition
Column was to be at Laviéville, the train at "D.18 central"
(north of Buire), the 59th Field Ambulance at Ebart's Farm,
the 57th Field Ambulance at Laviéville, and the 58th at Bresle.

The Divisional Artillery was already in the line, mostly
holding gun positions between the Becourt–Albert and La
Boiselle–Aveluy roads, i.e., behind Tara and Usna Hills and
in Tara and Usna Valleys.

An onlooker has thus described the breaking of "Z" day:
"Even in the trenches the dawn of the 1st of July seemed calm
and sweet, at least till the full chorus of the guns opened at
6.30. The field on both sides of the line now dissembled under
a soft mist, above which here and there a high spire or lofty
tree just peeped out."

Just before "Zero" hour the officers from Divisional Headquarters partook of the Sacrament.

At 6.30 there was a sudden roar, an awful rending of the

---

[1]The 22nd Battalion Durham Light Infantry joined the 19th Division on
the 17th June and was attached to it until the 2nd of July, when it was
transferred to the 8th Division.

comparative stillness, which left men dazed and with that helpless feeling which comes with an intense thunderclap; the final hour of intense bombardment had begun. All along the line the closely-packed trenches showed little movement; all were awaiting anxiously the close of that final hour of the greatest bombardment ever witnessed (up to that time) of the enemy's defences. Before the hour of attack arrived several mines were exploded, and clouds of smoke were released as the hands of watches moved slowly nearer "Zero."

"7.30!"

With almost as great a violence as when they began at 6.30 a.m., the guns suddenly ceased, long lines of khaki-clad figures leapt from their trenches and began to move quickly across No Man's Land. Immediately the sharp barking of scores of machine-guns filled the momentary silence as the guns lifted off the German front line, and in many places the advancing lines of troops were almost swept away. The first waves were followed closely by others, in many places suffering the same fate. South of Fricourt the attack went splendidly and rapid progress was made. Between Fricourt and La Boisselle the 21st Division, attacking from north of the village, after stubborn fighting swept the enemy back to his support trenches. But on the left of the 21st Division the 34th Division, attacking north and south of La Boisselle, succeeded only in penetrating the enemy's front line south of the village; little or no headway was made north of it. The 8th Division, on the left of the 34th, fared even worse. By mid-day but little real progress had been made and no impression had been made on La Boisselle itself. The fighting had been of an extremely confused nature and no one could tell how far the troops had got, how much of the enemy's trench system had been captured or where exactly anybody or anything was, though subsequently some of the 34th Division dead were found beyond La Boisselle.

La Boisselle was still very strongly held by the enemy, and his machine-guns not only made any attack on either front most difficult, but absolutely dominated No Man's Land and all approaches to the village. Secure in their deep dug-outs the Germans had waited until the fury of our guns had lifted off the ruined village above them and then, rushing up to the surface, were able to mount their machine-guns and meet the first wave of our assaulting troops with a devastating fire. It

THE BATTLES OF THE SOMME, 1916: THE RUINS OF LA BOISSELLE UNDER HEAVY BOMBARDMENT PREVIOUS TO THE 1ST JULY

did not matter that the enemy's machine-gun emplacements had been swept away; the lip of a shell-hole or crater, a heap of tumbled bricks, was enough shelter from behind which they shot down our men in dozens.

Yet, until La Boisselle was taken progress on the flank was impossible, and as the 34th and 8th Divisions had both suffered heavily, the 19th Division (Major-General G. T. M. Bridges) was called upon to capture the village.

The order to attack and capture La Boisselle was received late in the afternoon of the 1st of July, and at 7.14 p.m. brief orders were issued from Divisional Headquarters: "The 57th and 58th Brigades will attack at 10.30 p.m. to-night from the general line X.13 central–X.20 central, and will establish themselves on the line X.14.d.9.2–X.14.c.3.9.[1] The dividing line between brigades will be the La Boisselle-Contalmaison road." The 58th Brigade (Brig.-General A. J. W. Dowell) was to attack on the right and the 57th (Brig.-General C. C. Onslow) on the left, gaining touch with each other on the La Boisselle–Contalmaison road just east of the village. The 57th Brigade was to dig a trench to connect the westernmost corner of La Boisselle with the (then) first British front line.

Since the early morning the Division had moved forward and when the above order was received the three infantry brigades were situated as follows: the 58th Brigade was on the Tara–Usna line, i.e., between the Becourt–Albert and the La Boisselle–Albert roads; the 57th Brigade was on the left of the 58th holding the northern portion of the Tara–Usna line, having relieved the 56th Brigade (Brig.-General F. G. M. Rowley) during the afternoon, for the latter brigade has been placed under the orders of the G.O.C., 8th Division; and at 3 p.m. battalions began to move off to their allotted positions in the front line, support and reserve trenches of that Division, ready for an attack on Ovillers which had been ordered to take place at 5 p.m. But ten minutes before the attack was timed to begin, it was cancelled and an hour later the 56th Brigade was ordered to occupy its previous position in the Tara–Usna line.

An extraordinarily difficult task now faced the 19th Division. The whole area which had been held (and was still held) by

---

[1]X.13 central and X.20 central were points in No Man's Land, north-west of La Boisselle in Mash Valley and south-east of the village, and in Sausage Valley respectively. The line X.14.d.9.2-X.14.c.3.9. was a south-east to north-west line on the further side of the village.

the 34th Division was in a state of congestion. It could not have been otherwise after the hard fighting throughout the day. All communication trenches were blocked with parties of stretcher-bearers, slightly-wounded men, and the miscellaneous crowds of troops that result from a day's confused fighting such as the 34th Division had passed through. Parties of men were going up to the front line, others coming back from it, and no power on earth could have got the troops of the 58th and 57th Brigades into position to launch an attack at the time ordered.

The 58th Brigade had formed up on the Tara–Usna line, with the 9th Cheshires on the right, 6th Wiltshires on the left, 9th Royal Welch Fusiliers in rear and in support of the Cheshires, and 9th Welch Regiment behind the Wilts.

But only the 9th Cheshires (Lieut.-Colonel R. B. Worgan), or rather part of that battalion, succeeded in reaching the old British front line. Their orders were to take up position from Loch Nagar Street to Inch Street (just south of the La Boisselle salient). Proceeding slowly, with frequent blocks and checks in the line, the battalion pushed its way gradually forward by way of Northumberland Avenue, Scourinbourne Street, Ashdown Street and Loch Nagar Street, but on reaching Dundee Avenue received conflicting verbal orders, so that eventually part of "B" Company and part of "D" Company occupied the line as ordered, and the remainder of the battalion fetched up in Becourt Wood where they were assembled by Capts. J. L. Jackson and G. G. Symons.

From the conference Colonel Worgan hurried up to the front line to meet his battalion, but all he could find were parts of "B" and "D" Companies. At 9.40 p.m. he ordered them to reinforce troops of the 34th Division then holding the Green Line near the new crater. In the meantime the C.O. set out to find the remainder of the battalion and met Lieut. King, O.C., "A" Company, with details of two companies. Ordering him to join the men at the New Crater,[1] Colonel Worgan made his way back to Brigade Headquarters, and having reported the situation, returned to the battalion in the front line, meeting on his way down the communication trenches the Royal Welch Fusiliers who had not yet had their orders. On reaching the front line he ordered work on the defences to be begun immediately, but soon after received a telephone message

[1] The new crater was at the southern point of the La Boisselle salient.

that he was to attack the enemy without delay. The time was then 2.30 a.m. (2nd July). By 2.50 a.m. he had taken over the best part of his battalion into the Crater and old German front line adjacent to it. The Cheshires had to fight hard during the remainder of the night and throughout the morning to maintain themselves in their position, but they did it very gallantly.

When dawn broke on the 2nd of July the situation of the Division was roughly as follows: the 56th Brigade was in a reserve line south of Albert; the 57th Brigade was in the front line opposite the northern end of the La Boisselle salient, having been unable to carry out the attack owing to the state of the trenches and the impossibility of organising the attack; the 58th Brigade was in the front line opposite the southern end of the salient, with the better part of the 9th Cheshires in the German front line on the fringe of the village and the New Crater. North of the 19th Division the 12th Division had relieved the 8th Division and everything was ready for a fresh attack. But on a reconnaissance being made of the position, it was clear that no attack could be carried out with any chance of success until the afternoon, and it was definitely postponed until 4 p.m.

During the early afternoon "C" and "D" Companies of the 7th East Lancashires of the 56th Brigade (that battalion being then in the reserve line south of Albert), with two sections of the Regimental bombers, were lent to the 34th Division to attack "Heligoland"—a redoubt in the German front line some 700 yards south-east of the New Crater. These two companies (under Capt. House) fought magnificently, and not only captured their objective but about 1,000 yards of the German front and second lines, together with fifty-eight prisoners, suffering only a few casualties. The party was later congratulated by the G.O.C., 101st Brigade (34th Division) on its excellent work.

For the attack at 4 p.m. the 58th Brigade disposed the 6th Wiltshires on the right and 9th Royal Welch Fusiliers on the left; the 9th Cheshires were on the right of the Wiltshires; the 9th Welch had received orders to provide carrying parties, the Battalion Bombers being attached to the Welch Fusiliers.

Half-an-hour before "Zero" a very intense bombardment of Ovillers took place, accompanied by a smoke barrage. It was intended to deceive the enemy as to the point of attack. The ruse succeeded, for the Boche put down a very heavy barrage in front of Ovillers, turning his attention to that part of the line where he imagined an attack was to be made.

The Wiltshires had received orders to secure the western point of La Boisselle up to the line 100 yards behind the church; the Royal Welch Fusiliers were to take the ground and German trenches on the south up to approximately the same line, the ultimate objective of the attack being the capture of the whole of the village and the consolidation of the line east of it.

Orders stated "La Boisselle will be taken this afternoon without fail and regardless of losses, as the success of the whole operation depends on its capture."

With all our guns bombarding Ovillers and not a single one firing on La Boisselle, the enemy's attention was rivetted on the former village, so that when "Zero" hour arrived and the Wiltshires, Royal Welch Fusiliers and Cheshires raced across No Man's Land, they did so with comparative freedom and with scarcely a casualty, though machine-gun and rifle fire met them. Nevertheless, the advance was made with great dash and two lines of trenches were taken and consolidation began immediately. For a short time all went well.

At 5 p.m. the attackers, having formed up afresh, the advance was carried on. Taken at first by surprise, the enemy rallied and before long any general advance was impossible until the way had been prepared by systematic bombing and clearing of dug-outs and hostile shelters.

However, the greater part of the immediate objectives in the village had been secured (within one and a half hours of the first attack); the western houses were in our hands and had been cleared of the enemy. Bombing parties were pushing forward to the centre of the village, casualties were not excessive. The records state that at this period "the spirits of the men had never been higher."

To the south the Wiltshires had penetrated the enemy's support line and were bombing him out of numerous "pockets" which still held out. The remainder of the Cheshires had gone over and had joined their companies who had fought so gallantly since the previous night (of the 1st).

By midnight substantial progress had been made and the Royal Welch Fusiliers, in the village, were holding the line they had set out to take. But this, for the time being, was the limit of the advance. The chief centre of the enemy's resistance was a trench which ran in a south-easterly direction from a point fifty yards beyond (east of) the church. From this trench, strongly protected and garrisoned, very heavy machine-gun and rifle fire had been kept up all day long, and just before midnight (2nd/3rd July) a determined counter-attack was launched from it against the Welch Fusiliers. Similar counter-attacks were made simultaneously from various points further south. With great gallantry (give them their due) the German bombers came on and on both flanks we were for the time being compelled to give ground. But tired out as our troops were, the attack was stopped, and after the 9th Welch (the reserve battalion of the 58th Brigade) had been sent up to reinforce, the enemy was repulsed. Our foothold in the village was as strong as ever, but in order to meet eventualities the 7th King's Own of the 56th Brigade were placed under the orders of the 58th Brigade and sent up to Brigade Reserve.

"The attack," records the Divisional Narrative, "so well begun, was prosecuted vigorously."

At 3 a.m. (3rd July) the 12th Division, on the left of the 19th Division, assaulted Ovillers, the 57th Brigade co-operating by launching an attack from the old British line just opposite the point of the salient upon the northern portion of La Boisselle. In this attack the 8th North Staffords were the first to go forward. Their narrative of the beginning of the attack was as follows: "Got the battalion down the front-line trench in the following order from right to left: battalion bombers, 10th Worcester Battalion bombers, 'D,' 'C,' 'B,' 'A' Companies. The last two Companies got a bit wiped up coming out of the C.T. trench, and some of the 8th Gloucesters got mixed up with us, they were following immediately behind us . . . . The first party to go over was one platoon of 'D' Company under Second-Lieut. C. J. Hunter. They went over about 4.5 a.m. and seized the crater in front of the La Boisselle salient before the bombers entered. The battalion swept up the village and trenches fairly easily at first, up to a point about three-quarters way up. Having reached this point the bomb supply began to give out, although Battalion Headquarters men formed a carrying party. By this time about 100 of the enemy had surrendered."

On the left of the North Staffords, the 10th Worcesters with great dash had advanced and captured their line of trenches. Small parties of the battalion had also penetrated right through La Boisselle, but they also ran short of bombs and were forced back again.

A small party of Worcesters under Lieut. R. W. Jennings had penetrated the German third-line trenches. This party was driven back by a counter-attack during which Lieut. Jennings was wounded in the arm and also had his leg shattered. But No. 20572, Private T. J. Turrall, on his own initiative, stayed behind for three hours with his officer, though under heavy fire from machine-guns and bombs. Finally, he succeeded in carrying him back to our lines. The enemy actually occupied the position in which Lieut. Jennings was wounded, and at one time he and Private Turrall were completely cut off from the battalion until a counter-attack drove the Germans back again. Having carried Lieut. Jennings to the Battalion Aid Post, Private Turrall returned at once to his company and continued to fight with great gallantry until the battalion was withdrawn.

For his conspicuous bravery and devotion to duty Private Turrall was awarded the Victoria Cross, the first gained by the 19th Division in France.[1]

After the North Staffords and Worcesters the 8th Gloucesters and 10th Warwicks had to be sent in to join them.

By 5.30 a.m. excellent progress had been made and the Staffords had reached a line of trenches which ran roughly just in front of the church, in touch with the 58th Brigade on their right. The other three battalions of the brigade were in the village, clearing up the ground that had been gained. The 7th South Lancs. of the 56th Brigade had been placed at the disposal of the G.O.C., 57th Brigade, and were in Brigade Reserve.

At 6 p.m. the G.O.C., accompanied by Major Haskard, G.S.O.2., visited the village. Colonel Carton de Wiart was ordered to take command of all troops in La Boisselle.

Meanwhile the 58th Brigade had also been fighting hard. The 9th Royal Welch Fusiliers had attacked simultaneously with the 57th Brigade on their left. They encountered very strong opposition but managed to push forward to a line well in front of the church where they gained touch with the North Staffords as already related. On the right of the Welch Fusiliers the Wiltshires and Cheshires bombed their way forward to the enemy's second line.

The whole of La Boisselle, with the exception of four houses on the eastern edge of it, had now been captured, and at about

---

[1] For citation from *London Gazette* of 9th September, 1916, see Appendix.

8.10 a.m. Divisional Headquarters received a report that the village was clear of the enemy.

If this was so (and there is undoubted evidence that snipers and bombers were still lurking in dug-outs and amidst the ruins of the village) the enemy had not then relinquished his hold on La Boisselle, for at about 8.30 a.m. there began a series of fierce counter-attacks which led to what was probably the most intense fighting the Division had up to that period experienced.

The attack fell first upon the 58th Brigade and the Wiltshires, Cheshires and Welch Fusiliers were forced to give ground, the two first-mentioned battalions falling back from the German second-line trenches they had taken, to their starting point. The 9th Welch were at once hurried up and thrown into the contest, and after bombing contests of the most desperate nature the lost ground had been regained by 12.30 p.m.

Meanwhile the Germans, considerably reinforced, had attacked the 57th Brigade at about 11 a.m. in the northern end of the village, and the North Staffords, Worcesters and Gloucesters were forced back to a line about half-way through the village. The situation at this period (about 12.30) was desperate, for the 57th Brigade then held the line of a hedge where very hard fighting took place. Indeed, had the line given way at this point the enemy might have recaptured the whole of the village. That he did not do so was largely owing to the gallantry of Lieut.-Colonel A. Carton de Wiart (4th Dragoon Guards), commanding the 8th Gloucesters. The Commanding Officers of the 8th North Staffords (Major C. Wedgwood) and 10th Worcesters (Lieut.-Colonel G. A. Royston Pigott) had already been killed, and Lieut.-Colonel R. M. Heath, commanding 10th Warwicks, wounded, when Colonel Carton de Wiart took command of these battalions as well as his own. Thanks to his dauntless courage and inspiring example the troops of the 57th Brigade clung to their hedge and gave no more ground. He had lost an arm earlier in the war, and an eye in Somaliland in 1914, and but for his pluck and determination the day might have ended badly for the Division. Colonel Carton de Wiart was awarded the Victoria Cross for his conspicuous bravery[1]—the second Cross won during the battle.

[1] For citation from the *London Gazette* of the 9th of September, 1916, see Appendix.

Holding steadfastly to their hedge the 57th Brigade gave no more ground. For a time, however, further advance was impossible. The enemy, in considerable strength, held a trench running along the northern side of La Boisselle, which, without reorganisation (which the obscure position did not permit), it was impossible to attack.

By the evening of the 3rd of July the whole of La Boisselle was not yet in our hands. In the eastern end several "pockets" of Germans still held out, offering the stoutest resistance. But the 58th Brigade was by now practically exhausted and badly in need of relief. The 7th King's Own of the 56th Brigade were, therefore, moved up from Support to take over the line from the worn-out battalions of the 58th Brigade; the G.O.C., 56th Brigade, then assumed command of the front line.

Throughout the night of the 3rd/4th sporadic bombing continued.

At 8.30 a.m. on the 4th another attack (destined to be the last) was launched by the 56th and 57th Brigades; the final objective was a line of trenches some 200 yards beyond the eastern exits of the village, which was only to be attacked and captured if the whole of La Boisselle was absolutely and indisputedly in our hands.

On the right (the 56th Brigade front of advance) the King's Own, supported by the 7th East Lancs. and 7th Loyal North Lancs., attacked the enemy with great pluck and determination. To advance across the open was impossible and the fight became a series of bombing contests between British and Boche, the former having to bomb their way, assisted by machine-guns and trench-mortars, almost step by step, up communication trenches.

The advance was slow, not only on account of the fighting above ground, but because the enemy's dug-outs, often thirty feet below ground, had to be searched thoroughly. These dug-outs were indeed an "eye-opener" to our men, who, as they searched every hole and corner for lurking Boches, ceased to wonder why it was that the terrific shell-fire to which the enemy's trenches and positions had been subjected in the preliminary bombardment, had failed to wipe out every German within range of the shell bursts. The heaviest shells had failed to penetrate to the depths of these underground fortresses.

Much time, therefore, had to be spent in clearing out the

enemy, but by 2 p.m. substantial progress had been made, and at 2.30 p.m. the North Lancs. passed back a message that "with the exception of two streets at the eastern end, La Boisselle is clear of the enemy." But further advance to the objective was impossible, for a terrific machine-gun fire from the north-east held up all attempts to push on, and a line 200 yards short of it but well clear of the village, was consolidated.

In the meantime the 57th Brigade, on the left, assisted by the 7th South Lancs (of the 56th Brigade), had been fighting very hard. Their task was difficult. The trench running along the northern side of the village was "stiff" with Boche, who held a group of four houses. There were also several shell-holes manned by parties of the enemy with a machine-gun, which formed a formidable obstacle.

All four Battalion Commanders of the 57th Brigade had been either killed or wounded when Lieut.-Colonel C. R. P. Winser, commanding 7th South Lancs., took command of the brigade front, and it was greatly due to his resource and gallantry that the northern portion of the village was cleared of the enemy.

By 10 a.m. the group of houses already mentioned had been cleared at the point of the bayonet, and our troops were reported at two points on the road just beyond. A heavy bombing fight up the trench on the northern side of the village, which had previously given so much trouble, was in progress, but by mid-day here also the enemy had been cleared out.

By 3 p.m. the whole of La Boisselle was in the hands of the 19th Division.

It was inevitable that in fighting of the nature described the losses of the attackers would be heavy. The Division had lost about 3,500 all ranks. The captures consisted of some 350 prisoners, 6 machine-guns, and a few *minnenwerfer*.

The village itself, when finally taken, was unrecognisable as ever having been the habitation of human beings. "Its strength," said General Bridges, "lies underground, in a complicated series of dug-outs twenty to forty feet deep, all connected with each other, that no artillery can touch and no charge clear, however recklessly pressed home. If the attackers go too fast and leave garrisons in any of these holes unaccounted for, machine-guns rise from the bowels of the earth behind them and shoot them in the back. If they go too slow there is the danger of exhaustion before the objective can be reached. In La Boisselle such strongholds were particularly numerous."

Of gallant acts there were many. Two spectacular incidents are worth recording. One was that of an officer seen walking along the top of a parapet with a revolver, protecting from molestation a party of his own bombers who were advancing along the trench. The other was a dramatic bombing duel between a British soldier and a German. Each combatant stood on the parapet of a trench, about twenty-five yards apart, in full view. No one interfered or fired a shot at these gallant fellows but let them fight it out. They had exchanged three throws each, but the last bomb thrown by the British soldier knocked the German out.

Towards dusk the enemy's shell-fire slackened and the line gradually became quiet. But still there were spasmodic attacks here and there, though the position generally remained the same.

On the 5th fighting continued throughout the day and there was much bombing activity, especially on the left of the divisional front. At 2 p.m. the 7th East Lancs. made a bombing attack and were very ably assisted by "D" Company and the battalion bombers of the 7th Loyal North Lancs. "C" Company of the latter battalion had already been sent up on the previous evening, in reserve. But owing to some misunderstanding the left of the 7th East Lancs. withdrew to the old German front line and the old British front line. The Germans then tried to take advantage of this retirement, but "C" Company of the 7th Loyal North Lancs. were at once ordered to charge and regain the lost ground. They went "over the top" in fine style and retook the line vacated—a fine performance.[1] On the left Lieut. T. O. L. Wilkinson (7th Loyal North Lancs.), seeing that the East Lancs. in their retirement had left a Lewis gun behind, rushed forward and with the help of a couple of his men got the gun into action and held up the Germans who were advancing down the trench, until relief arrived. Subsequently, during a bombing attack, the advance being checked, this gallant officer forced his way to the front and

[1]This statement is taken from the Diary of the 7th Loyal North Lancs. Regt. In the 57th Brigade Headquarter's Diary, however, it is stated that the line retaken by the North Lancs. was not the original line held by the 7th East Lancs. and from which they had retired.

found men of four or five different units stopped by a solid block of earth over which the enemy was throwing bombs. The situation was critical, but Lieut. Wilkinson, with great courage and presence of mind, got a Lewis gun into position on the top of the parapet and dispersed the enemy bombers. Later in the day Lieut. Wilkinson made two attempts under heavy fire to bring in a wounded man lying some fifty yards in front. At the second attempt he was unfortunately shot through the heart just before he reached the wounded man. For his conspicuous gallantry, initiative and resource, he was awarded the Victoria Cross—the third gained by the 19th Division at La Boisselle.[1]

At 9 p.m. on the 5th orders were issued for several reliefs to take place. The 57th Brigade was to be relieved by troops of the 12th and 25th Divisions and move back to Albert; the 58th Brigade was to relieve the 69th Brigade of the 23rd Division in a line of trenches newly captured from the enemy. The 56th Brigade was to remain in the line.

By 12.30 a.m. on the 6th of July the 57th Brigade had been relieved and all ranks were located in Albert, with the exception of the Machine-Gun Company and Trench-Mortar Battery who remained in La Boisselle until later in the day.

The 58th Brigade completed the relief of the 69th Brigade (23rd Division) at about 9.10 p.m., the newly-captured line running from 41–00–79–49–01; this position was taken over by the 9th Welch Regiment and portions of the 58th Machine-Gun Company and Trench-Mortar Battery. The 56th Brigade should have been on the left, holding the line between the left of the Welch Regiment and La Boisselle, but they had been counter-attacked and had not regained all their line, which then ran 76–80. They were, however, engaged in a bombing fight with the enemy and by 7 a.m. on the 7th had reached the line 92–72–33, touch being obtained with the 58th Brigade at 92–01.

At 8 a.m. on the 7th the 19th Division, in conjunction with the 23rd Division on the right and 25th Division on the left, again attacked the enemy. After a heavy bombardment the 58th Brigade (right) and 56th Brigade (left) began their advance and made steady progress. In the centre, so eager were the troops to get on that at one time they ran into the divisional barrage and were held up. Three times during the day the left

---

[1] For citation from *London Gazette* of 26 September, 1916, see Appendix.

E

of the Division was attacked by the enemy, who came on with great gallantry, but on each occasion he was repulsed. By 9.35 p.m., in spite of determined efforts by the enemy to beat us off, the final objective (an east to west line from 81–52) was reached and consolidation was at once put in hand.

Throughout the 8th there was little activity. The line gained on the 7th was further consolidated and also slightly extended to the right. In the evening another advance was made and the next line of German trenches (81-53-46-82) was taken without difficulty and consolidated.

During the night of the 8th/9th the 58th Brigade was relieved by a brigade of the 34th Division and moved back to billets in Albert. Three battalions of the 57th Brigade proceeded to Millencourt, the 8th North Staffords remaining in the trenches, attached to the 56th Brigade.

The 9th was uneventful and during the night of the 9th/10th the 56th Brigade was relieved also by troops of the 34th Division.

On the 10th the 19th Division moved to Millencourt for a well-deserved rest, Divisional Headquarters and the 57th Brigade being located in the village, the 56th Brigade in Henencourt Wood and the 58th Brigade at Basieux.

But for the hard-worked artillery there was no relief, for when all three infantry brigades of the 19th Division had moved back out of the line, the divisional artillery came under the orders of the 34th Division, whose front they proceeded to cover as efficiently and devotedly as they had covered their own infantry.

The capture of La Boisselle was indeed a triumph for the 19th Division—one of which any division might well have been proud. Before the Division had come out of the line the Fourth Army Commander (Lieut.-General Sir H. Rawlinson) had visited General Bridges and had congratulated the latter on the fine performance of his officers and men.

It was a "Soldier's Battle"—the Divisional Memorial stands there—where so many gallant deeds had been performed!

To use a phrase common during the war, "the infantry were always in the limelight!" It was so in the capture of La Boisselle by the 19th Division; and yet without the devoted support of the divisional artillery, the fine work carried out in consolidation and digging trenches by the 5th South Wales Borderers (Pioneers) and Field Companies, R.E., the gallant

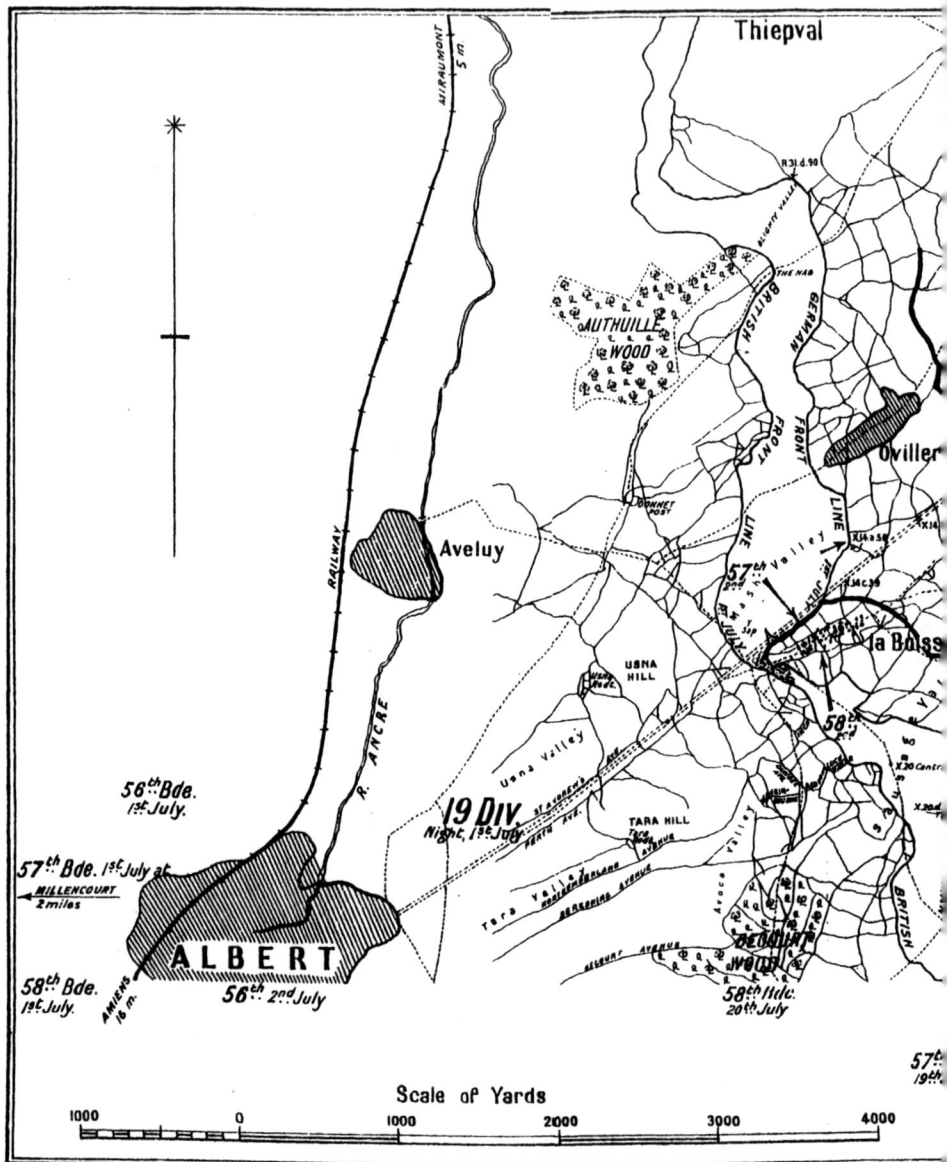

Thiepval

Authuille Wood

Oviller

Aveluy

Usna Hill

Usna Valley

19 Div
Night, 1st July

Tara Hill

la Boiss

ALBERT

56th Bde.
1st July.

57th Bde. 1st July at
MILLENCOURT
2 miles

58th Bde.
1st July.

56th 2nd July

58th Bde.
20th July

AMIENS 16 m.

R. ANCRE

RAILWAY

ALLIRAUMONT

5 m.

Scale of Yards

1000   0   1000   2000   3000   4000

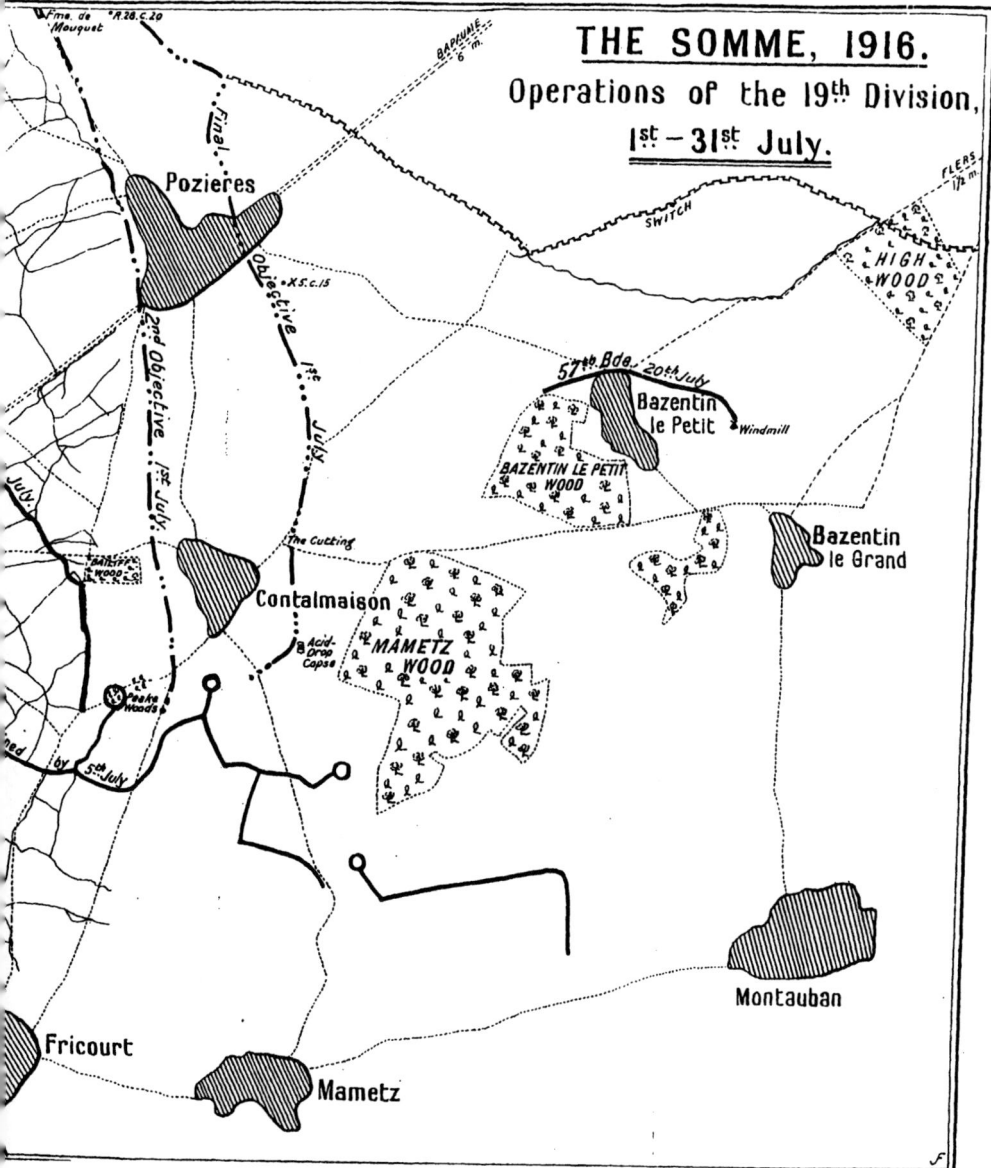

THE SOMME, 1916.
Operations of the 19th Division,
1st – 31st July.

way in which the Machine-Gun Companies and Trench-Mortar Batteries assisted by machine-gunning and trench-mortaring the German trenches, posts and strongholds, the splendid way in which the Army Service Corps and supply columns kept the troops supplied with rations (often brought up under heavy fire), the fine devotion to the wounded and dying by the medical units, and finally the cheering influence of many a British padre, who though non-combatants, were always to be found very near to, if not in the front line of battle, the infantry might not have done so brilliantly.

Victory was to that division in which co-operation between all ranks and units was as near perfect as human nature could make it.

CHAPTER VII
HIGH WOOD: 20TH/26TH JULY

WITH the exception of the artillery, still in action covering the front of the 34th Division, the 19th Division remained resting and training in the Millencourt area until the 19th of July. On that date, however, during the afternoon, the following orders were issued: the 56th Brigade was to relieve the 98th Brigade (33rd Division) in the line that night, *via* Fricourt, where guides would meet the relieving battalions and conduct them to the front line, then roughly in front of Bazentin le Petit. The 57th Brigade was to move from Millencourt to a bivouac area just west of Fricourt in the old British line. The 58th Brigade was to move to Becourt Wood on the 20th, upon which date also the 57th Brigade was to take over the sub-sector held by the right brigade of the 33rd Division. On completion of these reliefs the 57th Brigade on the right, and the 56th on the left, would hold a line from the Windmill due east of Bazentin le Petit to the railway line from Bazentin le Petit to Martinpuich. But the line just north of the village appears to have been very sketchy for, being recently captured, no definite trench system had yet been dug and the troops held the line in holes, short lengths of trench, and wherever they could dig themselves in. The state of the ground in the neighbourhood of Mametz Wood and Bazentin at the time of the operations near those places was terrible. Everything was smashed beyond recognition. The whole area was a mass of shell craters, and it was difficult in the extreme to recognise trenches which had been battered hopelessly.

Near the top end of Mametz Wood lay a number of dead horses which stank so much that passing them was almost more unpleasant than passing over heavily-shelled ground.

The 56th Brigade set out for the front line at 7 p.m., but it was 11 p.m. before the leading battalion (7th Loyal North Lancs.) reached Fricourt, the way up being blocked by traffic and particularly by Anzac troops who cut across the line of advance of the Brigade. The 7th East Lancs. had been detailed, with the 7th Loyal North Lancs. to take over the front line of the 98th Brigade, the 7th Royal Lancasters to be in support and the 7th South Lancs. in reserve.

The actual relief was a very slow process and was not completed until about 4.30 a.m. on the 20th. The 7th Royal Lancasters, the supporting battalion, had a terrible time. "The guides supplied by the 98th Brigade," records the Brigadier of the 56th Brigade, "did not altogether excel themselves, especially in the case of the 7th Royal Lancaster Regiment . . the four guides took the battalion right up into the *front line*. As, of course, there was no battalion there for them to relieve, the 7th Royal Lancaster Regiment were eventually marched back to their exact position." The mistake was costly, for the Battalion lost two officers and forty other ranks, killed or wounded.

The North Lancs. had difficulty in getting settled in the line as the Argyll and Sutherland Highlanders of the 98th Brigade were then attacking the enemy; and, having captured a trench (which the former Battalion would have to take over), were still in occupation of it, consolidation having begun: it was after dark on the 20th before the North Lancs. took over this new trench.

On this night also the 57th Brigade[1] moved up into the line on the right of the 56th Brigade and occupied a front described as from "S.C.3.4.4. along road to S.8.b.6½.8," which interpreted means a line running along the road between the northern exits of Bazentin le Petit village and the north-western corner of High Wood, the right of the Brigade being about half-way between the two points. The trench line here was almost "Z" shaped and obviously of a temporary nature.

Thus the two Brigades had reached the front line and were at once employed in digging themselves in more securely and in improving whatever defences and trenches existed. The Boche shell-fire was heavy and his snipers were everywhere, the continual crackle of machine-guns warning the troops to get well into the ground as quickly as possible.

During the day orders had been issued for the 19th Division,

---

[1] On the 20th of July Brig.-General C. C. Onslow was sick and Lieut.-Colonel W. Long, Wiltshire Regt., assumed command of the 57th Brigade until the arrival on the 22nd of Brig.-General G. D. Jeffreys, who had been wounded in April.

in conjunction with the 33rd Division on the right and 1st Division on the left, to attack the German Switch Line on the 22nd of July.[1]

The objective of the 19th Division was the German Switch Line (or rather that portion of it in the Divisional area), which ran from the enemy's trench system east of Pozières in an easterly direction to the north-eastern corner of High Wood, thence in an east by south direction to Morval. Along the Divisional front it cut across the triangle formed by Martin-puich (north), High Wood (east) and Bazentin le Petit (south).

Some idea of the difficult nature of the line taken over by the 56th and 57th Brigades may be gathered from the fact that the better part of the 21st was spent in locating the front line correctly.

The difficulties were enhanced by the continuous and heavy artillery and machine-gun fire, which rendered movement by day almost impossible and tried the endurance of the troops to the utmost. Headquarters of the 57th Brigade were in an old German dug-out in Mametz Wood, through which ran a straight ride much used as an avenue of communication towards the front line. This ride also was continuously shelled, causing a good many casualties, but a "by-pass" ride was cut through the undergrowth and by using this, instead of the main ride, many casualties were avoided.

With a view to discovering the strong points in the enemy's line, the ground out in front of the line was reconnoitred. This reconnaissance revealed a line of German trenches running between the Divisional front line and the Switch Line, but it was not clear whether it was held by us or by the enemy.

Corps and Army Headquarters would not at first believe in the existence of this "intermediate line," but in spite of numerous attacks it was not completely captured until more than a month later. Owing to disbelief in its existence it was ignored in the Artillery Fire Plan, with fatal results. After dark on the 21st patrols went out, and soon discovered that these trenches were not in our possession, but were held by the enemy. It was, therefore, fixed as the first objective of the attack.

At 12.30 a.m. (23rd July) the 56th and 57th Brigades

---

[1]The 51st Division took over the line from the 33rd Division on the 22nd, and the former was, therefore, on the right of the 19th Division.

attacked the enemy, but very little progress was made owing to the heavy machine-gun fire from the front and from the right flank. By 6.55 a.m. the attacking troops were back in their original trenches. At the last minute the 10th Royal Warwicks had to be put in to relieve the 10th Worcesters: this eleventh-hour relief and the presence of the "intermediate line" had much to do with the failure of the attack.

The remainder of the day was spent in reorganising and in strengthening the defences of the front line. At 9 p.m. the 58th Brigade began the relief of the 56th and 57th Brigades, the former moving back to Mametz Wood and the latter to Becourt: the relief was completed at about 10.25 p.m.

On the night of the 23rd/24th the 5th South Wales Borderers dug a new trench from north of the Windmill (east of Bazentin le Petit) in a north-easterly direction to connect up with one dug by the 51st Division (on the right of the 19th Division), the right of which entered High Wood.

Throughout the 24th the enemy shelled the Divisional trenches heavily at intervals and barraged the communications. At one time Germans were reported assembling for an attack, but no attack materialised. At night the troops in the front line, ably assisted by the Pioneers and Royal Engineers, were hard at work digging a new line of trenches to connect up with the 51st Division on the right, but owing to the enemy's shell and rifle fire this trench was not dug deep enough for occupation. The 25th[1] and 26th were occupied in digging and the general improvement of the defences.

On the 28th the 57th Brigade was ordered to relieve the 58th Brigade during the latter part of the 29th. The relief began at 5 p.m. and was completed without incident by about 9.30 p.m. On completion of the relief the following units came also under the orders of the G.O.C., 57th Brigade: 5th South Wales Borderers, 9th Cheshires (58th Brigade), 7th King's Own (56th Brigade), 82nd Field Coy. R.E., and two machine-guns of the 56th Brigade Machine-Gun Company in High Wood.

At 4 p.m. on the 29th, previous to going into the line, the 57th Brigade, with attached troops, was ordered to attack and

---

[1]Officially the "Attack on High Wood" ends on 25th July, but the Battle of Pozières Ridge began on the 23rd of July and continued until the 3rd of September. The areas of these two operations overlap and the 19th Division is entitled to both Battle Honours.

capture the German intermediate line between Pozières and High Wood along the Brigade front. "Zero" hour for the attack was 6.10 p.m. on the 30th.

The morning of the 30th was fairly quiet and the assaulting battalions of the 57th Brigade Group were able to complete their preparations. During the afternoon final positions were taken up and, as the hour of attack drew near, battalions were disposed as follows: on the extreme right the 7th King's Own (attached *vice* 8th N. Staffords), then came the 10th Royal Warwicks, 10th Worcesters and 8th Gloucesters; the 81st Field Company R.E., and 5th South Wales Borderers had been attached for consolidation purposes.

At 6.9 p.m. an intense barrage by field guns was put down on the enemy's trenches, under cover of which the first wave of the King's Own and Warwicks crept out under the barrage and lay down in No Man's Land waiting for the guns to lift. Both these battalions report that this operation was carried out, but the Worcesters and Gloucesters make no such statement.

At 6.10 p.m. the guns lifted and the attackers rushed forward. So far as the King's Own and Warwicks were concerned they were into the German line before the Boche had time either to man his trenches or bring his machine-guns into action: thus the two right battalions of the attack reached their objectives quickly. But the Worcesters and Gloucesters failed in their attempt: they advanced about one hundred yards and were then caught in a terrific flanking machine-gun fire and had to fall back to their original line. Prisoners and machine-guns were captured during this attack.

Aided by the 81st Field Company R.E. and the Pioneers (5th South Wales Borderers) consolidation proceeded rapidly and although the enemy launched counter-attacks against that portion of the line he had lost, all were repulsed. On the 31st the 57th Brigade Group was relieved by a brigade of the 34th Division.

The most valuable lesson learnt by the infantry from this attack was that of keeping close behind the barrage. By so doing it was possible to get into the enemy's trenches before he could get his machine-guns into action or man his line properly. The success of this method led to the adoption of what was to be known in the future as the "creeping barrage," though the latter was not officially known as such until September, 1916.

Casualties in this attack were heavy The King's Own had

LA BOISSELLE: THE 10TH WORCESTERS ESCORTING CAPTURED GERMAN PRISONERS

7 officers and 113 other ranks killed, wounded or missing; the Warwicks lost 9 officers and 148 other ranks; the Worcesters 2 officers and 87 other ranks, and the Gloucesters 9 officers and 160 other ranks.

The 10th Warwicks were commanded in this attack with great gallantry by Captain H. W. Dakeyne, a young regular officer of the Royal Warwickshire Regiment, whom the death of the C.O. in the night attack on the 22nd/23rd had placed in temporary command of the Battalion. He remained with the 19th Division to the end of the War and became one of its most experienced C.O.'s.

It was during this action that the fourth Victoria Cross was gained by a member of the 19th Division.

After the 7th King's Own had captured the German position and while the Battalion was consolidating, No. 12639 Private J. Miller was ordered to take an important message and bring back a reply at all costs. To do this he had to cross the open under heavy shell and rifle fire. On leaving the trench he was shot almost immediately in the back, the bullet coming out through his stomach and causing a portion of his bowel to protrude. In frightful agony, yet mindful of his mission, Private Miller, compressing his stomach with his hand, successfully delivered his message and returned with the answer, falling in a state of collapse at the feet of the officer to whom he delivered it. For this action of "most conspicuous gallantry, determination and self-sacrifice" Private Miller was awarded the Victoria Cross.[1]

----

[1] For citation from *London Gazette* of 9th September, 1916, see Appendix.

CHAPTER VIII

AN INTERLUDE

TRENCH WARFARE: AUGUST, SEPTEMBER AND OCTOBER, 1916

FOR the time being the 19th Division had been withdrawn from the Somme battlefields and was due to move north to the trenches south-east of Ypres—a comparatively quiet part of the line—where a certain amount of rest and recuperation could be afforded the tired troops who had passed through the strenuous days of July.

Speeded on its way by a kind message from General Sir Henry Rawlinson,[1] the infantry brigades of the Division entrained on the 2nd of August and on the 3rd arrived in the following areas: 56th Brigade—Gorenflos; 57th Brigade—Vauchelles; 58th Brigade—Pont Remy: the 5th South Wales Borderers were at Long with Divisional Headquarters. This was an intermediate stage, Vauchelles being in the Somme Valley between Amiens and Abbeville; in it were very comfortable billets. It was from this area that the Division entrained for the north. The artillery had not yet arrived.

On the 4th orders were received to relieve the 50th Division (V Corps) in the Spanbroekmolen-Wytschaete sector, both the infantry and artillery to be relieved by the night of the 9th/10th of August. The three infantry brigades arrived at Bailleul on the 6th and on detrainment relieved reserve battalions of the 50th Division.

All three brigades of the Division went into the front line, the 57th and 58th relieving battalions of the 50th Division on the night of the 7th/8th August in the right and left sub-sectors respectively, the 56th Brigade taking over the centre of

---

[1]In this letter Sir Henry Rawlinson said: "In capturing La Boisselle and in the trenches in the neighbourhood, as well as during the hard fighting in which they were engaged near Bazentin le Petit, the Division showed a determination and fine soldierly spirit which was wholly admirable. The co-operation of the artillery, as well as the dash of the infantry, indicates that a high standard of training has been reached and their success is very largely due to the careful and thorough system of training which has been carried into effect."

the line on the night of the 8th/9th. On the latter night the 19th Divisional Artillery began the relief of the 50th Divisional Artillery. Divisional Headquarters were at Westoutre.

In these days all men lived by comparison and, compared with the Somme battlefields, the Division found its new sector uneventful and almost a rest area. Yet the amount of work to be done and carried out was tremendous. The defences were always in need of repair, patrols were constantly out examining the enemy's wire and trenches; artillery, machine-guns and trench-mortars "carried on," more or less active as occasion demanded. During the period—roughly two months—spent away from the Somme, there is little of outstanding importance to record.

The Spanbroekmolen-Wytschaete frontage was held barely a month and then, on the 6th of September, the Division took over a new sector from the 36th Division between the Lys and Douve rivers, the 58th Brigade taking over the right, the 56th the centre and the 57th the left sub-sectors.

Raids and fights in No Man's Land were more frequent in this sector and on the 15th of September the 9th Cheshires (58th Brigade), 7th East Lancashires (56th Brigade), and 8th Gloucesters and 10th Worcesters (57th Brigade) all raided the enemy's trenches with successful results.

The 7th Division relieved the 19th between the 19th and 21st of September, and on the 22nd the three infantry brigades were disposed in the following areas: 56th—Outtersteene; 57th—Pradelles; 58th—Merris, where the training of new drafts, refitting and recuperating kept all ranks busy for the next ten days.[1] Orders had already been received at Divisional Headquarters to return to the Somme area, and on the night of the 4th/5th of October the entrainment of the Division began. By the 6th all units had reached billets in the Marleux area, and on the 7th the 56th and 58th Brigades took over the front line from the 152nd Brigade (51st Division), which ran from about six hundred yards north of John Copse to the

---

[1] During this period of training the 57th Brigade was reviewed near Borre by H.M. the King of the Belgians on October 3rd. It was a notable parade, in which the Brigade presented a fine appearance. The King and the Divisional Commander lunched at 57th Divisional Brigade Headquarters, and the King expressed himself as greatly pleased with all he saw. The 57th Brigade had been doing a good deal of drill and had been inspected by General Sir H. Plumer commanding II Army on September 27th.

sunken road east of Hébuterne. The 56th Brigade was on the right and the 58th on the left. Each brigade held its front line with one battalion.

The Division held this sector for only a few days, for by the middle of the month the 31st Division had taken over the line and on the 17th the 56th Brigade was located at Vadencourt, 57th Brigade at Warloy, 58th Brigade at Herissart and the 5th South Wales Borderers at Bauchelles. These locations were temporary, for on the 21st of October the 56th and 57th Brigades moved to the Brickfields, 58th to Bouzincourt and the 5th South Wales Borderers to Toutencourt.

The following day a new sector of the front line was taken over, the 57th Brigade relieving troops of the 25th Division in Hessian Trench and Stuff Redoubt, and the 56th Brigade taking over the western portion of Hessian Trench and also Schwaben Trench from the 39th Division. This line lay immediately south of the Ancre in front of which was the village of Grandcourt.

CHAPTER IX
THE BATTLE OF THE ANCRE, 1916:
13th-18th NOVEMBER

ON the 23rd of October orders were received that operations on a large scale were to be undertaken by the Reserve Army, the attack to be delivered not only eastwards from north of the Ancre, but northwards also from south of the river. The II Corps (to which the 19th Division now belonged) was to attack northwards. The attack was originally designed to take place before the end of the month, but had to be postponed on account of the bad weather which greatly hampered preparations.

Winter had set in on the Somme and the low-lying country in the Ancre valley had begun to fill with water, the heavy rains turning trenches into waterways and the ground round about into spongy morasses. As the days grew shorter and greyer the desolation became more pronounced. The roads were thick with mud, the tracks across country mere mud walks and the pock-marked ground, churned up by shells of all calibre, exuded water which filled the shell-holes and polluted the air with nauseating smells.

But at present the 19th Division held ground which overlooked the river, for behind the 56th and 57th Brigades, which held the front line, were the ruins of Thiepval, which stood on a ridge, and in the distance, between them, was Grandcourt, which was in their line of attack to take place as soon as the weather allowed.

At 5 a.m. on the 26th the enemy, after a heavy bombardment, attacked the 56th Brigade, but was repulsed with heavy loss, leaving one warrant officer and forty other ranks prisoners in our hands.

Each night the ground between the opposing lines was patrolled by both Brigades and much information as to the enemy's defences and strength was obtained.

On the 26th, the 58th Brigade relieved both the 56th and 57th Brigades, but on the 29th the two latter took over the line again, each holding the same sector as before, *i.e.*, 57th on the right, 56th on the left.

The bad weather persisted, and on the 7th of November the Divisional Diary records: "Owing to a continuance of bad weather conditions the major operations mentioned on the 1st are now postponed indefinitely and orders have been issued that all efforts are to be directed towards consolidating the present system of trenches and improving accommodation and communications."

Between that period (1st to the 7th November) the artillery of both sides was extremely active. Again and again, especially during the time the 58th Brigade was relieving the 56th and 57th Brigades, the enemy's artillery, in response to the rocket signals sent up from his front line, placed an intense barrage on the whole front line of the 19th Division. The Stuff and Zollern Redoubts received the heaviest shelling. Yet in every instance the guns of the Division effectively stopped the enemy's barrage.

On the 8th the 57th Brigade relieved the 56th Brigade and on the 11th, as the weather had improved, the following reliefs were to take place in preparation for offensive operations which had once more been ordered: the 58th Brigade was to relieve the right and centre battalions of the 57th Brigade on the 11th, the remaining battalions of the latter Brigade (left and centre) being relieved by the 56th Brigade on the night of the 12th/13th November.

The fine weather continued, but although the scope of the operations of the Fifth Army remained the same, the attack was to be carried out by stages, the first on "Zero" day and the second on "Zero" plus two days.

In the first stage the II Corps was to capture a line about eight hundred yards in depth along the front of the 56th Brigade and the enemy's trench system along the southern bank of the Ancre up to, and including, the Hansa Line facing the 39th Division. This meant that only the left half of the Corps was to advance during the first stages of the operations, the 57th Brigade (19th Division) and 18th Division remaining stationary during the attack.

Of the 56th Brigade the 7th East Lancs. were on the right and the 7th Loyal North Lancs. on the left.

The 13th had been fixed as "Zero" day and 5.45 a.m. as "Zero" hour.

The attack went splendidly. On the right, the right company of the East Lancs. almost immediately gained its objective, and later the left company also reported that the line had been gained. The Loyal North Lancs., on the left, reached their objective in ten minutes, the men keeping close up to the barrage.

The enemy had been taken by surprise. The morning was misty, which aided the attack. The East Lancs. lost 7 officers killed, wounded and missing, and 96 other ranks; the Loyal North Lancs. 5 officers and 81 other ranks. Two officers and 98 other ranks were captured: they were from four different German regiments.

After the capture of the objective line the enemy showed little activity, though during the afternoon his guns shelled the lost positions heavily.

During the night of the 15th/16th the 58th Brigade relieved the 56th and the latter took over the line on the left of the Division previously held by the 118th Brigade, 39th Division.

On the 16th, at 6.30 p.m., the 19th Division was ordered to co-operate in an attack by the II Corps on the enemy's positions on the western outskirts, and south-east of Grandcourt; the 18th Division was attacking on the right of the 19th, while the V Corps, across the Ancre, was also taking part in the operations.

The 57th Brigade (right) and one battalion of the 56th Brigade (left) were to carry out the attack of the 19th Division. The battalion of the latter Brigade was to advance along the Hansa road (a road which ran from the south-west through the centre of Grandcourt) to the eastern outskirts of Grandcourt, and then consolidate a line north and south of the road: the 57th Brigade was to capture the German trenches running in a south-easterly direction from the objective of the 56th Brigade.

The attack was to take place on the 18th of November at 6.10 a.m.

But, as frequently happened, the scope of the operations was altered almost at the last moment, for the Divisional Diary records that at 12.45 a.m. on the 18th the operations were extended: after a short halt on gaining the first objective a further advance was to be made in an easterly direction through Grandcourt by the 56th and 57th Brigades, the second objective being roughly a north and south line through the eastern end of the village. After the capture of the second objective the 56th Brigade was to attack Baillescourt Farm.

Tanks were to assist the attacks on all objectives.

Baillescourt Farm lay just north of the Ancre, which could only be crossed by trestle bridges, thrown across the river by the Divisional Royal Engineers, on the capture of the second objective.

Operation Orders, issued by 57th Brigade Headquarters (Brig.-General G. D. Jeffreys) stated that the 8th North Staffords would attack on the right, the 10th Royal Warwicks in the centre and the 8th Gloucesters on the left. Three companies of the 10th Worcesters were detailed as "clearing-up" (or "mopping-up") parties: the remaining company was to form up in Stuff Redoubt in reserve.

The 57th Machine-Gun Company was to send two guns to follow closely in rear of the left of the 8th North Staffords, four guns to take up positions in Stuff Trench in order to cover the advance by overhead fire, and four guns to positions between the Lucky Way and the left of the Brigade boundary (about the junction of Irwin Trench and Hansa Lane) for a similar purpose.

The 82nd Field Company, R.E., was to construct three strong points along the captured objectives.

Orders issued from 56th Brigade Headquarters (Brig.-General F. G. M. Rowley) detailed the 7th South Lancs. as the attacking battalion, the advance to be carried out as follows: two companies up the Hansa road to the objective line on the western outskirts of Grandcourt: one platoon to move along the line of the railway from Beaucourt Hill to the extreme left of the objective, i.e., north-west of the village, to gain touch with the V Corps: three platoons to form carrying parties and establish a dump at the western outskirts of Grandcourt: one company in reserve.

Something should be said here of the strength of the 7th South Lancs., who were very weak in numbers: "A" Company numbered 88, "B" Company 77, "C" Company 89 and "D" Company 70; 49 other ranks were at Battalion Headquarters. Thus the battalion had a fighting strength of only 324 other ranks.

At 6.10 a.m. the barrage opened and the attack began under the worst possible conditions. Sleet was falling and at "Zero" it was still dark. Nevertheless battalions moved forward immediately, got right under the barrage and went forward with it. But once beyond the immediate neighbourhood of their own trenches the attackers were lost to view and the observers could see nothing.

It should be noted that ever since the 21st of October the plan of attack had been that the 57th Brigade should attack on the right of the Division and battalions had carefully reconnoitred their allotted fronts. When after many postponements, owing to the appalling conditions of weather and ground, the attack was eventually decided upon, the 57th Brigade was "side stepped" to the left so that the frontage on which it had to attack was new to it and unreconnoitred.

Battalions moved into their assembly positions after dark on the 17th, therefore they had never seen the ground over which they were to attack at daybreak on the 18th.

It was the sudden change to hard frost on the 15th/16th that decided the Higher Command to carry out the attack. It was still hard frost when the 57th Brigade went into the line on the night of the 17th, but by daybreak it was thawing again and the ground was once more a sea of mud: at "Zero" it was pitch dark and half-snowing, half-raining.

Under the circumstances the wonder is that the Gloucesters actually got into Grandcourt and stayed there, capturing a gun and prisoners, and that the left of the Warwicks reached the second objective.

The 8th North Staffords, in recording this attack, state: "After commencement of operations all touch seemed to have been lost with the battalion." No records exist of what happened to this unfortunate battalion, but its attack was a failure and the survivors made their way back as best they could to the old British line from which they had started. The Diary of Divisional Headquarters gives the following statement: "The 8th North Stafford Regiment, on the right, got across the first German line without serious opposition, but the cleaning-up party allotted to this trench went astray and as this was held by the enemy the battalion was cut off. A party of seventy of the battalion came back afterwards up Battery Valley but nothing has since been heard of the remainder." The Battalion Diary gives the casualties as 17 officers and 317 other ranks.

Lieut.-Colonel Parish, commanding the 8th North Staffords, had been "shell shocked" some days previously and evacuated. Lieut.-Colonel Anderson, a South African officer who had quite recently arrived as second-in-command, took over command of the battalion. This officer visited General Jeffreys after the War and told him that on the 18th, at

F

"Zero," the battalion went straight ahead and in the darkness passed over the enemy's front-line trench without recognising it (the Germans in it were lying low to avoid our barrage). The battalion went right on and was eventually held up by the German reserve line. Meanwhile the Germans in their front line had cut off all communication to the rear and the battalion was eventually compelled to surrender.

Of the 10th Royal Warwicks, in the centre of the 59th Brigade attack, the two right companies were apparently cut off and very few returned. "The 10th Royal Warwickshire Regiment," records the Divisional Diary, "got off too far to the left at first, but later on parties of them reached O.G.1 and bombing fights ensued. After a time, however, it became evident that these parties were isolated parties of the two right companies which had entirely disappeared. The left of the 10th Royal Warwickshire Regiment and the 8th Gloucestershire Regiment edged off a little to their left, but reached the objective in the northern portion of O.G.1."[1]

On the left, the attack of the 56th Brigade was more satisfactory, though considerably affected by the ill-luck attending the 57th Brigade. Only one battalion of the 56th Brigade attacked: the left battalion of the 57th Brigade (8th Gloucesters) had further to go and was the most successful of any, actually getting into Grandcourt. The left of the centre battalion (10th Royal Warwicks) also got forward a considerable distance and was in touch with the Gloucesters.

The 7th South Lancs. advanced well, but when some two hundred yards from their objective, came under heavy machine-gun fire from the north of the river. Yet, in spite of this, they reached and captured the objective and joined up with the 8th Gloucesters on their right.

Both the South and East Lancs. now sent bombing parties into Grandcourt village but, owing to the failure of the attack of the 57th Brigade, they had to be withdrawn later. During the afternoon, as the situation on the right was still obscure, the 9th Cheshires of the 58th Brigade were placed at the disposal of the 57th Brigade. At 5 p.m. the Cheshires attacked Sight and Desire trenches, between the Stump Road and Lucky Way.

---

[1] O.G.1 and O.G.2 were trenches which ran in a south-easterly direction and almost parallel with one another, from the western outskirt of Grandcourt to the Lucky Way.

But again, owing to the darkness, direction was lost and, failing to take any ground, they were recalled.

With regard to the above operations, which may be regarded as unsuccessful, it is only fair to the 19th Division to record the fact that the Divisional Commander from the first strenuously opposed the plan, both at Corps and Army Headquarters. The whole trench system held by the Division was a quagmire and men arrived exhausted in the front line and were in no state to attack. But more important still, the artillery had to fire over a steep hill and form a barrage on the downward slopes, the efficacy of which was more than doubtful. At the Corps Conference the G.O.C. predicted the failure of this portion of the attack owing to these conditions and asked that the attack should be only in the nature of a demonstration.

None of the Tanks allotted to the 19th Division advanced over the front line, and only one got to within two hundred yards of the Headquarters of the 57th Infantry Brigade.

When it was finally decided to abandon further offensive operations for the winter the 8th Gloucesters and 7th South Lancs. were withdrawn from the positions they had captured and a line about a thousand yards further back was consolidated.

As a result of the day's operations only the northern portion of O.G.1 to the left objective on the railway at the western end of Grandcourt had been captured and was in process of consolidation.

Late that night the 19th Division was ordered to be prepared to renew the attack on Grandcourt at a later date, but the next morning it was stated that: "The attack will not now be renewed and every effort will be made to improve the trenches in the front line." But work in the line was hardly resumed before the Division was relieved, for on the 20th the 11th Division was ordered to the relieve the 19th, the relief to be completed by 6 a.m. on the 23rd.

By the 30th of the month Divisional Headquarters were established at Bernaville, the 56th Brigade[1] at Fienvillers, 57th Brigade at Gezaincourt and the 58th Brigade at Mon Plaisir; and the Divisional Diary stated that: "The Division has now arrived in its new area where it will remain probably

---

[1] On the 20th of November Brig.-General W. Long, from the 6th Wiltshire Regiment, assumed command of the 56th Brigade vice Brig.-General F. G. M. Rowley.

for six weeks for purposes of training before taking the field again."

The story of the Battle of the Ancre, 1916, makes dismal reading: it could not be otherwise seeing the terrible conditions under which the attack took place. No troops in the world could have advanced more gallantly to the attack, but no troops in the world could have kept direction in the midst of a snow storm, intense darkness, and over ground that was thick in mud, pock-marked with shell-holes and with little or nothing to guide them to their objectives.

The four battalions which took part in the actual attack were the only ones in the Division which could in any way be called "fresh." For five months the Division had been fighting and, to their lasting credit, those who advanced to the attack on the 18th of November did so without a moment's hesitation against a very strong position, held by an enemy with all the courage of desperation.

Not since the 19th Division arrived in France had such appalling conditions been met with. The grimness of the Ancre battlefield became graven on the mind—the cold, the rain and snow, the ghastly gloomy country, the ceaseless shell-fire, the clinging mud into which men and horses sank sometimes with fatal results. All units suffered alike. Every round the artillery fired had to be carried up by pack transport, and the poor animals not infrequently collapsed and sank dead into the all-enveloping mud. The R.A.M.C., in bringing back wounded men, had a terrible time: the Sappers, the Pioneers, all seemed to wallow in mud.

Mud, mud, mud! such was the Ancre Battlefield in 1916.[1]

---

[1]General Sir G. D. Jeffreys adds the following interesting note: "The conditions then were, I think, the worst I ever remember in the war. The shell-fire was continuous, the ground was a mass of slimy mud which, in such trenches as there were, was up to and sometimes above the men's knees. There were shell craters full of water in which a man could easily be drowned, yet with it all, somehow or other, the men managed to keep an extraordinary good spirit and put up with the hardships, dangers, and the filth in a spirit which was extraordinarily different from that which is sometimes described in some, to my mind, very bad war books which have been appearing of late. What was unfortunate was that the Army Commander and the personnel of Army Headquarters could not realise the state of affairs in the front line, and the exhaustion which was produced in merely staying in the line in such conditions of ground and weather was wellnigh intolerable. If they had been able to realise it, I feel that the attack of the 17th November would never have been ordered. The marvel to me is that the Gloucesters and Worcesters ever got as far as they did."

CHAPTER X
THE WINTER OF 1916-1917

BACK in the Bernaville area the "Butterflies," having scraped and rid themselves of the awful mud of the Somme, began combined training. The word "combined" is used in the sense that not only were military exercises and drill carried out, but recreational training formed part of the daily programme carried out by all ranks. By means of competitions the keenness of all ranks for the reputation of their own particular unit was fostered and kept to the fore. If a man can be taught to play hard it is almost certain that he would train hard and fight hard. Bodily fitness is a fine antidote to bodily fear or morbidity. December was spent in training, absorbing reinforcements, refitting and in getting ready for the next tour in the line.

General Jeffreys adds the following interesting note on the system of training adopted by him when he took over command of the 58th and 57th Brigades (1st January and 22nd July, 1916, respectively), and later when he assumed command of the 19th Division in September, 1917.

"When at rest out of the line I borrowed from the Guards Division a number of good instructors who were employed during the period of rest in training officers and senior N.C.O.s in drill, etc. I also succeeded in getting two experienced Guards' ex-N.C.O.s as commissioned officers in the Brigades. These, combined with some lectures which I gave to all officers and senior N.C.O.s on discipline and organisation, laid the foundations of a much improved state of things.

"A further step I took when in the 58th Brigade was to introduce the custom of standing orders for duties in the trenches which I took direct from those in use in the Guards Division. These were adapted for the 19th Division as a whole by General Bridges and had the effect of greatly raising the system of vigilance, discipline and sanitation in the line. All the above I did with the full approval and concurrence of General Bridges.

"When I took over the command of the 19th Division in September, 1917, I continued the process and obtained more

Guards' ex-N.C.O.s as officers, eventually providing one at least to each battalion of the Division. The influence of these ex-Guardsmen was very great indeed. Practically all of them were employed as adjutants to their battalions and did first-rate work in that capacity. Some were kept as instructors pure and simple. With their aid I reorganised the Divisional School and Reinforcement Camp, which I placed under the command of Captain Snook, Adjutant of the 8th North Staffords, an ex-Company Sergt.-Major of the Grenadier Guards. Through the School was passed a large number of officers and N.C.O.s, who were instructed there, not only in drill and discipline, but also in bombing, Lewis gunnery and minor tactics. I cannot speak too highly of the work which the School did for the Division. As the G.O.C., 37th Division, said to me: 'There are a lot of good divisions in the Army, but there is only one which can be compared with the Guards for discipline and smartness, and that is the 19th.' "

During the last month of the year Brig.-General G. D. Jeffreys left the Division to assume command of the 1st Guards Brigade (Guards Division), and was succeeded in command of the 57th Infantry Brigade by Brig.-General C. R. Ballard.

Lieut.-Col. P. M. Davies, A.A. and Q.M.G., left the Division on appointment to XVIII Corps and was succeeded by Lieut.-Col. P. L. Buxton.

On the 5th of January, 1917, orders were received for the 19th Division to return to the front line and relieve the 31st Division in the Hébuterne sector during the 10th and 11th.

The move forward began on the 9th *via* Marleux, and was continued on the 10th[1] when the 57th Brigade, proceeding by bus and lorry, relieved the 93rd Brigade in the left sub-sector of the Divisional front, and the 56th Brigade took over the Reserve Brigade area from the 92nd Brigade. The following day the 58th Brigade proceeded also by bus and lorry to the right sub-sector, relieving the 94th Brigade of the 31st Division.

At noon on this date General Bridges assumed command of the Hébuterne sector, which ran approximately from Nairn Street, a communication trench on the northern edge of John Copse, to a point opposite the western apex of Gommecourt

---

[1] On the 10th of January Brig.-General A. E. Glasgow arrived and assumed command of the 58th Brigade *vice* Brigadier-General A. J. Dowell.

Park. Along both right and left sub-sectors the front line was held by posts.

On the 12th the 5th South Wales Borderers, who had been temporarily detached for work under the 7th Division, rejoined the 19th Division, and at 12 noon the C.R.A., 19th Division, took over the artillery defences of the sector from the C.R.A., 31st Division, though the relief of the artillery was not completed until the 15th.

With the exception of an intermittent bombardment carried out by the 19th Divisional Artillery, to which the enemy replied vigorously, causing a considerable amount of damage to the front-line and communication trenches, little happened on the 12th of January.

The enemy's infantry were very quiet, the General Staff Diary of the 19th Division describing his attitude as "inoffensive." Poor "Fritz," how he would have objected to that term!

Hardly had the Division taken over the line when extraordinarily severe weather set in. Hard frosts, freezing the ground to a depth of from twenty to twenty-four inches, accompanied by frequent and heavy falls of snow, caused the greatest discomfort. In the trenches and the shell-hole posts, which constantly needed repairing and strengthening, it was almost impossible to get a spade or pick into the ground: working parties had a terrible time. Yet, in spite of the very severe weather, the medical arrangements against "trench feet" were so effective that comparatively few casualties were incurred from that distressing affliction.

The only operation during the remainder of January was a raid by the 9th Welch of the 58th Brigade on German posts just south of The Point. The enemy, however, was on the alert, and none were captured although casualties were inflicted on him. The raid took place at 2.15 a.m. on the 31st.

A great loss was sustained by the Division on the 28th by the death of Brig.-General W. Long, who was killed in the trenches near the junction of Yankee Street and the Red Line in front of Hébuterne village. This very gallant officer knew no fear and it was while inspecting the front-line trenches that he met his death. He was succeeded in command of the 56th Brigade by Brig.-General E. Craig-Brown, who arrived on the 1st of February and took over from Colonel Trower who, for the time being, had assumed command.

On the 1st of February also H.R.H. The Prince of Wales inspected the 8th North Staffords at Courcelles au Bois.

On the night of the 3rd of February, the 7th Royal Lancs. and the 7th Loyal North Lancs., both of the 56th Brigade, raided the enemy. Only the latter entered the enemy's trenches and after thirty-five minutes, having seen no enemy, returned: the former were spotted by the enemy and were unable to penetrate his line.

A word about these raids: the Army Commander had notified General Bridges on the 29th of January that he wished the 19th Division to make one or more raids. It was essential to keep touch with the movements of the enemy's troops, for important events were to happen in 1917 and, as will be seen later, that year was to witness great fighting by the British forces in France and Flanders. The necessity was, therefore, urgent to keep a close watch on the enemy's defences, his strength, and to secure identifications from every sector along the whole line.

The first two raids have already been mentioned. The third, by the 10th Worcesters of the 57th Brigade, took place at 11.15 p.m. on the 11th of February. The strength of the raiding party was from 180-190 all ranks. Of the three parties the right and left entered the German trenches but the centre was unable to get in. Few Germans were seen and no identifications were obtained.

The barrage put down by the Divisional Artillery caused great damage to the hostile trenches, but the extent of the Boche casualties could not be ascertained.

There was one comment on the raid by the C.O. of the 10th Worcesters (Lieut.-Colonel D. M. Sole) which deserved (and no doubt received) attention. He said: "It is more apparent than ever that if the rank and file are to take active part in operations they must have more training at their work, and their own officers must get more chance of handling them, otherwise the fighting all falls on a few gallant men."

It should be noted that raids did not become such carefully-planned and highly scientific affairs as they were in later stages of the War, until 1917. Here and there, divisional, brigade and battalion commanders, with a genius for "raiding," had carried out successful raids, but generally it was not until the following year that the subject was studied more carefully and almost every unit of a division included in the operations.

Beyond the usual trench warfare nothing occurred until the latter part of February, when not only the great thaw came, but there was also a strange restlessness in the trenches on the opposite side of No Man's Land. The air was full of rumours which presently became certainties that the enemy intended the evacuation of a large portion of his front line north and south of the Somme.

CHAPTER XI

THE GERMAN RETREAT TO THE HINDENBURG LINE

ESPECIALLY in the neighbourhood (north and south) of the Ancre it is difficult, if not impossible, to distinguish the official defining line between the British Advance and the German Retreat to the Hindenburg Line in 1917. The exact point where the former ended and the latter began is beyond recognition, for even the German date of the Retreat (the 16th of March) is obviously inaccurate. Therefore, so far as the 19th Division is concerned, the two operations are narrated as one.

The official despatches state that "As soon as active operations again became possible, proceedings were commenced to drive the enemy from the remainder of the Beaumont Hamel Spur." But only the 3rd, 11th and 7th Division were engaged. The 19th Division held the sector from Hébuterne to opposite Serre until the 19th of February, when the 31st Division took over the northern portion of the line, leaving the 19th Division a front extending from Flag Street to Nairn Street (south to north). This was a distinct gain for the Division, for it meant that only one brigade need be in the front line, while the other brigades could devote time to training—an absolute necessity.

By the third week of February, however, although the 19th Division had not been engaged in the operations, the Beaumont Hamel Spur, Beaucourt, Grandcourt and Bailleul Farm and the Serre Spur had all been taken from, or evacuated by, the enemy.

The first mention of the Boche retirement occurs in the 19th Divisional General Staff Diary on the 24th of February: "Patrol report of 21st Manchesters received from 7th Division. Patrols advanced at 6 a.m. to western outskirts of Serre without opposition and saw no signs of enemy. Serre believed evacuated." At 9 p.m. that night there is a further reference: "G.301 from V Corps. Indications point to enemy having retired along all front of V Corps. Touch with enemy to be regained to-night. Division to push out patrols and arrange to bring up supporting troops."

The report was true. On the 24th Pys, Miraumont and Serre were evacuated by the Boche and were at once occupied by us.

The enemy's abandonment of position which he had (let it be admitted) fought most gallantly to retain, is thus explained in the words of General Ludendorff :

"The decision to retreat was not reached without a painful struggle. It implied a confession of weakness bound to raise the *morale* of the enemy and lower our own. But as it was necessary for military reasons, we had no choice: it had to be carried out.

". . . On February the 4th orders were given to carry out 'Alberich' according to plan. The first 'Alberich' day was February 9th. The retreat was to begin on March 16th, *but under enemy pressure might start at any earlier date.*"

The actual details of the "Alberich" plan were as follows: "Under the rubric 'Alberich' the Army Group of the Crown Prince Rupprecht had worked out a programme for the work of clearance and demolition, which was to be spread over five weeks. If an attack on the part of the enemy made it necessary we could at any moment interrupt this programme and begin our retreat. Our first object was to avoid a battle, the second to effect the salvage of all our war material and technical and other equipment that was not actually built into the positions, and finally the destruction of all high roads, villages, towns and wells, so as to prevent the enemy establishing himself in force in the near future in front of our new positions."

The new powerful line of defences, known as the Hindenburg (or Siegfried) Line ran from the northern banks of the Aisne between Crouy and Vailly in a north-westerly direction, to just west of St. Quentin, thence to just east of Arras. All the enemy's positions west of that line were to be abandoned.

The 57th Brigade, the only one of the three brigades of the 19th Division then holding the front line, records that on the 24th "news [was] received in afternoon of evacuation of Serre," and orders were issued immediately to the 8th Gloucesters to occupy Rhine Trench on the morning of the 25th.

When dawn broke on the 25th a dense fog shrouded the trenches of friend and foe alike. The fog was in our favour inasmuch that it rendered movement over open ground possible, yet it was likely to make the keeping of direction extremely difficult.

The 8th Gloucesters before 7 a.m. on the 25th had reached Walter Trench, just west of Serre, but several parties of the battalion lost their way in the fog and found themselves isolated. About midday, therefore, the situation was so unsatisfactory that reorganisation was carried out in the Brigade old front line and the Gloucesters moved off once more to occupy the Serheb road, which ran north-west from Serre. Here, during the evening, they were relieved by the 8th North Staffords, who then took up the advance and when darkness fell companies of that battalion held the following positions: one company at the junction of Wing Trench and Serheb Road (in touch with the 7th Division), one in Kaiser's Lane, one about Serheb Road, and one in support in Walter Trench.

Thus Serre had fallen at last, almost without a shot, though during the day the enemy had subjected his old front line to artillery fire. The fog during the morning had robbed him of the power of inflicting casualties by long-range rifle and machine-gun fire. In the evening, however, when the North Staffords attempted to advance on Puisieux they were held up by violent machine-gun fire from the village.

"By the evening of the 25th of February," record the official despatches, "the enemy's first system of defence from north of Gueudecourt to west of Serre, and including Luisenhof Farm, Warlencourt, Eaucourt, Pys, Miraumont, Beauregard Dovecot and Serre had fallen into our hands."

During the night of the 25th/26th the North Staffords pushed forward to Rhine Trench, and at 6 a.m. on the 26th held a line from the junction of Serre Alley and Rhine Trench, thence north along the latter to south-east of Star Wood, the Wood and Slim Trench to La Louviere Farm being also held by the Battalion. The advance on Puisieux was not (under Corps orders) to be made until afternoon unless the village was found unoccupied. The Staffords, however, found it possible to occupy Hock Trench whence patrols were sent forward to Box Alley.

At 1.30 p.m. the 19th Division received orders from the V Corps to occupy Knife and Fork Trenches as far as our artillery fire permitted. Orders also stated that when Puisieux and Rossignol Trench were occupied the 19th Division would probably be withdrawn from the line.

At about 5.30 p.m. the 10th Royal Warwicks moved forward to Rhine Trench from the old British front line, where they had been waiting all day, and relieved the 8th North Staffords, pushing on during the night of the 26th/27th into Box Wood and Rossignol Trench which they occupied with three companies, the fourth company remaining in Star Alley; the Staffords withdrew to Euston Dump. The position in Rossignol Trench was not, however, a sinecure, for the enemy was on both flanks. A German post of five men was captured by the Warwicks, but while the latter were establishing posts about fifty of the enemy rushed a Lewis-gun team, killing one man and wounding two. A block was then established in the trench. Touch with the 7th Division on the right and 31st Division on the left could not be obtained, though progress was made on the right.

During the evening of the 27th, the 10th Worcesters relieved two companies of the Warwicks in the front line. By this time the Warwicks had extended their right to the road junction in the north-western corner of Puisieux, though Knife and Fork Trenches, and Berg Trench on the left, were held in force by the enemy, who also had numerous troops in Rossignol Wood.

The general situation at the close of the 27th of February is thus described by Sir Douglas Haig: "The enemy's rear-guards in Puisieux-au-Mont were driven to their last position of defence in the neighbourhood of the church, and to the north-west of the village our front was extended to within a few hundred yards of Gommecourt. That evening our patrols entered Gommecourt village and park, following closely upon the retreating enemy, and by 10 p.m. Gommecourt and its defences had been occupied."

On the morning of the 28th the capture of Puisieux was completed. At dusk the Warwicks rushed Knife and Fork Trenches from the Puisieux-Bucquoy Road.

That evening the 9th Welch, of the 58th Brigade, arrived and relieved the 10th Warwicks and two companies of the 10th Worcesters, who moved back to Euston Dump.

At midnight, 1st/2nd of March, the 9th Welch attacked and gained possession of St. David's Trench—an hitherto unnamed trench north-east of Rossignol Trench—after a fight with the enemy in which they sustained 37 casualties. During the whole advance, however, from the 25th of February, casualties had been small, for the enemy resistance was mainly by rearguards, plentifully supplied with machine-guns.

Late on the 2nd, the Welch were relieved by the 6th Wilts.

and moved to Courcelles. During the night of the 2nd/3rd the Wilts. also improved their position by advancing their right and left flanks and establishing a line of posts in front of the main line of defence. Good patrol work was also carried out by the battalion. By 3.10 a.m. on the 3rd the 58th Brigade had reached the objective allotted to it.

On the night of the 3rd of March the 58th Brigade was relieved and moved back out of the line, the whole of the 19th Division having thus been withdrawn.

At 6 a.m. on the 4th of March Divisional Headquarters were at Couin, under orders to move to Bus: the 56th Brigade was at Bus, Lealvillers and Vauchelles, the 57th Brigade at Louvencourt, Courcelles and Arqueves; and the 58th Brigade at Courcelles, Couin and Bus. The Divisional Artillery Headquarters were at Couin (also under orders to move to Bus), and the 5th South Wales Borderers (Pioneers) at Courcelles.

The 19th Division had been in the line for nearly two months during exceptionally severe weather, and was in need of rest and refitting. But it was rather hard that, having helped to drive the Boche out of his positions, the Division had not the satisfaction of chasing him right back to the Hindenburg Line.

The stay in the Bus-en-Artois area was, however, but temporary, for on the 7th orders were received from V Corps Headquarters stating that the Division was to be transferred to the Second Army, and on the 9th the first stage of the march was carried out, *via* Beauval, Bouquemaison, Ramecourt (St. Pol), Pernes, Norrent Fontes, Steenbecque and Merris: the Division reaching the Fletre area on the 20th of March.

During March, Lieut.-Col. P. M. Johnson, G.S.O.I., left the Division and was replaced by Lieut.-Col. E. Hewlett, Devon R.

CHAPTER XII
IN THE YPRES SALIENT
TRENCH WARFARE AND PREPARATIONS FOR THE FLANDERS OFFENSIVE OF 1917

THE 19th Division now formed part of the IXth Corps of the Second Army under General Sir Herbert Plumer, who at this period was busily engaged in preparing for the coming Flanders Offensive.

According to orders the Division was to take over the Diependaal sector at the end of March from the 16th Division, but one Infantry Brigade (57th) was to relieve the 124th Brigade (41st Division) on the 22nd March, the 56th Brigade moving to an area near Recques, and the 58th Brigade to Caestre, where both Brigades were to begin training.

The G.O.C., 57th Brigade, assumed command of the sector on the 22nd. The front taken over by the Brigade on that date ran from the Vierstraat-Wytschaete road on the right to the Diependaal Beek (half a mile south-west of St. Eloi) on the left—a frontage of some 1,800 yards. The 8th Gloucesters and 8th North Staffords went first into the line, being relieved by the 10th Worcesters and 10th Royal Warwicks on the 27th. But the tour ended on the 30th when the 58th Brigade took over the front line, the 57th moving to the Meteren area.

Of that first tour in the line the 57th Brigade Diary records: "Nothing of importance occurred while the Brigade was holding the line. Two patrols from both battalions in front line went out on patrolling every night. The German front line in the Hollandscheschuur salient was entered on several occasions, but was always found to be unoccupied."

On the 31st General Bridges assumed command of the sector, Divisional Headquarters being established at Westoutre where the C.R.A. and C.R.E. also had their Headquarters.

The move of a division into a new sector in 1917 was by no means an easy task. First the whole of the area had to be reconnoitred, the state of the existing defences noted, and orders issued for their improvement or the construction of new trenches. Then every unit had to understand the "Defence Scheme"—usually a complicated business. The formation of all sorts of dumps, the selection of suitable positions for the artillery (if the incoming C.R.A. was not satisfied with existing positions): sites for the mounting of machine-guns: the selection of transport and wagon lines, for artillery, battalions, Army Service Corps and Field Ambulances. There were telephone wires to lay and signalling posts to be established.

The out-going division was supposed to hand over all these details to the relieving division, but every divisional and brigade commander had his own idea as to the suitability of positions, and changes were frequent. Thus, taking over a new sector was a somewhat strenuous and complicated business.

The new Divisional front was not an ideal position. The front line was dominated by the Boche positions on the Wytschaete Ridge, which overlooked not only our trenches but also our communication trenches, which were in full view of the enemy. The Vierstraat Ridge (in our lines), which commanded the front-line trenches, was itself defended by G.H.Q. second line. The Ridge offered a good line of observation and nearly all the 19th Divisional Artillery was located on or behind the high ground. The portion of the Ridge within the Divisional area was about 1,500 yards in rear of the front line and ran from the direction of Kemmel, past the cross-roads north-west of Vierstraat and Ridge Wood, thence to Scottish Wood. The possession of this Ridge would not have been of much importance to the enemy unless he used it for observation purposes in conjunction with other attacks on Kemmel Hill.[1]

When the Division first took over the front line it consisted of breastwork trenches. In places they were in bad repair and offered so little protection that they could not be occupied. The support trenches ran, on an average, about one hundred yards in rear of the front line: they were mostly derelict, though portions (mostly off the main communication trenches) were habitable. There was a new reserve trench which ran from Poppy Lane through the Bois Carre into Chicory Lane, thence in rear of the Bois Confluent. This line had a good field of fire, but being on the forward slope of the Ridge could be observed from the enemy's positions. Some three hundred yards behind the new reserve trench ran the old reserve

[1] He did so in 1918.

trenches (between Poppy Lane and Bois Carré) which were well sited and in good condition.

The Bois Carré had strong points at its southern, eastern and western corners, but when the 19th Division took over the sector the value of these redoubts was considered negligible, while Strong Point 7, situated in a small copse, was also in bad repair.

No sooner, therefore, had all these deficiencies been noted than a memorandum on the "Organisation of War" was issued and all units were soon busy on the defences. But almost simultaneously came the issue of lengthy instructions entitled "Work to be undertaken in preparation for Offensive Operations," which involved the provision of assembly trenches for the two Brigades.

The truth was out: the 19th Division had been transferred to a new sector in order to train and prepare to take part in a great attack upon the enemy—the Flanders Offensive of 1917.

On the 1st of April the 58th Brigade held the Divisional front line with two battalions (9th Cheshires right and 9th Royal Welch Fusiliers left), the 6th Wilts. in Ridge Wood Camp and the 9th Welch in Murrumbidgee Camp. The 56th Brigade was in the Cocoue area (7th North Lancs—Mentque, 7th South Lancs.—Nordausques, 7th Loyal Lancasters—Tournehem, 7th East Lancs.—Zouafques). Of the 57th Brigade, Headquarters with the 10th Royal Warwicks and 10th Worcesters were at Caestre, and the 8th Gloucesters and 8th North Staffords in the Meteren area. The Pioneers (5th South Wales Borderers) were just south-east of Scherpenberg. The machine-gun companies were with their respective brigades, also the trench-mortar batteries. The 81st, 82nd and 84th Field Companies, R.E., were at Tournehem, Baldoyle Camp and an R.E. camp north of Scherpenberg respectively. The three field ambulances, 57th, 58th and 59th, were at Recques, La Clytte and Westoutre, the A.D.M.S. having his headquarters in the latter village. The Train was at Frontier Camp. The Artillery was, at that date, moving into new positions.

The 58th Brigade held the front line until the night of the 17th/18th, though the 56th Brigade began to take over the sector on the 12th. From the diaries of all four battalions of the former brigades during that period, it is possible to deduce two things: that trench warfare was normal and that all battalions,

G

whether in or out of the front line, were continually at work on the defences, large working parties being supplied from those units in support and reserve for the purpose of preparing for the coming offensive.

The divisional artillery and the trench-mortars were continually engaged in wire cutting and in shelling the enemy's trenches in order to keep them in poor condition: that they did this successfully is evident from patrol reports. Patrolling was very active and small parties often succeeded in getting into the Boche trenches, gaining much useful information concerning his defences. Occasionally the enemy bestirred himself to action, as on the night of the 10th of April, when he raided some advanced posts of the Cheshires, capturing two men, besides killing an officer and one other rank, and wounding three more. And on one occasion at least he shelled the Divisional front line heavily after his trenches had been raided by the 16th Division on the left of the 19th, the former taking fifty prisoners.

Generally, however, trench warfare was normal, though the word "normal" must not be misunderstood. At all times life in the forward trenches was at the best a chance existence. Death claimed his victims by night and by day from shell-fire, trench-mortaring, machine-gunning or sniping: rare indeed were occasions when absolute peace reigned. Quietude on both sides of No Man's Land gave one an uncanny feeling that something was about to happen, and usually it did happen.

The above conditions describe "normal" trench warfare: for abnormal trench warfare there was only one word—it was "Hell!"

The 56th Brigade completed the relief of the 58th at about 7 a.m. on the 18th. But again there is little to record with the exception of violent shelling of the Divisional front line on the night of the 20th. The Boche was raiding the 16th Division on the left and followed the usual practice of shelling the flanking units. His artillery had a particular liking for Ridge Wood, which at all times of the day and night received the unwelcome attention of his guns. This wood was a wretched place: it was (as already explained) a mark for the enemy's guns, had few defences and these of an inadequate nature. The 7th South Lancs. thus described the place: "Ridge Wood is by no means a pleasant place to stay in. Like most other woods, it gets periodically shelled and the so-called dug-outs would hardly keep out a cricket ball thrown at them." Indeed, it was the practice to leave the wood when the Boche opened fire on it and take shelter in neighbouring trenches and dug-outs.

Throughout April the 57th Brigade did not go into the front line but spent the month in the Caestre, Hazebrouck, St. Omer, Westoutre and Scherpenberg areas where training and attack practices were carried out.

Towards the end of April orders were received at Divisional Headquarters for a move to the Hooge and Hill 60 sectors, where the 19th Division was to take over the line held by the 23rd Division. The 57th Brigade was to march first to Ouderdom and there relieve the 70th Infantry Brigade in the Hill 60 sector, while the 58th Brigade moved to Ypres to relieve the 68th Brigade at Hooge. The 56th Brigade was to be relieved by a brigade of the 16th Division on the 1st/2nd May.

On the 29th at 1.45 p.m. the 58th Brigade set out on the march to the Lindehoek Farm area, Brigade Headquarters being established at Poperinghe. The next day the Brigade began the relief of the 68th Brigade in the Hooge sector, the four battalions taking up the following dispositions: the 9th Cheshires took over the right sub-sector of the front line near Zillebeke, the 9th Royal Welch Fusiliers going into the left sub-sector: the 9th Welch were in support at Zillebeke and the 6th Wilts in Brigade Reserve in Ypres.

An officer of the 9th Welch thus describes the move from St. Lawrence Camp (between Poperinghe and Vlamertinghe) to the support trenches: "We moved by train which decanted us just short of Ypres. We marched through Ypres by night (leaving 'C' and 'D' Companies in Ypres) through the Lille Gate, past Shrapnel Corner, and relieved a battalion of the 23rd Division in close support of the Zillebeke sector of the line, having our headquarters at the Tuileries.

"So much has been written of Ypres that our opinions are hardly called for. Everyone who passed through the town formed his own opinion of the place, but all agree that it was an uncanny place. To us, on our move up to the line, though it was a bright moonlight night, it seemed a city of the dead. Not a soul was met in the streets and the only sound was the whine and crash of an occasional shell followed by a clatter of falling bricks and masonry. Troops we knew were billeted in the city, but none were about by night. In the moonlight the city had a peculiar beauty of its own. Shells by the thousand had fallen among its buildings and yet in the dim light little damage appeared on the exterior, but when one looked closely at the houses one saw that only shells remained—the interiors were gutted.

"By day the City looked gaunt and evil: from a distance the buildings seemed to be undamaged, but as one got closer, windows and doors showed charred and black interiors *like the sunken eye-holes of a rotting corpse.*"

On the night of the 2nd/3rd of May the 57th Brigade left Ouderdom for the Hill 60 sector, three battalions of the Brigade relieving the 70th Brigade (23rd Division) in the front line. The 10th Royal Warwicks took over the right sub-sector, the 10th Worcesters the centre, and the 8th North Staffords the left: the 8th Gloucesters were in support in Railway Dug-Outs.

An instance of that uncanny quietude which somehow always preceded considerable "activity" occurred on the night of the 8th/9th of May. The Diary of the 10th Royal Warwicks records that that particular night was "unusually quiet." The next morning the enemy's trench-mortars broke out furiously against the right of the Battalion's sector. In the afternoon observers reported unusual movement in the Boche lines and certain indications that a raid was imminent. Brigade Head-quarters were informed, also the units on the right and left of the battalion. At about 9.30 p.m. violent artillery activity developed and the enemy's guns literally plastered the line with shell of all calibre, but complete telephonic communica-tion was maintained between Battalion Headquarters and companies, and also with battalions on the right and left. The utmost vigilance was observed. But there was no action by the enemy's infantry on the Battalion front and at 11.10 p.m. all ·companies were told they might "stand down," though they were warned to maintain the closest watch on the enemy. At about 3.30 a.m. on the 10th, the enemy's guns again broke out into a furious bombardment and placed an intense barrage on the trenches of the Warwicks, chiefly on those held by the right company: the left company's support line, companies in support, dug-outs and Battalion Headquarters were also shelled violently. Efforts made by Battalion Headquarters to communicate by telephone with companies were unsuccessful excepting with "C" Company which, however, having replied "O.K." immediately "went off." Thus communication with the front line was completely severed. Scouts sent out reported that the support lines of both front-line companies were all right. An S.O.S. was sent up and the Divisional Artillery responded immediately and effectively.

When the enemy's barrage ceased, however, it was found that one of "D" Company's posts (No. 2, held by six men and a Lewis-gun) was missing, but some German grenades were found where the post had been. Nobody saw the Germans "come over." The remaining posts of "D" Company were very much knocked about, but otherwise intact. "C" Company's posts were untouched, though their support line had been badly blown in and they sustained a number of casualties.

There is no doubt, however, that the vigilance of the Battalion on the previous day and at nightfall was instrumental in nipping in the bud a big raid on the centre sub-sector held by the 8th Gloucesters, who had relieved the Worcesters on the night of the 6th/7th.

After the Warwicks had been relieved (on the night of the 10th/11th of May) the Brigadier visited them in Montreal Camp on the 12th and congratulated the Battalion on its work in the Salient, particularly on the night of the 9th/10th.

The 8th Gloucesters record that at 6 p.m. on the 9th they received from the 10th Worcesters the following message: "Much movement has been observed to-day in the enemy's front and support lines. Two officers were seen on The Caterpillar with maps and a large sheet of paper on which they appeared to be sketching our lines. This was at 1.50 p.m. They were seen again at 2.55 p.m. and at 5.10 p.m., and are still in position. In front of The Caterpillar some sand bags are visible which have a large white blob on: also two trees are marked in a similar manner. The white faces our lines. Several men were seen carrying planks in front line at 4 p.m. in front of Caterpillar."

The Caterpillar was a mound resembling a caterpillar in shape, some two hundred to three hundred yards south of Hill 60 and on the southern side of the Ypres-Comines railway: Hill 60 was north of the railway.

Immediately on receipt of this information the O.C. 8th Gloucesters ordered the Battalion to "stand to" for the night. What happened is told in the Battalion Diary in the following words:

"At 9 p.m. the enemy opened a heavy fire on our front line.

This fire extended to the battalions on the right and left. The enemy also opened machine-gun fire on the front-line parapet. There appears every probability that he was on the point of raiding the sector. The artillery opened fire on the S.O.S. lines and a heavy machine-gun and rifle fire was opened from our front line. The raid was completely checked. At 4 a.m. the enemy repeated his tactics, his fire, if anything, being heavier than before. Clear indications of a raid were noticeable. Much movement was heard behind the enemy's line and the rattle of metal (presumably tools) was distinctly heard before the enemy's barrage started. Our artillery opened again on the S.O.S. line and the raid was again checked before the enemy could get clear of his own lines."

On the night of the 11th/12th the Gloucesters were relieved by the 12th Durham Light Infantry, for the front held by the 19th Division was being taken over again by the 23rd Division, the former having been ordered to move back to the Diependaal sector.

The 56th Brigade moved by march route from Poperinghe to camp in the Scherpenberg area and relieved the 49th Brigade in the old front line on the night of the 9th/10th of May; the 57th Brigade moved also to the Scherpenberg area, but on the 11th, and began training; the 58th Brigade was the last to leave the Ypres Salient and it was the night of the 12th/13th before the 70th Brigade of the 23rd Division took over the line. The 58th Brigade then moved to Poperinghe and on the 13th to Berthen.

The G.O.C., 19th Division, assumed command of the Diependaal sector on the morning of the 12th of May.[1]

The remainder of May passed without any incident of outstanding importance taking place. Two raids were made during the month, one by the 7th North Lancs. at 2 a.m. on the 17th, on Object Trench, which was unsuccessful in

---

[1]The 19th Division was now commanded by Major-General the Hon. A. R. Montagu Stuart-Wortley, C.B., D.S.O., Major-General G. T. M. Bridges, C.B., C.M.G., D.S.O., having been appointed to accompany the British Mission to the United States of America on the entry of that country into the War: he had left for England on the 6th of April. On this date also Brig.-General C. R. Ballard, C.B., G.O.C., 57th Infantry Brigade, proceeded to England, Brig.-General T. A. Cubitt assuming command of that Brigade. On the 25th of May, however, Major-General the Hon. A. R. M. Stuart-Wortley left to command the 32nd Division and Major-General C. D. Shute arrived to take command of the 19th Division.

obtaining identifications, the other by the 10th Worcesters on the crater at Nag's Nose on the 27th, during which several prisoners were taken belonging to the 33rd Fusilier Regiment.

All units were now leading a very strenuous existence: in the front line patrol work was constant: extraordinary precautions were necessary to prevent the enemy discovering the presence of mines, which were to form a special feature in the forthcoming operations. These mines had been completed some nine months previously. The enemy's wire, the whole of his front-line defences, the movement of his troops—all needed a vigilant watch. When out of the front line the amount of work to be done was prodigious and no battalion was free from the necessity of providing large working parties.

But, beyond all this preparation for the great battle, nothing of outstanding importance happened until just before "Zero" day, *i.e.*, the day upon which the offensive was launched.

At 3 p.m. on the 5th of June one company of the 9th Royal Welch Fusiliers (58th Brigade), right, and one of the 7th King's Own Royal Lancaster Regiment (56th Brigade), left, carried out a raid on the enemy's trenches for the purpose of securing identifications and as many prisoners as possible: the raid was in conjunction with a practice barrage by the artillery and was a splendid success.

Under cover of the barrage the two companies crossed No Man's Land and had no difficulty in entering the enemy's trenches, which had been almost demolished by our guns. The Germans had either betaken themselves to their dug-outs or else were found crouching close against the walls of their battered trenches in a demoralised state. The Royal Welch Fusiliers took 37 prisoners and killed at least 15 of the enemy; the King's Own Royal Lancasters captured 1 officer and 40 men. Having carried out their orders both companies threw smoke bombs and retired rapidly to their own lines under cover of the smoke cloud and barrage.

The King's Own lost 3 officers wounded, and 1 man killed and 5 wounded; the Welch Fusiliers 1 officer seriously wounded, 2 men killed and 9 wounded.

This highly successful raid—the largest made by the 19th Division up to that date—drew many congratulations.

CHAPTER XIII

THE BATTLE OF MESSINES, 1917

THE capture of the Messines-Wytschaete Ridge, which lies about midway between Armentieres and Ypres, was necessary before the offensive could be launched further north in the Ypres salient. The Ridge is situated on the eastern end of a range of abrupt, isolated hills dividing the valleys of the Lys and the Yser rivers, linking up that range with the rising ground which, from Wytschaete, stretches north-eastwards to the Ypres-Menin road, thence northwards, *via* Passchendaele, to Staden.

Messines, situated on the northern spur of the Ridge, commanded a wide view of the valley of the Lys, enabling the enemy to enfilade the British lines south. Wytschaete, situated on the highest part of the Ridge, commanded even more completely the town of Ypres and the whole of the old British positions in the Ypres Salient.

The German front-line trenches ran along the western foot of the Ridge in a deep curve from the Lys opposite Frelinghien, nearly to the Menin road; it then turned north-west past Hooge and Wieltje. The enemy's second line of defence followed the crest of the Messines-Wytschaete Ridge, forming an inner curve. In addition, two chord positions crossed the base of the salient from south to north; the first, known as the Oosttaverne Line, lay slightly east of the village of that name; the second, the Warneton Line, crossing the Lys at Warneton and running parallel with the Oosttaverne Line, but a little more than a mile east of it.

For more than two years the enemy had devoted the greatest skill and energy to developing the natural advantages of his position, and not only Messines and Wytschaete but numerous woods, farms and hamlets had been organised as main centres of resistance.

The actual front selected for the attack extended from a point opposite St. Yves to Mount Sorrel (right to left)—a distance of between nine and ten miles, the final objective being the Oosttaverne Line, which lay between those two points.

At the moment of assault, fixed at 3.10 a.m. on the 7th of June, nineteen deep mines were to be exploded beneath the enemy's trenches—a feature without parallel in land mining: over a million pounds of explosives were used in the charging of these mines.

The front of attack allotted to the 19th Division was bounded on the south by the Vierstraat-Wytschaete road, and on the north by the Diependaal Beek. The 16th Division was attacking on the right and the 41st Division on the left of the 19th Division.

Operation orders for the attack cover many foolscap sheets of typescript which, condensed, give the following essential points: the 58th Brigade, on the right, and the 56th, on the left, were to capture the three first objectives, i.e., Red, Blue and Green Lines; the 57th Brigade was then to pass through and capture the fourth objective—the Black Line—and subsequently push forward an outpost line.

The attack was to be made not only under an artillery barrage but, for the first time, the Division was to employ an organised machine-gun overhead barrage.

The Divisional R.E. and the Pioneers were not only to construct strong points on the captured objective lines, but were to prepare one overland track in each brigade area as far forward as the Green Line, fix signboards in the German trenches, search for possible sources of water and dug-outs, and render dug-outs which had been partially destroyed serviceable.

Of the 58th Brigade the 6th Wilts, on the right, and 9th Royal Welch Fusiliers, on the left, were to capture the Red Line; the 9th Welch, on the right, and the 9th Cheshires, on the left, were then to pass through and capture the Blue and Green Lines.

The 56th Brigade was to attack with the 7th King's Own Royal Lancasters on the right, and the 7th Loyal North Lancs. on the left, to capture the Red Line, and the 7th East Lancs. (right), and 7th South Lancs. (left) to capture the Blue and Green Lines.

The Green Line having been captured the four battalions of the 57th Brigade were to attack and capture the Black Line in the following order from right to left: 10th Worcesters, 8th Gloucesters, 10th Warwicks and 8th North Staffords; they were then to push forward outposts.

The attacking infantry were to be covered by six brigades of Field Artillery[1]—in all 108 18-pdrs., and 36 4.5 in. howitzers. The "Heavies" were also to co-operate.

The Royal Engineers and 5th South Wales Borderers (Pioneers) were alloted to brigades as follows: 81st Field Company, R.E. (less two sections) and two platoons of "D" Company, 5th South Wales Borderers to the 56th Brigade 74th Field Company, R.E. (less two sections) and two platoons of "D" Company, 5th South Wales Borderers, to the 58th Brigade, 82nd Field Company, R.E., "A" Company, 5th South Wales Borderers, to the 57th Brigade. These troops were to construct strong points in the captured lines. They were to follow in rear of the assaulting troops. The remaining two sections of the 81st and 94th Field Companies, R.E., and "B" and "C" Companies of the Pioneers were to be employed directly under the C.R.E. in order that pack and wheeled transport could be sent forward quickly.

During the night of the 6th/7th of June the various units of the Division moved to their assembly positions without a hitch—only six casualties occurred in the whole Divisional area, and by 2.45 a.m. on the 7th everyone was ready for, and anxiously awaiting, "Zero" hour.

The thing which held everyone in the grip of expectancy was the great explosion of mines at "Zero" hour. On the 19th Divisional front these were to "go up" beneath the Holland-scheschuur Salient, that portion of the enemy's line opposite the right front of the Division of which Nag's Nose formed part.

As "Zero" hour approached Kemmel Hill and every point of vantage behind the front lines for miles around had its little group of Staff Officers and others whose immediate duties did not demand their presence in the forward area.

It was still dark as the hands of synchronised watches drew nearer and nearer the hour, and then at last touched "Zero," i.e., 3.10 a.m.

Immediately the ground trembled and shook as if a violent eathquake was in progress. There was an ear-splitting roar which numbed the senses for the first few seconds, leaving the

[1]The 87th and 88th Brigades, R.F.A. (the 19th Divisional Artillery) were supplemented by the 77th, 150th, 155th and 232nd Brigades, R.F.A. For the reorganisation of the 19th Divisional Artillery during 1916 and 1917, see Appendix.

THE BATTLE OF MESSINES: A CAPTURED GERMAN TRENCH IN WHICH WAS A TELEPHONE EXCHANGE
THE TRENCH WAS RENAMED "OBLIGE TRENCH"

body incapable of movement and the brain inactive from the violent concussion. The sudden sheets of fire which shot up into the air resembled flaming water spouts. Clouds of smoke and dust hung over the enemy's trenches while the mangled bodies of Germans were flung about in all the ghastly contortions of a violent death. Little wonder that Sir Douglas Haig referred to the explosion of the nineteen mines as "without parallel in land mining."

As the mines "went up" so our artillery barrage fell on the German trenches, or the tumbled and troubled earthworks which had once been a carefully-dug and well-organised trench system.

"Covered by a concentrated bombardment which overwhelmed the enemy's trenches and to a great extent neutralised his batteries, our troops," the despatches state, "swept over the German foremost defences all along the line."

The infantry of the 19th Division got across No Man's Land well up to time. The enemy left alive in the front-line and front-line support trenches surrendered immediately; their power of resistance had gone, the awful holocaust which had passed over them had left them incapable of further resistance. Their own artillery lent them but feeble support, for the German guns had been "smothered" by our fire. One hostile battery only was firing on Bois Carre, while a few shells were falling near the new reserve line. At 3.50 a.m. the 56th Brigade was reported to be through the German second lines, and going on to the Red Line, which the 7th Loyal North Lancs. reported they had taken, with 40 prisoners, at 3.45 a.m., the message reaching Brigade Headquarters at 4.10 a.m. Next, at 4.27 a.m., the 58th Brigade was also reported on the Red Line, where the Wilts. had taken 5 machine-guns, 3 trench-mortars and 179 prisoners, the 9th Royal Welch Fusiliers, on their left, taking 5 machine-guns and 80 prisoners.

The Red Line was then in process of consolidation.

At 4.48 a.m. a message from 58th Brigade Headquarters reached Divisional Headquarters that the 9th Cheshires had passed over the Red Line at 4.15 a.m., and were advancing towards the Blue Line, which they appear to have taken by 4.50 a.m., also capturing many prisoners; touch was obtained on the left with the 9th Welch Regiment. The 56th Brigade reported that the 7th South Lancs. were on the Blue Line at

5.5 a.m., that battalion having captured Catteau Farm, in which were found two machine-guns. By 5.32 a.m. consolidation of the Blue Line was in progress.

From 4.50 a.m. the enemy's shell-fire was reported to be very heavy: his long-range and heavy guns and field-guns, off which our counter-battery fire had lifted, had come into action again. Yet casualties were not heavy.

After passing the Blue Line some parties of men advanced through the protective barrage and pushed forward to the Green Line. Fortunately, however, it was possible to recall these parties before the barrage fell on the Green Line.

The infantry were timed to reach the latter line at 7.20 a.m. and at 7.30 a.m. a message reached Divisional Headquarters from the "Heavies" that not only had the Green Line been captured but also a portion of the Black Line.

The early morning mist had lifted and the sun was shining when the advance from the Blue Line began.

Both the 9th Welch and the 9th Cheshires (58th Brigade) were on the Green Line up to time, when they began at once to consolidate.

Of the 56th Brigade, the 7th East Lancs. and the 7th South Lancs. reported taking the Green Line according to schedule.

At 7.50 a.m. the whole of the Green Line was reported to Divisional Headquarters as having been captured.

The advance of the 57th Brigade began at 8.10 a.m., the pre-arranged time. But again there was little resistance from the Germans, who either ran forward to surrender or (if they could do so) ran away: very few of them put up a fight. The four battalions, *i.e.*, the 10th Worcesters, 8th Gloucesters, 10th Warwicks and 8th North Staffords, then began the work of consolidation, each having first sent a company forward, according to orders, to occupy the Mauve Line which ran roughly along the eastern edge of Oosttaverne Wood. At 10.15 a.m. all battalions of the 57th Brigade were reported to have occupied the Black and Mauve Lines.

But at 12.40 p.m. Brigade Headquarters received orders from the Division (which had received them from Corps Headquarters) that the task of the Brigade had been extended, and that at 3.10 p.m. Oosttaverne Village and Oosttaverne Line, from Polka Estaminet to about seven hundred yards east of Odonto Trench, were to be attacked and captured. The barrage was to open at 2.55 p.m.

Time was short to organise a fresh attack, but fortunately telephonic communications had held and were excellent. The 58th and 56th Brigades were ordered to relieve the 57th on the Black Line immediately, and the latter to concentrate three battalions north-west of Oosttaverne Wood to carry out (as already stated) the assault of Oosttaverne Village and the Oosttaverne Line.

The Divisional Narrative then states "that the assault succeeded, reflecting the greatest credit on all ranks of the 57th Brigade, as it was impossible to get any detailed orders to company or platoon commanders in the time available."

The 8th Gloucesters attacked on the right, the 10th Warwicks on the left, the 8th North Staffords were in support, and the 10th Worcesters in reserve.

The 57th Brigade Narrative of this advance states that it was "a great gamble owing to the short time available for preparation." The Gloucesters and North Staffords, however, followed the barrage as closely as possible and, owing to skilful leading and the complete disorganisation of the enemy, captured their objectives with small loss. In conjunction with the 82nd Field Company, R.E., and "B" Company of the 5th South Wales Borderers (Pioneers), consolidation was begun, touch being established on the right with the 3rd Australian Division, and on the left with the 24th Division.

At 5 p.m., however, an unlooked-for event happened: our barrage began to fall short and the 8th North Staffords, 10th Warwicks and 8th Gloucesters (having suffered considerable casualties), were eventually forced to fall back to the Odonto Line, where they started to dig in afresh. But at dawn on the 8th they again went forward and occupied their original line. Early in the morning each battalion sent out a raiding party, bringing back a number of prisoners from various farms and dug-outs on their immediate front.

The total casualties suffered by the 19th Division from the 7th of June to noon of the 8th of June were approximately 51 officers and 1,358 other ranks killed, wounded and missing. The number of prisoners taken was 1,253, and in material the captures were 14 guns, 14 machine-guns, 36 trench-mortars, but the Division reported that: "There is much more material which will be found and brought in later."

The great success which had attended the attack of the 19th Division drew from Corps and Army Headquarters many congratulations. That success was due not only to the excellent arrangements made by all commanders and the hard work of all units in preparing for the offensive, but also to the very efficient artillery preparation and splendid leading by battalion and company commanders. There was not one unit of the Division which did not contribute to the fine results obtained. The machine-gunners handled their guns with great ability: for the first time the machine-gun companies fired an organised machine-gun overhead barrage—a new form of covering fire which proved a great success. Those units whose work lay both behind and in the forward areas, *i.e.*, the medical units, whose gallant doctors and stretcher bearers first attended to, and then picked up the wounded at the aid posts, and carried them back to the dressing stations, thence to be evacuated along the whole chain of communications, and the Army Service Corps, who were responsible for the supply of rations and water, the Divisional Ammunition Column, who were responsible for the transport of ammunition, the hard-worked signallers, whose devotion kept telephonic communication open, the Field Companies, R.E., and the 5th South Wales Borderers, who carried out valuable work in consolidating the objectives gained—all shared in the success of their Division.

Messines, 1917, was one of the 19th Division's[1] greatest triumphs.

---

[1] In "Sir Douglas Haig's Despatches" (Boraston) there is a mistake. The 19th Division is given as being commanded by Major-General G. T. M. Bridges. The Division was actually commanded by Major-General C. D. Shute, who had taken over command from Major-General A. R. Montagu Stuart-Wortley on the 24th of May until General Bridges, who had been to America as the Military Member of Mr. Balfour's Mission to the United States on the entry of that country into the War, and did not again take over command of the 19th Division until the 19th of June, 1917, *vide* Appendices.

The Battle of Messines, 1917.
7th June.

Red Line shown thus ∘∘●●●●∘∘
Blue ......„...........„.........„... ▫▭▫▭▫
Green ...„............„........„.... ▭▭▭▭▭▭▭▭
Black ..„............„........„... ▬▬▬▬▬▬▬▬
German Front Line ..„....... ⌐⌐⌐⌐⌐

41ST

Left Bde.

+35

Right Bde.

Ze Woo

Zero-Ho.

16TH Div.

+35

+1·40

Black Cot

Wytschaete

Sca

100 0 100 200 300 400 500

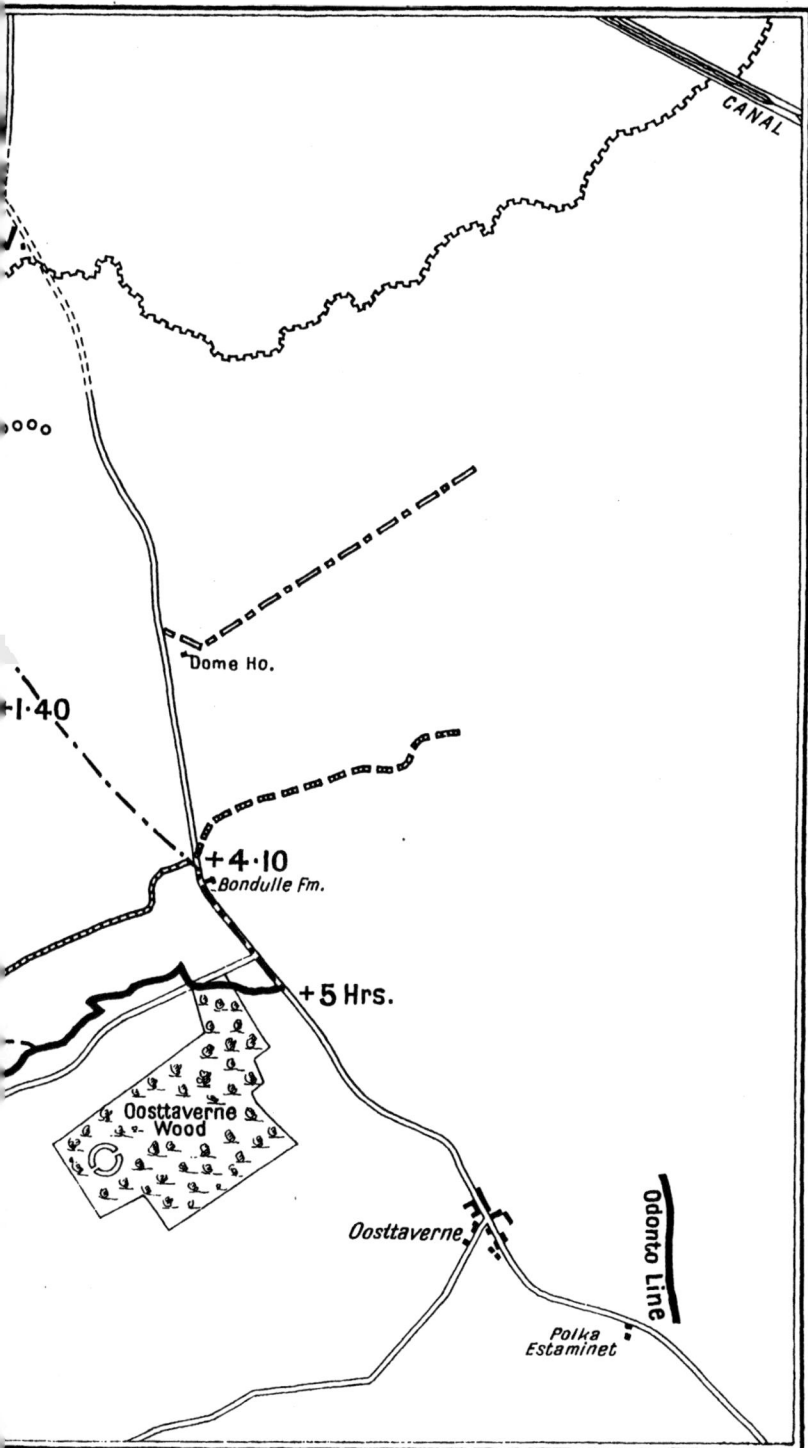

CANAL

Dome Ho.

+1·40

+4·10
Bondulle Fm.

+5 Hrs.

Oosttaverne
Wood

Oosttaverne

Odonto Line

Polka
Estaminet

Yards

2000

CHAPTER XIV
THE BATTLES OF YPRES, 1917

THE general results of the Battle of Messines, 1917 (the first stage of the Flanders Offensive) were the complete capture of the Messines–Wytschaete Ridge and the advancement of the British line on practically the whole front, from the River Warnave to Klein Zillebeke. Final preparations and dispositions for the main offensive east and north of Ypres were then taken in hand. That offensive was due to begin on the 31st July.

In the meantime the 19th Division was busily engaged in strengthening the defences of the newly-captured Oosttaverne Line, in digging new trenches, and in the thousand-and-one jobs necessary in order to make the line secure.

The Division was due for relief on the night of the 19th/20th of June, but before handing over command a successful demonstration raid was carried out by the 56th Brigade on Verhaege Farm and some neighbouring houses. The raiding party consisted of one-and-a-half companies each from the 7th East Lancs. and the 7th South Lancs. Regiments.

The report by Brigade Headquarters is as follows: "14th June. 7.30 p.m. 'Zero' hour, excellent barrage to which the enemy replied within twenty seconds by shelling the village, forward trenches and in front of front line. Battalions had no difficulty in reaching their objectives and searching them thoroughly, but only a few of the enemy were found. As a demonstration the operation was apparently successful, having regard to the amount of hostile shelling which was drawn to it. Casualties reported rather heavy: 7th East Lancs., 35 other ranks; 7th South Lancs., 1 officer, 14 other ranks."

On the 19th of June Major-General G. T. Bridges returned from the U.S.A. and re-assumed command of the Division.

On the 20th of June, at 10 a.m., the G.O.C., Division, handed over command of the line to the 36th Division, and the same afternoon Divisional Headquarters opened at St. Jan's Cappel, to which area the three infantry brigades had moved back for a short period of training. Early in July the Division returned to its old sector, the Oosttaverne Line. The 57th

Brigade was first in, having begun to move forward to the support area on the 1st of July. On the night of the 2nd/3rd the Brigade relieved a brigade of the 37th Division in the front line, and at 10 a.m. on the 3rd of July the G.O.C., 19th Division, assumed command of the line.

The situation in the front line was one of considerable activity. Patrolling by both sides was constant, and raids were frequent. The Division had been ordered to assume an aggressive policy and push forward whenever possible, nibbling (so to speak) bits of the enemy's front line by continually throwing out posts and consolidating them as well as capturing farms and houses which came in the line of advance. These small actions kept the fighting spirit of the troops tuned up to the highest pitch, and many gallant deeds were done. In particular there was the extraordinary bravery of a private of the 10th Worcestershire Regiment (Private T. Stevenson).

During the afternoon of the 5th of July the 10th Worcesters sent out two patrols, both being very heavily fired on. One was unable to get any distance, but the other, consisting of one N.C.O. and two men, crossed a road out in front of our outpost line and apparently penetrated the enemy's line of posts. They had only gone a short distance when the N.C.O. was shot down and one of the other men wounded. The third man, Private Stevenson, under heavy fire, then began to make his way back by jumping from shell-hole to shell-hole. Unfortunately, he jumped into a hole containing six Germans, by whom he was taken prisoner. His captors took him back to a dug-out containing a machine-gun and a team of six men. After a time two of the Germans went out, and, waiting his opportunity, Stevenson attacked the remaining four men, and after knocking out two of them, succeeded in escaping from the dug-out. Though heavily fired on and bombed this gallant man reached his own lines.

The 10th Warwicks slightly advanced their line on the night of the 5th, and the 8th Gloucesters and 8th North Staffords also pushed forward their front on the night of the 9th. On the 10th General Cubitt (commanding 57th Brigade), who went up to see the new front line, reported that the advance on the 9th was "an extraordinarily good show."[1] On the 17th the

---

[1] In recognition of the skill and gallantry displayed by the 8th Gloucesters in capturing Druid's Farm on this occasion, the Divisional Commander gave that battalion the right to wear the Divisional Butterfly on the sleeve of the service jacket.

9th Cheshires of the 58th Brigade attacked and captured Junction Buildings, which, however, were lost again on the 18th. Another counter-attack was launched by the 58th Brigade at dawn on the 19th, and by 3.35 a.m. the Buildings had been taken, but two hours later the enemy came on again in greatly superior numbers without artillery preparation, and, taking the captors by surprise, drove them out. The 56th Brigade next attacked the place (on the 22nd), and Junction Buildings were, for the third time, wrested from the enemy. The cost had, however, been so heavy that the Brigade Commander ordered a withdrawal near to the original line. Junction Buildings thus remained in the enemy's hands until the Battles of Ypres had begun.[1]

On the night of the 27th/28th, a party of the enemy, belonging to the 31st R.I.R. and Fourth Army *Sturm Truppen*, attacked the 8th Gloucesters with the object of blowing up Wall Farm. They were repulsed with considerable loss. A few Germans obtained a footing in a post but were at once ejected by a well-led counter-attack. All men of the 8th Gloucesters were accounted for. The battalion suffered two officers and about sixty-five other rank casualties in repelling the raid.

Towards the end of July preparations for the opening of the offensive were nearing completion. The great attack was to be launched on the 25th, then on the 28th, but owing to the French, on our left, not having all their guns in position (the French had only just taken over the line on the left of the Fifth British Army), a further postponement was agreed to until the 31st of July.

THE BATTLE OF PILKEM: 31st JULY–2nd AUGUST

In this, the first of the Battles of Ypres, 1917, the allied front of attack extended from the Lys River, opposite Deulemont, northwards to and beyond Steenstraat, a distance of over fifteen miles. The main attack, however, was to be made by the Fifth Army from the Zillebeke–Zandvoorde road to Boesinghe, a front of roughly seven and a half miles. The task of the Second Army was to cover the right of the Fifth and advance only a short distance, its principal object at this stage being to increase the area threatened by the attack and so compel the

---

[1] On the 19th of July the 246th Machine-Gun Company joined the 19th Division from England.

H

enemy to distribute the fire of his artillery over a greater portion of our front line. On the left of the Fifth Army, the First French Army was to advance its right in close touch with the former and so secure it from counter-attack from the north.

The left division of the Second Army (41st Division) was to attack astride the Ypres–Comines Canal. This Division was on the immediate left of the 19th Division; the 37th Division was on the right of the 19th.

In the "General Plan" which formed the preamble to 19th Divisional Operation Orders it is stated that: "These operations, which will be preceded by several days' bombardment, should create the impression of a serious attempt to capture the Warneton–Zandvoorde Line," though, as a matter of fact, the objectives allotted to the 19th and 37th Divisions were only from 1,000 to 1,500 yards in depth.

The X (41st Division) and IX Corps (19th and 37th Divisions) were to capture the Blue Line, which, in the area of the 41st Division, included Hollebeke, and along the 19th Divisional front ran from Bee Farm on the south to just east of Forret on the north. Two battalions of the 63rd Brigade (37th Division), on the immediate right of the 19th Division, would be attached to the latter for the first phase of the operations; they were to capture the Blue Line from July to Bee Farms. In the second phase of the attack the two battalions of the 63rd Brigade were to come again under the orders of their own division, and the latter was to attack at a later hour from south of July Farm.

The 56th Brigade had received orders to carry out the attack along the front of the 19th Division on a three-battalion frontage.

The 7th Royal Lancs., on the right, 7th East Lancs., in the centre, and 7th North Lancs., on the left, were the assaulting battalions; the 7th South Lancs. were in support.

The three attacking battalions were to assemble in the brigade front line and in the line of supporting posts in rear; all four companies of the support battalions were to assemble in the old British line and at "Zero" advance in artillery formation and occupy the front-line system, which by that hour would be vacated by the three assaulting battalions.

The latter were each to have all four companies in the line, each company on a frontage of two half platoons.

"Zero" hour was fixed at 3.50 a.m. on the 31st of July.

There is with the Diary of 56th Brigade Headquarters a document entitled, "Notes on Conference given by the Divisional Commander to the officers of 56th Brigade, 26/7/17," one paragraph of which, concerning the attack, reads: "There are two phases of the attack—(*i*) getting there; (*ii*) staying there. The attack in prospect is a new proposition for the brigade. There is no position or line of trenches to be attacked, only strong points supporting each other, and an enemy scattered in shell-holes and short lengths of trenches. Simultaneous pressure in the attack is the way to deal with this. The troops must not be 'sticky' but keep up to the barrage. The attack on strong points must be organised beforehand. They must, if possible, be rushed at the point of the bayonet, and bombing fights should be avoided as they cause delay. Platoons must help each other whatever battalion they belong to, and where one is held up others must push forward and envelop or surround the obstacles which will then be mopped up by the units detailed for the purpose."

The above quotation gives a fair summary of how the attack was actually carried out.

In co-operation with the attack by the 56th Brigade, one battalion of the 58th Brigade—the 9th Royal Welch Fusiliers —with two sections of the 58th Trench-Mortar Battery, were to assemble in trenches east and west of Oosttaverne (Oronto Trench and Mauve Line) by "Zero" hour. Two companies of the Fusiliers were then to replace the support battalion of the 56th Brigade in the centre of the old British front line. The remaining two companies were to be in Oronto Trench.

The 58th Brigade was to support the 56th and assemble in Ridge Defences and area as far west as the Grand Bois; the 57th Brigade, in reserve, was to move to the camp in the Divisional Support Area vacated by the 58th Brigade, arriving there by 10 a.m.

The attack was to be supported by the 19th Divisional Artillery Group, the left Group of the 37th Divisional Artillery and two six-inch batteries of the IX Corps Heavy Artillery. The guns were to form creeping, searching, and flank barrages. Covering fire and a protective barrage during consolidation were to be provided by the 57th and 58th Machine-Gun Companies, and six guns of the 19th M.M.G. Battery.

The 81st and 82nd Field Companies, R.E., and two Companies of the Pioneers (5th South Wales Borderers) were to be affiliated to the 56th Brigade to assist in consolidation and provision of communications forward.

The 56th Brigade took over the front line from the 57th Brigade on the night of the 29th/30th of July.

The 7th King's Own Royal Lancs. took up their assembly positions without incident and were in position by 3.20 a.m. on the 31st. The order of Companies was "A," "B," "C," and "D," from right to left; the battalion had a combined strength (Battalion Headquarters and companies) of 20 officers and 422 other ranks. The centre battalion—the 7th East Lancs.— formed up in position along the western edge of Green Wood without interference from the Boche. The 7th Loyal North Lancs. at first had difficulty over getting their stores up until a platoon of the support battalion was placed at their disposal. Their companies assembled (right to left) in the following order: "A," "C," "D," and "B." The 7th South Lancs. moved to Godsell Post and Rose Wood during the evening of the 30th.

The enemy, along the front of the 19th Division at least, seems to have been unaware of the impending attack.

It was still dark on the 31st when the barrage fell punctually at 3.50 a.m. and the advance began.

On the right the 7th King's Own secured all their objectives rapidly, the enemy offering very little resistance. Junction Buildings, which had already been the scene of desperate and bloody fighting and from which much trouble was expected, fell quite easily, and three German officers and eighteen other ranks surrendered. Tiny and Spider Farms were also speedily captured, each producing its quota of prisoners. The Middlesex and Lincolnshire of the 63rd Brigade, on the right of the King's Own, captured Rifle Farm and all their objectives, and formed a defensive flank as ordered.

At 4.10 a.m. the right company of the King's Own reported that they were on the Blue Line in touch with the Middlesex, but this was the last heard of the company. For during the advance a gap of some three hundred yards was created between one and a half companies on the right and the remainder of the battalion.

At 4.30 a.m., therefore, the situation was as follows: one and a half companies of the King's Own (on the right of the Divisional front) were on their objective in touch with troops of the 37th Division on their right; there was then a gap of three hundred yards opposite Wasp Farm and Fly Buildings; from west of Fly Buildings the remaining two and a half companies of the King's Own were on the Blue Line with the 7th East Lancs. on the left of the latter. Only two right companies of the North Lancs. had, however, reached their objective, the two left companies being thrown back south and south-west of Forret Farm.

The attack had surprised the enemy, though prisoners stated that it had been expected to take place later in the day. Not until several minutes after "Zero" had the hostile barrage descended on the old British line and communications—even then it was not heavy.

The darkness made mopping up difficult, though consolidation proceeded with little interference.

At about 5.30 a.m. the enemy's artillery fire increased, and men could be seen dribbling into Pillegrem's Farm, east of the point where the 37th Division joined up with the 19th Division; twenty-three prisoners came into our line about Rose Wood.

Between 5 a.m. and 6 a.m. the two companies of Royal Engineers and two of the Pioneers moved up. The former began the construction of strong points, whilst the South Wales Borderers continued Oboe and Preston Avenues between the jumping-off trench and the objective.

The Royal Engineers and Pioneers worked splendidly, though the former had to discontinue their labours after two hours owing to the severity of the enemy's shell-fire. In the meantime, however, they had constructed and wired a strong point at Tiny Farm, which proved invaluable. The Pioneers continued their work until 11 a.m., when about 250 yards of each communication trench had been dug to a depth of from four to five feet.

From 5.30 a.m. onwards small groups of Germans could be seen approaching the right flank from the direction of Lake and Bab Farms; they were seen creeping along the hedge north of Fly Farm.[1] Hostile rifle and machine-gun fire now became intense, and at about 6.40 a.m. a considerable quantity of smoke was observed in the neighbourhood of the junction between the 19th and 37th Divisions.

Under cover of the smoke the enemy attacked the junction of the two divisions, and at 6.45 reports were received that Rifle

[1] Marked on the map as "Fly Buildings."

Farm (which had been captured by the 37th Division) had been lost.

At 6.50 a.m. the Middlesex and Lincolnshires of the 63rd Brigade (37th Division) came again under the orders of their own brigadier, and a counter-attack was ordered by the latter and launched at 7.50 a.m.

Five minutes earlier, however, the enemy launched a counter-attack from the direction of Fly Buildings. This was repulsed by the two left companies of the King's Own, but apparently it made headway against the one and a half companies on the right, which were broken up, only one officer and twelve other ranks succeeding in fighting their way back to Tiny Farm, where they occupied a strong point. The enemy drove through the gap, but although their right flank had been turned the two left companies ("C" and "D") of the King's Own, with fragments of "A" and "B" Companies, held on to their front line and inflicted heavy casualties on the enemy with rifle and Lewis-gun enfilade fire.

One company ("C") of the 7th South Lancs. had been placed at the disposal of the O.C., 7th King's Own, and at 8.10 a.m. the O.C. of that battalion ordered the company to reinforce the front line, i.e., the one and a half companies on the right. But at 10.25 a.m. the O.C., company, sent a message to the O.C., King's Own, stating that as soon as he attempted to reach the old British line he had been met by heavy machine-gun fire and suffered such heavy casualties that he did not think it advisable to proceed unless guides could be sent him to show a better way up to the line. The right of the King's Own (as already stated) had by this time been broken and the O.C., "C" Company, South Lancs., was then ordered to form a defensive flank from Jill Farm northwards along the old British line, thence east to Spider Farm (or Spider House) and the right flank of the two companies of King's Own which were still holding on to the line. Apparently this order never reached the South Lancs. and the defensive flank was finally formed by a company of the 9th Royal Welch Fusiliers (58th Brigade) who had come up to reinforce "C" Company of the South Lancs. The O.C., "B" Company, South Lancs., led the Welch Fusiliers and two platoons of his own company forward and occupied the hedge running east from Tiny Farm, where he faced south, Welch Fusiliers in the front line, South Lancs. in support. Another company of the Welch Fusiliers moved up at the same time from the old British line and occupied the jumping-off line from a point west of Tiny Farm to the southern Divisional boundary, where touch was gained with the 37th Division and a Lewis-gun post established.

At 6 p.m. arrangements were made to co-operate at 8 p.m. with the 63rd Brigade in a fresh attack on Rifle Farm. The right company of the Royal Welch Fusiliers was ordered to send a platoon along the road which formed the southern Divisional boundary until touch was gained on the objective with the 63rd Brigade, and all front-line troops were ordered to endeavour to get up to the Blue Line at the same hour.

The attack by the 63rd Brigade was momentarily successful, but before the Royal Welch Fusiliers reached the objective the enemy again counter-attacked and drove the troops of the former back to their original line. An attack in greater strength might have been successful, but owing to the short notice received by the 19th Division of the impending attack and the difficulty in getting troops forward in daylight, it was impossible to lend more assistance.

In the meantime, on the extreme left of the Divisional front, the position remained unaltered. Forret Farm still held out, and the two left companies of the Loyal North Lancs. were repulsed, as earlier in the day.

At a Corps conference that night an attack at dawn on the 1st of August was discussed, but negatived owing to the difficulty which would undoubtedly ensue if fresh troops, not knowing the ground, were brought up to attack. At 12.45 a.m., therefore, on the 1st, orders were issued to consolidate all ground gained.

During the night of the 31st July/1st August, one officer and eleven other ranks of the 7th East Lancs., who had gone out on patrol, captured thirty-three Germans whom they encountered in No Man's Land.

Throughout the 1st, consolidation continued. The enemy's snipers were very active, but no infantry attack took place. The left company of the 7th King's Own was relieved by "D" Company of the 7th South Lancs., and went back to reorganise in the old British lines. Two companies of the 9th Welch (58th Brigade) were brought up to the old British line and replaced two companies of the Royal Welch Fusiliers who had been engaged in the fighting. The night of the 1st/2nd was spent in further consolidating the line and in connecting Tiny Farm with the jumping-off trench by a line of posts.

The 19th Division had captured up to this period, 3 officers and 130 ranks.

On the night of the 1st/2nd of August the Divisional front was re-adjusted, being divided into two sub-sectors, the 58th Brigade taking over the sub-sector south of Junction Buildings road from the 56th Brigade with two battalions, *i.e.*, 6th Wiltshires, on the right, and 9th Welch, on the left.

A projected attack by the 19th and 37th Divisions on the morning of the 3rd of August with the intention of recapturing the Blue Line from Rifle Farm northwards to the right of the former division, *i.e.*, the lost portion of the line, was rendered unnecessary (so far as the 19th Division was concerned) by the Wiltshires pushing forward their line to include the lost portion of the original objective. On the extreme left, also, the 41st Division (on the left of the 19th) during the night of the 1st/2nd of August captured Forret Farm, and on the following night the 7th Loyal North Lancs. pushed out posts to the Blue Line.

Thus the 19th Division, by the 3rd of August, had captured all the objectives allotted to it in the original operation orders.

The casualties suffered by the Division in this action were 13 officers and 205 other ranks killed, 25 officers and 566 other ranks wounded, and 3 officers and 58 other ranks missing.

On the night of the 3rd/4th of August the 57th Brigade relieved the 56th Brigade in the front line, the 10th Worcesters taking over the line from the road north-east of Junction Buildings to Gym Farm, and the 8th North Staffords from Gym Farm (exclusive) to Forret Farm (exclusive); the 10th Royal Warwicks were in support and the 8th Gloucesters in reserve.

Conditions in the front line were very bad, the only cover available being water-logged shell-holes. Troops had to be relieved every night.

During the 4th the line was comparatively quiet excepting a seven minutes' bombardment on S.O.S. lines by the Divisional Artillery, to which the enemy's reply was feeble.

At 5 a.m. on the 5th of August, however, the enemy attacked the 41st Division, on the left of the 19th, and gained a temporary footing in Hollebeke and Forret Farm.

He had opened with accurate and heavy shell-fire at 4 a.m. on the old British front line, Olive Trench and Switch, Ravine Wood and Ravine.

There was a thick mist at the time, and although four attempts were made to light S.O.S. rockets, they were damp and would not ignite. Visual signalling was impossible and the telephone wires had been cut in several places by the enemy's shell-fire.

The enemy, estimated at 100 strong, rushed Forret Farm on the 8th North Staffords' immediate left, and a section of trench to the north of it. When the attack took place Second-Lieut. Gough, 8th North Staffords, was visiting Nos. 1, 2, 3 and 4 (in that order from the north) and seeing the enemy were occupying Forret Farm he rallied elements of a battalion of the East Surreys and organised three posts, each of about twenty other ranks, as follows: right party, Company Sergt.-Major Amos; centre party, Second-Lieut. Gough; left party, under a company-sergt. major of the East Surreys (name unknown). A few orderlies and runners of the 8th North Staffords accompanied Second-Lieut. Gough and Company Sergt.-Major Amos.

By this time the Boche had placed a machine-gun in Forret Farm.

Sending a party to each flank and taking the centre party himself, Second-Lieut. Gough then attacked the Farm. On approaching the latter about fifty Germans put up their hands and shouted "Kamerad," but almost immediately lay down again and opened fire. The three parties then rushed the Farm, from which the Germans retired throwing hand grenades and, carrying their machine-gun with them. The Farm was re-occupied and several Germans and two wounded officers of the East Surreys were found in a dug-out. A Lewis-gun was then, brought into action with good effect.

In a little while the enemy again attacked but was driven back by Lewis-gun and rifle fire. Three patrols were sent out, and another prisoner was brought in.

Meanwhile, Capt. E. J. Colls (8th North Staffords) had moved forward with the supports of the left company and ordered Second-Lieut. Gough to remain in command of Forret Farm for the moment. Capt. Colls' party captured another five prisoners and sent back five more from those captured by the East Surreys in the Farm. Three or four more Germans were captured by a battle patrol sent out by the left support company, North Staffords (Capt. G. M. Eaton).

"One of these prisoners, a stretcher-bearer," records the

narrative in the Divisional Diary, "speaks fluent and very pertinent slang English."

Second-Lieut. Gough received reinforcements from his own battalion and remained in command of Forret Farm until relieved at about 11 a.m. by troops of the 122nd Brigade, 41st Division.

The mist had suddenly lifted about two hours previously revealing about a hundred Germans, fully equipped and dressed similarly to the captured *Sturm Truppen*, in the neighbourhood of The Twins, two houses out in front of the North Staffords. These were at once engaged with rifle and machine-gun fire and subsequently scattered by the Divisional Artillery, obviously demoralised.

On the night of the 7th/8th of August, the 19th Division was relieved, and during the following days moved back to the Lumbres area for training, the 56th Brigade being located at Colembert, the 57th at Nielles, and the 58th at Lumbres, where Division Headquarters were also at first situated, moving later to St. Jans Cappel.

The first of the Battles of Ypres, 1917, had been a distinct success for the 19th Division.

THE BATTLE OF THE MENIN ROAD RIDGE:
20TH–25TH SEPTEMBER

The 19th Division remained out of the line, engaged in training, until the night of the 11th/12th of September, upon which date the 58th Brigade (right) and 57th Brigade (left) relieved the 112th Infantry Brigade (37th Division) in the Klein Zillebeke sector: the reliefs were completed very early on the 12th.

The new Divisional sector was bounded on the right by the Ypres–Comines Canal, the front line running in a north-easterly direction through Opaque Wood, along the eastern outskirts of Imperfect Copse, thence to about 150 yards west of Greenburg Farm, the ruins of which lay half-way between the British and German trenches. Klein Zillebeke lay on the left rear of the Divisional front. In the German lines were the following well-known places:—Hessian Wood, Pioneer House, Potsdam and Jarrocks Farms, Belgian Wood, on the southern outskirts of which Wood Farm was situated, Princes House, Moat Farm and Top House; the Klein Zillebeke–Zandvoorde road ran through the left brigade sector.

On the 13th the 111th Brigade (37th Division) was placed at the disposal of the G.O.C., 19th Division, in order to relieve the 57th and 58th Brigades on the night of the 14th/15th. These two brigades were then to remain out of the line training and making final preparations for operations to take place on the 20th, until they took over their battle positions on the night of the 18th/19th of September.

The extent of the preparations and the need to give the ground time to recover from the heavy rains had rendered necessary a considerable interval between the Battle of Langemarck, 1917, which had taken place from the 16th to the 18th of August, and the operations about to begin on the 20th of September. By the latter date, however, everything was ready for the next attack.

The front selected was just over eight miles in extent, running from the Ypres–Comines Canal, north of Hollebeke, to the Ypres–Staden Railway, north of Langemarck. There were to be twelve divisions in the front line of attack, the 19th being on the extreme right. The main object of the attack of the IX Corps, to which the 19th Division belonged, was to secure the right flank of the X Corps (attacking on the left of the 19th Division).

Each brigade was to attack with three battalions in the front line and one in reserve: each battalion was to hold one company in reserve, or so arrange the formation of the attack that a company could be collected on the first objective for use during the later stages of the attack.

The 58th Brigade was to attack with the 6th Wiltshires on the right, 9th Welch in the centre, and 9th Cheshires on the left, the 9th Royal Welch Fusiliers being in reserve.

The 57th Brigade attack was to be carried out by the 10th Worcesters on the right, 8th Gloucesters in the centre, and 8th North Staffords on the left; the 10th Royal Warwicks to be in Brigade Reserve.

There were three lines, Green, Red, and Blue. On the 57th Brigade front the Green and Red were practically identical, but in the 58th Brigade area of attack the three lines on the left were separate objectives, though on the right (from Hessian Wood to the Cemetery) the Red and Blue Lines were identical.

The infantry advance was to be carried out under a creeping and steady barrage covering a depth of about 1,000 yards. The attacking troops were to follow as close to the creeping barrage (which would advance by lifts of 100 yards) as possible. After the creeping barrage had passed over the objective line it would form a protective barrage 200 yards in front of the objective. In front of the Blue Line (the final objective) the protective barrage was to remain at a distance of 200 yards until "Zero" plus two hours thirty minutes, when it was to lift another 200 yards. Battle patrols were then to be pushed forward under the barrage to clear the immediate foreground. Parties of sappers were to accompany these patrols with mobile charges to carry out any demolition required.

In studying the many closely-typewritten pages of instructions which make up the Operation Orders for this attack, the unusual advance in the science of making war at once becomes evident. Compared with the modest Operation Orders of 1914, when the great struggle first began, these pages of minute instructions are voluminous. The staging of a battle in 1917 required an extraordinary amount of thought and care, every unit had its ordered place in the scheme of operations; the artillery barrage maps and orders for the work of the gunners, instructions to the signallers, machine-gunners, Royal Engineers, Pioneers, Field Ambulances and administrative units generally are such as the old Army of 1914 could not possibly have dreamed.

The science of killing had indeed become a very complicated business.

After darkness had fallen on the night of the 19th/20th the Divisional area was full of activity. Troops were moving up to their assembly positions in the front line, others to their respective positions in the support and reserve lines. The gunners had amassed huge dumps of ammunition, for every known hostile strong point in front, or dug-out, was to be fiercely shelled; they had all been marked down days before, and had already suffered a merciless bombardment. Every fire and communication trench had for days been subjected to a tornado of shell—the guns had done their best to make the way easy for the infantry and were now only waiting to barrage the enemy's lines.

The difficulties encountered by the infantry battalions as they trudged on their way through and over all sorts of obstacles to their assembly positions cannot adequately be described. Loaded with all the impedimenta of warfare—rifles, 170 rounds of ammunition, equipment of all kinds, bombs, rifle grenades, sand bags, and either a pick or a shovel—no light weight to hump along in the dark over ground often a foot deep in mud.

Take for instance the forming up of the 6th Wiltshires of the 58th Brigade. Their assembly positions were in and in the neighbourhood of Opaque Wood. The Wood at this period was a mass of shell-holes, broken shreds of wire, and fallen trees lay about in all directions. To traverse this maze in the darkness was, to say the least, difficult. The possibility of German listening posts discovering unusual movement in the Wood, and the proximity of the barrage line, made assembly south of the Wood inadvisable. A direction tape was then laid through the Wood, running south, along which the battalion assembled in file, with the idea of deploying into the normal formation of attack on emerging from the Wood. The plan worked well owing to the careful reconnaissance of the platoon leaders.

The left battalion of the 58th Brigade, *i.e.*, 9th Cheshires, had anything but a comfortable night. This battalion left to move up to its assembly positions about Imperfect Copse at 8.30 p.m. The route had been clearly marked, but even so in the excessive darkness, over shell-torn ground, movement was slow and difficult. Then at midnight, heavy, drizzling rain began to fall, which went on until 5 a.m.

At 12.15 a.m. a message giving "Zero" hour was received; it was to be 5.40 a.m. The assembly operations had been completed by 1.45 a.m., so that out in the darkness and rain, which soaked all ranks through and through, the men lay on the wet and muddy ground hour after hour without even a tot of rum to keep their shivering bodies warm. However they did it was a marvel, but the Battalion Diary records that "silence was maintained and no movement made, the troops lying there confident and quiet."

The difficulties experienced by the Wiltshires and Cheshires were practically those of every battalion moving up to assembly positions on that wretched night.

As "Zero" hour approached all six attacking battalions were in line, *i.e.*, from right to left, 6th Wiltshires, 9th Welch, 9th Cheshires, 10th Worcesters, 8th Gloucesters, 8th North Staffords. The reserve battalion of the 58th Brigade—9th Royal Welch Fusiliers—were in the angle formed by the Battle and Fusilier Woods; the 10th Warwicks, the reserve battalion of the 57th Brigade, were in position just south of Ravine Wood.

Of the 56th Brigade (in reserve) the 7th King's Own Royal Lancs. were assembled along the northern bank of the Ypres–Comines Canal, south-west of Battle Wood; the 7th South Lancs. were in reserve of the King's Own; the 7th East Lancs. were at Bois Conluent, and the 7th Loyal North Lancs. at Bois Carre.

The G.O.sC., 57th and 58th Brigades (Brig.-Generals T. A. Cubitt and A. E. Glasgow), had their headquarters in the tunnel beneath Hill 60; Brig.-General F. G. Willan[1] and 56th Brigade Headquarters were on the canal bank north-west of the Bluff.

Towards dawn a heavy mist came down over the battlefield-to-be, but despite this disadvantage, all attacking troops, with the exception of two platoons of the 8th North Staffords which had lost their way, were in position by 4 a.m.

At 5.40 a.m. there was a crash as the barrage fell and the attacking troops of both brigades advanced.

On the right brigade front, during the first phase of the advance, *i.e.*, to the Red Line, considerable opposition was encountered from dug-outs south-west of Hessian Wood, Jarrocks Farm, Pioneer House, and from a small wood in front of the latter. From Hollebeke Château and the railway embankment also, the enemy's machine-gun fire was heavy. Despite this opposition, however, the Wiltshires reached their objective to time, but the Welch and Cheshires suffered heavy casualties, and temporarily lost touch on both flanks and with the barrage. But during the pause on the Red Line the Cheshires regained touch with their flanking units, completed "mopping up," and reorganised. It was then seen that the Welch were held up by machine-gun fire from the northern corner of Hessian Wood and had not reached their objective. The Wiltshires, therefore, formed a defensive flank on their left.

Of the left brigade the 10th Worcesters advanced well under the barrage and occupied the Red Line in good order, though opposition was encountered on their right. The Gloucesters and North Staffords had in front of them a stretch of extremely boggy ground which delayed their advance considerably, so

---

[1]Brig.-General F. G. Willan had taken over command of the 56th Brigade on the 5th September vice Brig.-General E. Craig-Brown.

that they were late in following the barrage. Both these battalions suffered heavy casualties from machine-gun fire chiefly from a line of dug-outs just north of Top House; owing to the difficulties of the ground, instead of being able to advance in extended order they had to go forward in "mass" formation—a better target for the enemy. In spite of the delays and losses mentioned above, the Red Line was occupied all along the front, and during the pause the two rear platoons of each attacking company moved up for the advance against the final objective; the ground in rear was also "mopped up."

The advance to the Blue Line—the second phase of the attack—began at 6.24 a.m. It has already been stated that on the right of the attack the Red and Blue Lines from Hessian Wood were identical; the Wiltshires, therefore, were already on their final objective, but the Welch were still held up in front of Hessian Wood. They had lost their Commanding Officer—Major J. A. Gibbs—and many other officers, and their casualties had been very heavy. Weak in numbers, they were unable to make headway and clear the wood. It was at this stage that a young officer of the 9th Cheshires—Second-Lieut. Hugh Colvin—went to the assistance of the Welch. All other officers of Lieut. Colvin's company ("D") had become casualties, and all but one of the officers of "C" Company had also been wounded. He assumed command of both companies and led them forward under heavy machine-gun fire with great dash and success.

It was then that he observed the predicament which had beset the Welch on his left. Taking a platoon with him he went to their assistance. "He then went on with only two men to a dug-out. Leaving the men on top he entered it alone and brought up fourteen prisoners. This is itself no small feat, but he went on with the two men to another dug-out which had been holding up the attack by rifle and machine-gun fire and bombs. On reaching the dug-out he succeeded in killing or taking prisoner the gun crew and captured the gun.

"He was then attacked by a party of fifteen Germans under an officer from another dug-out; one of his men was killed and the other wounded. Seizing a rifle he shot four of the Germans, and, using another as a shield, forced most of the survivors to surrender. He cleared several other dug-outs alone, and with one man taking about fifty prisoners in all."

As if that was not enough: "He then returned to his own front where he consolidated his position with great skill, and personally wired his own front under heavy close-range sniping in broad daylight, where all others had failed to do so. He was once completely buried by shell-fire, and his clothes and his equipment were several times struck and penetrated by bullets."

The complete success of the attack in this part of the line was mainly due to this officer's magnificent leadership, skill and courage.[1]

Second-Lieut. Colvin was awarded the Victoria Cross for his extraordinary bravery and gallant conduct.

The result of Lieut. Colvin's action was that the Welch were able to get into the northern edge of Hessian Wood and gain touch with the Wiltshires at the south-western corner.

Along the front of the 57th Brigade opposition was encountered at Wood Farm and in Belgian Wood. The latter was cleared by a fine bayonet charge, and the Blue Line was gained all along the front up to time.

In the meantime a liaison detachment, consisting of half a platoon of the 8th North Staffords, under Second-Lieut. G. S. Carver, with two Vickers guns and a detachment from the 57th Machine-Gun Company, had advanced with the 16th Notts. and Derby of the 117th Brigade (39th Division) on the left of the 19th Division. Lieut. Carver's orders were to put his machine-guns into position near North Farm. After a short and sharp fight, in which four machine-guns and twenty-nine prisoners were taken, the officer gained his objective.

At 8.10 a.m. the protective barrage on the Blue Line lifted to enable battle patrols to clear the immediate ground in front of the new line. In this way Moat Farm and Funny Farm were "mopped up."

The 9th Royal Welch Fusiliers were moved up to reinforce the Welch Regiment and support lines, the 7th King's Own (56th Brigade) taking over the position vacated by the Welch Fusiliers south of Fusilier Wood; the 7th East Lancs. replaced the King's Own in the canal dug-outs west of Pontoon Bridge.

The work of consolidation now proceeded, but the construction of strong points was much interfered with by heavy machine-gun fire from Hollebeke Château. Portions of trench were dug at once on the Green Line, the ground in front up to and including the Blue Line being held by posts in depth.

[1] From the official citation of award in the *London Gazette* of 8/11/17.

The enemy did not counter-attack until the evening, when, at about 7.30 p.m., hostile troops were observed advancing on the left against North Farm; they were annihilated by artillery, machine-gun and rifle fire.

Once more the 19th Division had captured all its objectives, though on this occasion also only after a stiff fight. The enemy had put up a most determined resistance, especially from his strong points—his losses were very heavy.

In prisoners the Division had captured 20 officers and 371 other ranks.

The total casualties suffered by the Division from noon on the 19th to noon on the 23rd of September were 15 officers and 325 other ranks killed, 58 officers and 1,265 other ranks wounded, and one officer and 269 other ranks missing, most of the latter being accounted for later as having been either killed or wounded, or evacuated by other divisional field ambulances.

The 19th Division had, however, lost its Commander. General Bridges, with his usual impetuous energy, had at about 5 p.m., visited the G.O.sC. of the 57th and 58th Brigades, whose headquarters were in dug-outs tunnelled under the famous Hill 60. As he came out of the tunnel a 5·9-in. shell burst close by, a fragment of which almost severed his right leg, which shortly afterwards had to be amputated.

On the 22nd Major-General G. D. Jeffreys, well known to everyone in the 19th Division, took over command.

On the night of the 21st/22nd of September, the 56th Brigade took over the front line from the 57th and 58th Brigades.

On the 22nd the following Special Order of the Day by Major-General T. Bridges was published: "The Army Commander most heartily congratulates all ranks of the 19th Division on the great successes gained by them in the recent fighting. He is proud to feel that he possesses in his Army officers and men who have not only given repeated proofs of their prowess in the past, but continue with every fresh endeavour to add to their splendid reputation."

It should, however, be remembered always that in winning great successes for their divisions, the infantry in the front line could not have done so had it not been for the splendid co-operation of all arms of the Division: the R.A., T.M. Batteries. Pioneers and R.E., Signallers, and medical units, were

I

constantly in the shell-swept area.   The services of D.A.D.O.S. and his personnel in replacing and repairing destroyed and damaged weapons and equipment during the operations, were simply immense. The Army Service Corps and the Veterinary Corps were invaluable.

And some had their exciting moments also.

Take for instance the 5th South Wales Borderers, the Pioneers; their Lewis-gun teams were engaged in anti-aircraft work during the battle, and highly successful they were too. The enemy's aircraft were very busy during the operations. At about 1.30 p.m. a hostile plane flew over the Lewis-gunners of the Pioneers, who promptly opened fire, one gun, worked by Private Hitchins (in Corporal Vaughan's team), bringing down the machine in flames. The following day a similar incident occurred when, between 12.30 and 1 p.m., another hostile plane droned down from a cloud and flew over the Pioneers. The Lewis-guns opened fire and Private Brown (Corporal Underhill's team) brought the plane down in flames. On another occasion the Lewis-gunners of the Pioneers broke up formations of hostile aeroplanes and drove them back over their own lines.

Very creditable work for Pioneers, whose duties usually consisted in digging.

There are some interesting items in the diaries of the medical units, i.e., 57th, 58th, and 59th Field Ambulances. Regimental Aid Posts were selected in Fusilier Wood and Battle Wood. There were Bearer Posts in Battle Wood and on the southern side of the Ypres–Comines Canal, north-west of Hollebeke. Advanced Dressing Stations were at The Mound and Norfolk Lodge, and to within 150 yards of the former there was a trench tramway which ran from one of the Bearer Posts south of the canal. This tramway was shelled heavily, the line being frequently broken by shell-fire. The Mound had also been marked down by the enemy's gunners, who obtained a direct hit on the Receiving Room. The room was crowded with orderlies, patients, and stretchers. The result of the shell-burst was that seven men were killed and eighteen wounded, two of the killed and ten of the wounded being patients waiting to have their wounds dressed.

Casualties were also sustained by the R.A.M.C. carrying stretchers through the barrage on the 20th.

The main dressing station was at Kemmel. The method of

dealing with "walking cases" is interesting, and the following is an extract from a report by the O.C., 59th Field Ambulance: "Our arrival cases had full particulars of identification entered on a field medical card. This the patient took with him into the dressing room, where the M.O. filled in the diagnosis and signed the card. The man was next passed into the anti-tetanic room, where he received his injection and had the fact noted on his card, finally passing into the clerical room, where full particulars were entered on A.F.W.3210 for record in the field ambulance books. The case was now ready for evacuation and waited in the evacuation shelter."

For several days the enemy's shell-fire was terrific, and in some reports among the numerous diaries and documents of the 19th Division there are statements that it was "unprecedented."

No further infantry attacks were made on or by the enemy to the close of the Battle of the Menin Road, *i.e.*, 25th of September.

IN THE LINE: 26TH SEPTEMBER–10TH NOVEMBER

After the Battle of the Menin Road Ridge the 19th Division made no further attacks upon the enemy in the Battles of Ypres, 1917. With conspicuous success the Division had taken part in two battles, had been out of the line training during another, and after the operations from the 20th to the 25th of September, remained in the line until the 10th of November. The Division, therefore, is entitled to the remaining battle honours, *i.e.*, the Battle of Polygon Wood (26th September–3rd October), Broodseinde (4th October), Poelcapelle (9th October), First Passchendaele (12th October), and Second Passchendaele (26th October–10th November).[1]

The right flank of the Second Army (to which the 19th Division belonged) had well carried out the task allotted to it; that flank had been sufficiently advanced and the actions of the battles now shifted to (and astride) the Menin Road, thence in a northerly direction. The part assigned to the 19th Division was to maintain its position in the front line,

---

[1]The official areas of the Battles of Ypres, 1917, according to the Report of the Battles Nomenclature Committee, ran on the right from the Ypres–Comines Canal as far as Voormezeele, thence the road to Vlamertinghe Château–Elverdinghe Château–Woesten–Bixschoote.

and the efforts of all units were turned to that purpose. For some six or seven weeks, therefore, actions along the Divisional front became individual as opposed to general; in other words, a period of trench warfare ensued.

The 56th Brigade (as already stated) relieved the 57th and 58th Brigades on the night of the 21st/22nd of September, and on the completion of the relief at 4.40 a.m., the former brigade held the line on a three-battalion frontage. An hour later the 7th East Lancs., who had taken over the line from the Cheshires and Worcesters, reported the capture of two Germans and a machine-gun, but no reference is made of the incident in the Battalion Diary of the first-named battalion. The 7th King's Own had taken over the front line on the right, the 7th East Lancs. in the centre, and the 7th South Lancs on the left; the 7th Loyal North Lancs. were in reserve.

The enemy's shell-fire was extremely heavy; the line he had lost was plastered with shell of every calibre, while the old British front line and the back area were swept by an almost continual storm of high-explosive and shrapnel. On the 23rd, for instance, within the space of an hour he dropped 500 shells on the railway cutting and around Hill 60. On this date the Divisional front was readjusted by the East Lancs. taking over the right and the South Lancs. the left.

Of the diaries of the four infantry battalions of the 56th Brigade, only that of the South Lancs. gives any idea of the difficulties and state of the front line immediately after fighting had finished on the 21st.

During the evening of the 21st the C.O. of that battalion had received orders to relieve the 8th Gloucesters and 8th North Staffords in the left of the new front line. Battalion Headquarters were then at the Spoil Bank, on the northern bank of the Ypres–Comines Canal, and companies crowded into dug-outs in the neighbourhood. Sending for the company commanders, the C.O. gave them detailed orders for the relief, and at about 8.30 p.m. "A" and "D" Companies began to file out of the dug-outs for the front line, followed by "B" and "C" Companies who were to be in support and reserve respectively. Battalion Headquarters followed at about 9.15 p.m. and eventually fetched up in an old German dug-out in Klein Zillebeke, Battalion Headquarters of the Gloucesters and North Staffords being in the same place.

The relief, a rather difficult one, was eventually over and the code word "Vellacott" was wired back to Brigade Headquarters.

The line taken over was a hastily-constructed series of shell-hole posts on the eastern outskirts of Belgian Wood and reaching as far north as Top House. All night long the enemy continued to shell this area and search the back areas for any troops on the way up to, or going back from, the front line. It was not a pleasant position; snipers were extremely active and the Boche machine-guns were apt to open bursts of fire at all times, in the hope of catching working parties out in front, strengthening the defences, putting up wire, etc., which frequently happened.

The night passed and dawn appeared, but still the enemy's guns continued their incessant fire.

The position of Battalion Headquarters of the South Lancs. had, apparently, not been well chosen, for the C.O. records that they were in full view from three directions, and everyone who came and went during the day brought down fire upon the dug-out. During the evening a dug-out, which had been the old headquarters of the 10th Worcesters, was shelled and fired by the enemy; it burned for a couple of days and acted as a guide to runners. Rations had to be brought up after dark by the surplus personnel and carried on to companies by head-quarters guides; they were frequently scattered by shell-fire and to find one another again and form up in the pitch black night was not an easy business.

A party of thirty sappers, who had been sent up to Battalion Headquarters under an officer to see what improvement they could make in the dug-out, met with a disastrous end. They had decided to work on a weak wall facing the enemy which needed strengthening, and had already begun their task when there was a blinding flash and a roar as a shell burst amongst the party. Nine were wounded, four of whom were flung against the door of the dug-out. They were carried down below, but two died before they could be got to the Aid Post.

The morning of the 23rd was foggy and the Boche guns were not very active until about 11 a.m. They then got to work in earnest and again swept the whole Divisional area with a perfect tornado of shell. The C.O. of the South Lancs. dryly records that they "selected targets to-day, and Battalion Headquarters was one of them." Previously the enemy's shell-fire was of a promiscuous nature, but on the 24th he only fired on definite targets.

The next morning another tragic incident is related; at daylight an artillery officer arrived at the entrance to headquarters dug-out: "He had scarcely reached the door when a shell burst at his feet and he was struck through the chest and died a little later in the dug-out."

The South Lancs. were relieved by the Loyal North Lancs. on the evening of the 25th. The enemy's shell-fire slackened somewhat during the afternoon, and in the evening died down altogether; the relief, therefore, passed off peacefully. Battalion Headquarters, with "C" and "D" Companies, went off to the dug-out tunnel near Hill 60, "A" and "B" Companies to similar accommodation in Buffs Bank and Gaspers Cliff on the canal: "These places give good shelter from artillery fire, but the atmosphere becomes very thick."

The Battle of Polygon Wood opened the following day—26th—but only the 19th Divisional Artillery and the Machine-Gun Companies co-operated by forming barrages; the artillery also formed a smoke screen to assist the 39th Division who were attacking on the left of the 19th Division.

The Divisional front line was lightly held during the opening stages of the attack. The Boche retaliation was at first heavy, but during the remainder of the day his shell-fire was intermittent and indiscriminate. The two front-line battalions do not record anything untoward.

No further incident of importance happened in the Divisional area before the end of September, and by the 3rd of October the fourth of the Battles of Ypres was over.

On the 1st of October the 19th Divisional Wing, Corps Musketry and Reinforcement Camp was opened. In addition to the ordinary training of reinforcements arriving at railhead, a series of courses of training platoon commanders and warrant officers of infantry battalions in drill and musketry, lasting eight days, was begun. The first class assembled at the Divisional Wing on the 27th and started work the following day.

The Battle of Broodseinde opened on the 4th, but again the infantry of the 19th Division was not called upon to attack the enemy, only the artillery putting down a barrage and smoke screen to cover the right of the 37th Division; the Machine-Gun Company also put down a barrage.

For the whole of October there is only one item to record of outstanding interest. Front-line battalions had a hard existence —mud was everywhere and some of the posts were almost impossible for habitation, yet men lived in them; their pluck and endurance were wonderful.[1]

Towards the end of the month it was necessary to obtain identifications from the enemy, and the 7th King's Own Royal Lancs. were ordered to carry out a raid on a group of dug-outs which lay almost opposite Bulgar Wood and on the eastern side of the Bassevillebeek. These dug-outs had been reconnoitred on the nights of the 29th and 30th of October; the raid was to take place on the 1st of November.

The raiding party consisted of two officers and twenty-eight other ranks of "B" Company. The battalion had been relieved on the 31st, and "B" Company, with Battalion Headquarters, had moved back to Hill 60. The raid was to be carried out under a box barrage, fired round the seven dug-outs which were to be raided and destroyed.

At 4.45 p.m. the raiders left Hill 60 fully equipped. Raiding parties generally presented a bloodthirsty appearance, and this was no exception. Orders stated that they were to be in "skeleton dress," which meant they were to go stripped of all equipment but that of the lightest character. Some carried bludgeons and revolvers, others rifles and bayonets; each N.C.O. had in his pockets three bombs, and carried an electric torch. Rifle magazines were charged with ten rounds.

By 6.45 p.m. they had passed through the outpost line and were making for the southern edge of Bitter Wood. Duck-boards, carried by the raiders, were placed across the Beek and a Lewis-gun mounted in position covered the crossing; two men were also left at the crossing with a whistle to attract the attention of the party when returning. The raiders crossed the Beek in small parties at ten minutes' intervals, and by 7.50 p.m. had successfully worked their way into a position of assembly about ten yards west, and parallel with, Rifle Road, which was about eighty yards from the line of dug-outs.

At 8.20 p.m. the barrage fell on the whole chain of dug-outs and Vickers guns opened fire on the flanks and the southern group of dug-outs which were not being attacked. For four minutes the guns placed a perfect tornado of shell on the northern group and then lifted to 150 yards east. Each party of the raiders then rushed forward to the objective.

[1]During October Lieut.-Colonel E. H. Hewlett (Devon R.), G.S.O.I., was transferred to the War Office and was succeeded by Lieut.-Colonel H. F. Montgomery, R.M.L.I.

Dug-outs Nos. 1, 2 3, and 5 were found to be unoccupied, but No. 4 was defended by a German machine-gun section. The latter, however, tried to escape but was driven into the barrage by an N.C.O. and his party, and must have suffered casualties. No. 6 dug-out was attacked by Second-Lieut. Holmes (O.C., raid), who found the entrance on the far side guarded by two sentries; these he promptly shot, their bodies falling and blocking the entrance through which the occupants of the dug-out were firing, thus preventing the raiders from entering. A bomb was, therefore, thrown in. A German machine-gunner, who opened fire through a loop-hole in front of the dug-out, was shot by one of the raiders firing through the aperture.

In the meantime an N.C.O. (Corporal Storey) was having a stiff fight with the occupants of No. 7 dug-out. Lieut. Holmes then went to his assistance, and eventually six German prisoners were taken from it.

A further attempt made by Second-Lieut. Conheery to enter No. 6 dug-out was held up by fire from within.

The object of the raid having now been accomplished, the O.C. raid signalled the withdrawal, and the whole party, plus the six prisoners, were safely across the Beek by 8.40 p.m.

The report adds: "Our casualties were nil," but one man was slightly wounded and one officer slightly gassed. The prisoners supplied valuable identifications, as their division had only come into the line the previous night from the Arras front.

This small operation was a great success, and drew many congratulations to the 7th King's Own Royal Lancaster Regiment.

On the 4th of November orders were received at Divisional Headquarters stating that the 19th Division was to be relieved by the 37th Division by 10 a.m. on the 10th; on relief the Division was to proceed to the Blaringhem area for training.

The 56th Brigade, having been relieved by the 57th Brigade on the 5th, came out of the line and moved from the support area on the 8th to the Locre area; the 58th Brigade on the same date moved to the Strazeele area. At 10 p.m. on the night of the 9th the 57th Brigade reported their line taken over by the 112th Brigade. By the 12th all moves were completed, 19th Divisional Headquarters being at Blaringhem and the three infantry brigades in the neighbourhood, i.e., 56th at Blaringhem, 57th Mont D'Hiver, and 58th at Ebblinghem.[1]

---

[1] In November Colonel J. A. Hartigan joined the Division as A.D.M.S. vice Colonel H. A. Hince, appointed D.D.M.S., VI Corps.

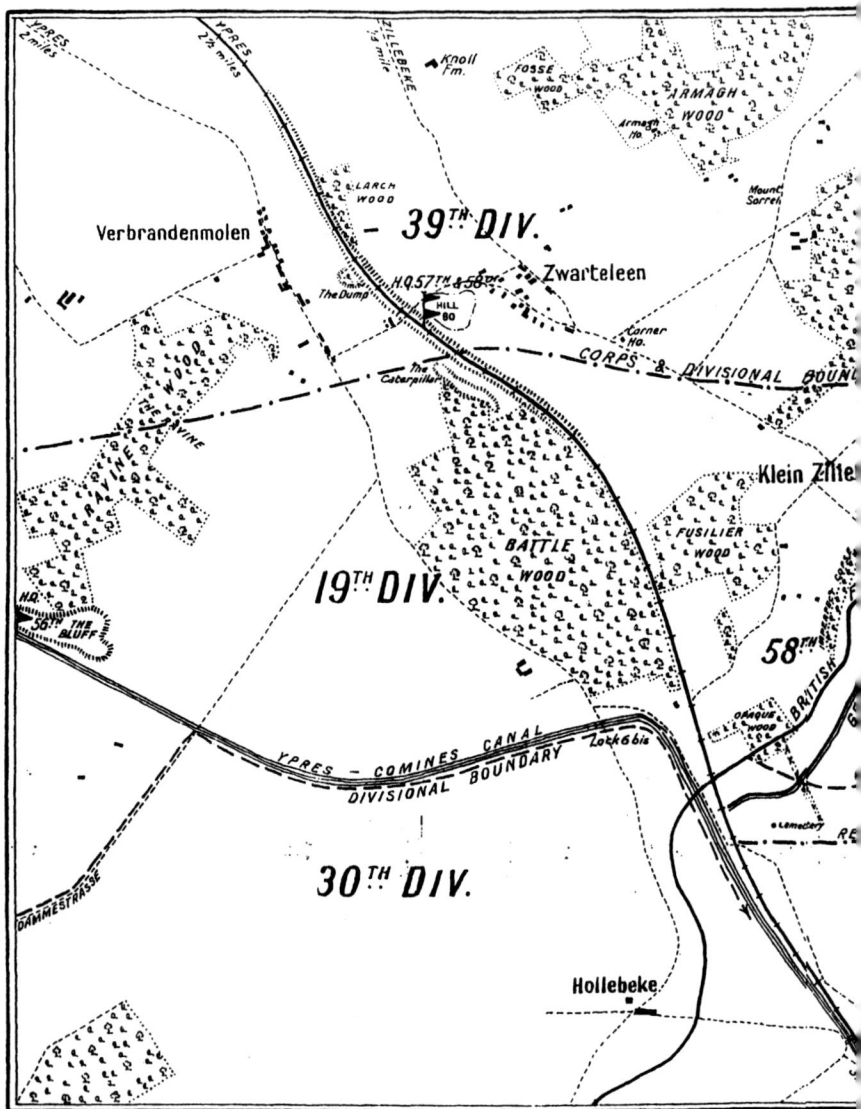

YPRES 2 miles

YPRES 2½ miles

ZILLEBEKE 1½ mile

Knoll Fm.

FOSSE WOOD

ARMAGH WOOD

Armagh Ho.

LARCH WOOD

Mount Sorrel

Verbrandenmolen

39ᵀᴴ DIV.

HQ 57ᵀᴴ & 58ᵀᴴ

The Dump

HILL 60

Zwarteleen

Corner Ho.

CORPS & DIVISIONAL BOUNDARY

The Caterpillar

Klein Zille

RAVINE

FUSILIER WOOD

HQ 56ᵀᴴ THE BLUFF

19ᵀᴴ DIV.

BATTLE WOOD

58ᵀᴴ

BRITISH

ANGUS WOOD

Lock 6 bis

YPRES — COMINES CANAL

DIVISIONAL BOUNDARY

Lame Cars

RE

DAMMESTRASSE

30ᵀᴴ DIV.

Hollebeke

YPRES, 1917.

Operations of 19th Division,
20th – 25th September.

Scale of Yards.

BURY FOREST

Jules Fm.

Groenenburg Fm.
(Greenburg Fm.)

North Fm.

201/X/17.

201/X/17.

MENIN RD
1 mile

GHELUVELT
1 mile

Top Ho.

Princes Ho.

Funny Fm.

BELGIAN
WOOD

Bassevillebeek

Easl Fm.

Wood Fm.

Pioneer Ho.

Potsdam Fm.

Moat Fm.

Rocks

BOUNDARY LINE

RED LINE

BLUE LINE

FINAL OBJECTIVE

May Fm.

Zandvoorde

Chalk Fm.

Basseville Fm.

Bassevillebeek
(8 ft. wide)

ollebeke
hateau

Gaverbeek

CHAPTER XV

THE LAST WINTER IN THE TRENCHES: TO THE EVE OF THE GERMAN OFFENSIVE, 1918

WINTER had begun in earnest when the 19th Division was withdrawn from the line and conveyed to the Blaringhem area. But when General Jeffreys handed over command of the Divisional sector on the 11th November the training programme had already been issued to all units.

In the first paragraph of that programme it was stated that, although it was impossible to forecast accurately the time available for training, it was anticipated that the Division might be out of the line for a period of from six weeks to two months. Nevertheless, it was possible that that period would not be continuous, for the Division might have to go back into the trenches for a short tour within the month.

It is not uninteresting to look back upon those periods of training and see how units were prepared for their work and heavy fighting in the front line; for the system under which all ranks received instruction was not always the same. There were times when there seemed no probability of an advance, when trench warfare was to the fore: on other occasions (such as while the German Retreat to the Hindenburg Line was taking place) training in open warfare engaged the attention of brigades and divisions out of the line.

General Jeffreys, an old Guardsman, who had been in command of a Guards brigade prior to his assuming command of the 19th Division, had brought with him his own system of training, and the programme mentioned above was based upon his own lengthy experience.

With prospects of some weeks out of the line, training began on progressive lines, *i.e.*, starting with elementary work and gradually working up to battalion and brigade training. For the first two weeks platoon training, including a large proportion of standing drill combined with specialist training, was to engage infantry battalions. Not less than four, and not more than five, hours' work a day (no training on Sundays) was to be carried out. Thus time was left for recreation—no less necessary than training; those divisions in France and Flanders who trained hard *and* played hard were generally considered the best fighting units.

Infantry instruction covered a wide range, *i.e.*, drill and rifle exercises to inculcate smartness and discipline, musketry and fire discipline, bayonet fighting, Lewis gunnery, bombing and rifle bombing, tactical work and wiring, and anti-gas training.

The machine-gun companies, in addition to their specialist work, were also to carry out drill and arm drill. Similarly the light trench-mortar batteries, which were to be affiliated to infantry battalions for musketry, practised bayonet fighting and bombing. This, in addition to their own training in the use of their mortars.

Signalling at this period of the War had become almost a high art, and the signallers were to be exercised in the use of amplifiers, power buzzers, the organisation of runner relay posts, the use of the Fullerphone, visual signalling with the Lucas lamp, and the employment of pigeons.

All transport, *i.e.*, men, horses, vehicles and harness, were to be inspected for condition and cleanliness.

One of the most interesting features of this training was the construction of a "show ground" where the various types of trenches, strong points, wire entanglements, revetments, and trench devices were to be seen and studied.

Of great importance was the training in tactical work, in which single attack schemes in the form of warfare then in vogue were carried out. In the first instance these schemes were carried out by platoons, special attention being given to the encouragement of initiative of platoon commanders in dealing with unexpected situations.

The following extract from the "Training Programme" is given, as it practically describes exactly what happened in attacks when in the front line:—

"In the later stages of training, attacks behind a barrage by one or more companies working together will be practised, one platoon being held up and having to dispose of the opposition and regain its place behind the barrage. Platoons must be practised in getting forward under their own covering fire of rifles, Lewis-guns, and rifle bombs, supposing the barrage to have been lost.

"In all these exercises the repulse of counter-attacks by rifle and Lewis-gun fire must be constantly practised. Men must be taught to regard a counter-attack after a successful assault as a certainty, and to welcome it as the best scheme they can have of killing Germans. The best method of ensuring that rifles and Lewis-guns are in a fit condition for use on arrival at an objective after an attack over heavy ground, is one that requires special attention.

"Instruction in night patrolling and marching by compass bearing will be frequently carried out. Schemes for such exercises will be set by the C.O. or the second-in-command. They should not involve keeping men out late or for a long time. Enemy patrols or listening posts should always be represented."

It was probably due to this careful training which the several G.O.s commanding the 19th Division laid down for their officers and men, that success in operations in the field so frequently attended the efforts of the Division. Certain it is that the quotations given above covered every "situation" likely to arise, and which did so often arise when attack was being made on or by the enemy.

And so the Division set to work. The weather was good on the whole, though during the remainder of the month there were one or two wet days. But it was the 2nd of December before white frost lay on the ground, and thereafter frosty days and nights, followed by snow, proclaimed the depth of winter.

The Division was out of the line for not quite a month, for on the 4th of December a wire arrived at Headquarters ordering the Division, less artillery, to be prepared to leave the Second Army and proceed by rail, on or after the 6th, to join the Third Army on the Somme.

Once again the "Butterflies" were to live up to their reputation for flitting from place to place. The reason was significant: some divisions were more highly trained than others, and as a consequence their successes were more frequent. The 19th Division was always looked upon as a fine fighting unit, and was amongst those divisions which were changed about from one part of the line to another, where the fighting was heaviest, or a stubborn defence, or an intrepid advance necessary. There had been heavy fighting at Cambrai when the enemy, on the 30th November, had launched a great counter-attack after our initial successes between the 20th and that date.

Operation orders for the move were issued on the 5th of

December, and the following day the Division entrained for the Third Army area.

Into details of all the preliminary moves it is unnecessary to go, but on the 10th the 57th Brigade relieved the left brigade of the 6th Division in the Ribecourt sector: on the 12th the 58th Brigade took over the right sub-sector, the 56th Brigade being in Divisional Reserve. Divisional Headquarters were then at Etricourt, but were moved subsequently to Neuville Bourjonval.[1]

That part of the line which the 19th Division had taken over was a portion of the Flesquières Salient (known to the enemy as the Cambrai Re-Entrant)—a salient formed by the positions we had taken up after falling back from the Masnières–Noyelles–Bourlon Wood–Mœuvres line as a result of the heavy counter-attack launched by the enemy on the 30th of November. The area comprised the two dominating heights of Highland Ridge and Premy Chapel Ridge, and two deep valleys radiating from Marcoing towards Couillet Wood on the right, and Ribecourt in the centre. These valleys, especially the Couillet Wood Valley, afforded the enemy avenues of approach which necessitated special vigilance and efficient wire and machine-gun defence in order to render them secure against a surprise attack. Owing to the ground falling towards the north-east, the enemy was able to obtain observation over practically the whole of the front and intermediate systems of defence of the Divisional front, from Nine Wood and the high ground south and east of Marcoing.

The Divisional front ran from the most westerly of four sunken roads south of Marcoing in a north-westerly direction to east of Flesquières. Ribecourt was included in this sector. The old Hindenburg Support Line was the Divisional support and reserve line; a line of posts formed the outpost line; the whole front was 4,500 yards in extent.

---

[1] The following note by General Jeffreys is an interesting comment on the Neuville Bourjonval area:—"Neuville Bourjonval and other villages were little better than ruins. Some houses, however, were capable of being restored, and one of these latter was occupied by the Headquarters of the Division, the walls being fairly sound and a new roof, doors, etc., having been provided. The Reserve Brigades were mostly in Nissen huts (some in tents) amid a sea of mud, and in these conditions it was difficult to keep the health and spirits of all ranks at the high pitch which one would have liked to have attained. The whole width of the devastated area and the Somme battlefield lay between the troops and any undestroyed towns, villages, or country, so that throughout the winter the men never saw civilians nor anything which could be described as comfort."

Behind the front-line system there was an intermediate line, also consisting of outpost, front and support lines; Ribecourt lay between the two systems.

In the Divisional Defence Scheme, issued as soon as the line was taken over from the 6th Division, the following paragraphs occur:—

"The policy is to hold on to the Hindenburg Support System by a defence in depth. As, however, the trenches of this system are very close together and only partially wired, and, in many places only partially dug, it is necessary to push forward an additional trench to serve as a front-line trench so as to give depth.

"Further, in order to keep the enemy back on the commanding Premy Ridge as far as possible, and to gain command of the exits from Marcoing, and of the valley north-west of the Premy Ridge, a further line has been thrown forward forming a marked salient on the ridge."

The trenches in the Marcoing Valley were liable to become waterlogged and drainage was at once begun; the valley was also to be strongly wired and defended by cross-fire from Lewis and machine-guns.

The holding of a salient was always a dangerous and uncomfortable business, and the greater part of the Ribecourt sector was not only exposed to enfilade fire, but to reverse fire from the direction of La Vacquerie, on the right of the salient and just east of the Welsh Ridge.

The Boche was vigilant. He had been taught a sharp lesson on the 20th of November, and was not again likely to be taken by surprise in this sector of the front line. But he was little better off than we were, in that both sides had to make new defensive lines as well as improving existing trenches.

The battalion diaries, however, for the remainder of December are practically bare of interest. Only one, that of the 7th Loyal North Lancs., refers to what might be termed the "atmosphere" in the Divisional area. This particular battalion, in a few short sentences, gives the situation generally, though particularly referring to its own portion of the line: "This sector appears very quiet, but great keenness and alertness are necessary owing to the probability of the enemy attempting to regain his lost position."

It *was* at one time thought that he would attack, and indeed he did launch a small attack against the 63rd Division, on the right of the 19th, at the end of December, gaining a temporary advantage, but he was counter-attacked and lost most of his gains, which were inconsiderable.

The Loyal North Lancs. also state that "Great importance is laid on patrolling, since the dispositions and intentions of the enemy have not yet been ascertained and even identifications are lacking."

A German stretcher-bearer, however, wandered into the Divisional lines and was captured, and provided a valuable identification; he belonged to a division lately transferred from the Russian front; it was evident that the enemy was bringing troops back from the east, where the Russians had collapsed as a result of the revolution, as quickly as possible.

But not yet had he decided on making a heavy attack; his losses (like ours) had been prodigious during 1917, and rest and training was just as necessary for his troops as for ours. The remainder of December, therefore, along the Divisional front followed without incident of more than ordinary importance.

Yet for battalions in the front line there was always "something doing." The "Intelligence Reports" contain much information of active patrolling, the periodical capture of prisoners and patrol encounters, with subsequent fighting.

Take, for instance, the night of the 13th of December; a patrol went out and observed a large party of Boche lying in the open; one of them came out of a trench and challenged the patrol but was immediately shot. Four more of the enemy then ran out with their hands up, but this was deemed merely a trick and they also were shot down. An attempt was then made to surround the patrol, which, however, got safely away, and, firing as they retired, eventually got back to their own trench.

On another occasion a patrol was out to locate dug-outs and to secure identifications if possible. Several dug-outs were found and some were occupied, apparently, by about twenty-five Germans. They were bombed, whereupon the occupants made a bolt but only some of them escaped.

At times as many as a dozen patrols were out along the Divisional front on a single night, and by this means Divisional Headquarters were kept continually informed of the condition of the Boche trenches and wire, and of his dispositions.

On the 19th a patrol, split up into three groups of five, went out to capture a machine-gun post. Six prisoners (of whom two were wounded) and a machine-gun were brought back in this little venture.

The enemy's infantry, however, appears to have been rather quiescent, and there are no records of raids on the Divisional front nor of his patrols entering our lines. Excepting for artillery and machine-gun fire his attitude was not very aggressive.

The General Staff Diary of the 19th Division begins the year 1918 with the following laconic statement: "Division on left— 17th; Division on right—63rd; brigades in line—right 57th and left 58th."

Divisional Headquarters were at Neuville Bourjonval.

The most momentous year of the War began very quietly in fair, very cold, and frosty weather. For a week nothing occurred to disturb the comparatively even tenor of trench warfare, then on the 8th of January came a fluttering of the dove cots in the form of a warning letter from the V Corps Headquarters. The corps stated that the Germans would probably attack on the night of the 11th/12th. Troops were to be warned to be on their guard; wire was to be improved, and the machine-gun defences looked to. Divisional reserves were to be warned and the 2nd Division (then out of the line) kept ready to move up. Brigades were ordered to have counter-attack battalions in a state of readiness on the mornings of the 11th and 12th, while the 57th Brigade (in reserve) was to be ready to move at one hour's notice. All sentries were to observe special vigilance, and patrols pushed out before dawn to watch for hostile concentrations of infantry.

The following night (9th) the 58th Brigade, at 7.10 p.m., reported continuous streams of G.S. wagons and parties of Germans along the Cambrai–Masnieres and Cambrai–Noyelles roads, and on the Rumilly road, all moving in a south-westerly direction, Corps Headquarters immediately ordered the "Heavies" to shell the area Masnieres–Rumilly–Noyelles– Marcoing during the night, also the Cambrai road between Fontaine and the Sugar Factory; the 19th Divisional Artillery was to put down a heavy fire on the enemy's communications.

Another message on the 10th from Corps Headquarters repeated a report from the 17th Division that the enemy was seen massing in his trenches, coming in in parties of thirty: "about seventy parties seen." That morning hostile shell-fire increased on the front and support lines, though the back areas received only slight attention from the enemy's guns. But another suspicious sign was the registration of the support line in the centre of the Divisional forward area.

The 11th was anxiously awaited—nothing happened; and nothing happened on the 12th or 13th, nor, indeed, during the remainder of January or in February. But the scare was typical of the alarms which floated about, until rumours became actualities at dawn on the 21st of March.

In order, therefore, to understand the serious situation at the beginning of 1918 which led to the above alarums, the following quotation from Sir Douglas Haig's despatches is an admirable summary of the trend of affairs during the latter part of 1917 and early in the New Year, which led up to the great German Offensive of 1918 in which the 19th Division fought many a hard battle:

"The broad facts of the change which took place in the general war situation at the end of 1917, and the cause which led to it, have long been well known and need be referred to but shortly. The disappearance of Russia as a belligerent country on the side of the Entente Powers had set free the great bulk of the German and Austrian divisions on the Eastern Front. Already, at the beginning of November 1917, the transfer of German divisions from the Russian to the Western Front had begun. It became certain that the movement would be continued steadily until numerical superiority lay with the enemy. It was to be expected, moreover, that large numbers of guns and munitions, formerly in the possession of the Russian Armies, would fall into the hands of our enemies, and at some future date would be turned against the Allies. Although the growing Army of the United States of America might be expected eventually to restore the balance in our favour, a considerable period of time would be required to enable that Army to develop its full strength. While it would be possible for Germany to complete her new dispositions early in the New Year, the forces which America could send to France before the season would permit active operations to be recommenced would not be large.

"In view of the situation described above it became necessary to change the policy governing the conduct of the operations of the British Armies in France. Orders accordingly were issued early in December, having for their object immediate preparations to meet a strong and sustained hostile offensive. In other words, a defensive policy was adopted and all necessary arrangements consequent thereon were put in hand with the least possible delay."

To add to Sir Douglas Haig's difficulties an additional twenty-eight miles of front had to be taken over from the French as far south as Barisis, immediately south of the Oise.

The British line in France and Flanders at the end of January was 125 miles in extent—all active front.

The new defensive policy "necessitated a vast amount of work in the construction of defences. Old systems had to be remodelled and new ones created. All available men of the fighting units, with the exception of a very small porportion undergoing training, and all labour units were employed on these tasks. Training was hindered but the preparation of defensive systems was essential."

Another, and far more serious problem faced General Headquarters. The heavy fighting of 1917, when the British Army had practically borne the brunt of the great battles of that year upon its own shoulders, had resulted in an enormous casualty list. Many divisions were pitifully weak in numbers, reinforcements from England had dropped off, and there was nothing that could be done but to disband some units to bring the others up to strength. Accordingly, towards the end of January the reduction of infantry battalions in divisions from thirteen to ten[1] was ordered.

The 19th Division received these orders on the 24th of January; all four battalions of the 56th Brigade were to be disbanded and the brigade reconstituted as follows: 8th North Staffords from the 57th Brigade, 9th Cheshires from the 58th Brigade, and 1/4th King's Own Shropshire Light Infantry from the 63rd Division. The date from which the reorganisation was to take effect in the 19th Division was the 4th of February.

It is impossible to express adequately the heart-burnings which these changes created. All divisions were affected, some even disappeared for the time being and became cadres. The four Lancashire battalions of the 56th Brigade had served the Division well; they had taken part in many a hard fight and had done much towards its successes and great reputation. But what had to be could not be avoided.

---

[1] *i.e.*, including the Pioneer Battalions.

K

Sir Douglas Haig, in a personal letter to General Sir John Byng (commanding Third Army) said: "I know how deeply officers and men will feel the severance of the ties binding them to the units in which they have served and fought with such splendid gallantry and success, and with which they had hoped eventually to return home after the great struggle had been won and their task achieved. But I know also that since this reorganisation has to be, it will be accepted with the loyalty and devotion with which every trial has been met by British officers and men throughout the War."

A copy of this letter was given to every battalion coming out of the line and was communicated verbally to all ranks.

And the G.O.C., 19th Division, added these words: "I know that all ranks of the 19th Division join with me in deeply regretting the loss of old comrades and in wishing them good-bye and the best of luck wherever they may go."

The actual date of disbandment of the four Lancashire Battalions of the 56th Brigade appears to have been: 7th East Lancs. and 7th Loyal North Lancs. on the 6th of February; 7th South Lancs. and 7th King's Own Royal Lancaster Regiment on the 22nd.

The four machine-gun companies were also amalgamated into the 19th Battalion Machine-Gun Corps, and the 5th South Wales Borderers (Pioneers) were reduced to three companies.

No events of special importance took place during January, February, or the first fortnight of March. The enemy's shell-fire was not excessive, patrolling was very active but there were few encounters with the enemy and the trenches were better than the water-logged line of the Ypres Salient. The "rest" billets behind the line were, however, very poor, and the enemy's aeroplanes were continually busy at night, which made life out of the front line decidedly uncomfortable.

A great deal of demolition was carried out during this period by the Field Companies, R.E., chiefly of derelict tanks, dug-outs, and buildings in No Man's Land, in order to render them untenable by the enemy. The destruction of three large cellars at Dago House, about 400 yards in front of the Divisional outpost line, will be remembered.

But if there was "little doing" in the front line so far as actions with the enemy were concerned, there was a vast amount of work to be performed, and all ranks had a strenuous time in January and February strengthening existing defences and building new ones.

On the 15th of the latter month the 19th Division was relieved by the 63rd (Naval) Division, and moved back to the Haplincourt area. A course of progressive training was immediately begun, numerous counter-attack schemes forming a considerable portion of the training programme. These counter-attacks were practised in conjunction with No. 8 Tank Battalion.

By the middle of March the Division had attained that high standard of efficiency which showed itself during the next three months in the brilliant manner in which all ranks fought the Boche, in what has aptly been termed the greatest battle in the military history of the world.

CHAPTER XVI

THE GREY AVALANCHE
THE GERMAN OFFENSIVES OF 1918
I. IN PICARDY: 21st MARCH—5th APRIL

NO words can give an adequate picture of the tense feeling existing in the Fifth and Third Armies between the 1st and 21st of March, 1918. The Great German Offensive was expected—but when? The question held everyone, from G.O.C. to private, in a constant state of anxious suspense.

No operation along the Western Front, indeed no battle in the military history of the world, was of such gigantic proportions. Nor is that view exaggerated, for when all his plans for the attack had been made, General Ludendorff told the Kaiser that: "The Battle in the West is the greatest military task that has ever been imposed upon an army," and when, on the eve of the attack, the three great German Armies were preparing to advance, he said: "I reported to the Emperor that the Army was assembled and well prepared to undertake the biggest task in its history."

Only in one thing was the Chief of the German General Staff wrong, *i.e.*, his statement that preparations for the attack, the front upon which the German assault would take place, and the approximate date were unknown to us. For in his despatches Sir Douglas Haig states: "Towards the middle of February, 1918, it became evident that the enemy was preparing for a big offensive on the Western Front . . . By the end of February, 1918, these preparations had become very marked opposite the front held by the Third and Fifth British Armies . . . . As the 21st of March approached it became certain that an attack on this sector was imminent."

"Nor did the enemy discover anything by other means. I must assume this; otherwise his defensive measures would have been more effective and his reserves would have arrived more quickly."[1]

But more than half the British divisions in France and

---

[1] General Ludendorff.

Flanders were even then contained in the Fifth and Third Armies, for Sir Douglas Haig could not denude other parts of the front; every officer and man who could possibly be spared had been put into the line.

The German plan of attack was as follows: Three Armies, Seventeenth, Second, and Eighteenth (in that order from right to left[1]) were to attack the Third and Fifth Armies from La Fere to Croisilles, *i.e.*, the Seventeenth on the line Croisilles–Moeuvres, Second and Eighteenth between Villers Guislain and La Fere. "In these operations the Seventeenth and Second were to take the weight off each other in turn, and, with their inner wings, cut off the enemy holding the Cambrai re-entrant,[2] afterwards pushing through between Croisilles and Peronne. This advance was to be protected on the south flank by the Eighteenth Army in combination with the extreme left wing of the Second."

The Seventeenth Army consisted of twenty-eight divisions, the Second of twenty-two divisions, and the Eighteenth of twenty-six divisions. Thirteen divisions were holding the line on the morning of the 21st; twenty-eight divisions formed the first wave of the attack, nineteen divisions the second wave, and sixteen divisions the third wave.

Against this huge force there were eighteen British divisions in the line on the 21st of March and eleven in reserve, *i.e.*, from opposite La Fere to Croisilles.

Apart from the enormous superiority in infantry the enemy had an overwhelming preponderance in artillery—twenty to thirty batteries to each kilometre, without counting trench-mortars, of which there were a great number.

To meet this great attack the following preparations were made: "The general principle of our defensive arrangements on the front of these Armies (Fifth and Third) was the distribution of our troops in depth. With this object three defensive belts, sited at considerable distance from each other, had been constructed or were approaching completion in the forward area, the most advanced of which was in the nature of a lightly-held outpost screen covering our main positions."[3]

There were three "zones," *i.e.*, Forward, Battle, and Rear,

---

[1] Or from left to right facing us.

[2] Known to us as the Flesquières Salient.

[3] Official Despatches.

the outpost line being out in front of the first-named; there were also intermediate lines of defence between each zone.

The story of the German Offensive, so far as it concerns the 19th Division, is that of the operations on the V and IV Corps (Third Army) front, to which the Division belonged.

The V Corps on the 21st of March was holding the Flesquières Salient from about 1,500 yards north-west of Gonnelieu to south of Mœuvres. As already explained, the Germans hoped to "pinch off" the Salient by heavy attacks north and south of the re-entrant; the Corps front, therefore, was not subjected to violent infantry assaults on the 21st of March, such as took place against the Fifth Army and the remainder of the Third Army, but hostile shell-fire on the Corps area was just as severe as on other areas.

The five divisions forming the V Corps were the 47th, 63rd, and 17th holding the front line, in that order from right to left, and the 2nd (right) and 19th (left) in reserve in the Rear zone.

The 19th Division was located in the area Bertincourt–Velu–Haplincourt, having on more than one occasion during the early days of March received orders to relieve the 17th Division, which orders were subsequently cancelled owing to the Boche offensive seeming imminent. On the 11th, Corps Headquarters received an order from Third Army Headquarters that no reliefs were to take place until further orders, but late on the 18th the 19th and 47th Divisions were ordered to relieve the 17th and 2nd Divisions respectively, between the 22nd and 24th of March.

Meanwhile, in the rear zone the 19th Division had carried out a good deal of work on the battle zone and rear defences. Variouss chemes for counter-attacks in conjunction with Tanks and contact aeroplanes were prepared, and localities reconnoitred. These schemes aimed at the re-capture of definite localities:—Havrincourt, Hermies, Doignies, Louverval, and Beaumetz. Places of assembly were allotted to brigades in the event of any of these counter-attacks being necessary.

The 56th Brigade was located at Beaulencourt, the 57th at Barastre, and the 58th Brigade on the Haplincourt–Bertincourt road. Divisional Headquarters were at Haplincourt, on the Haplincourt–Bertincourt road.

During the third week in March it became more and more certain that the attack was almost due. Opposite the IV Corps area (on the left of the V Corps) no fewer than 120 new battery positions were counted; new divisions were identified, and prisoners definitely stated that the offensive would begin on the 21st or 22nd.

Throughout the period from the 8th to the 21st vigorous "counter-preparation" was carried out each night by the field and heavy artillery along the whole Army front. Bursts of fire were opened for short periods during darkness and from half an hour before dawn, until it was evident that no attack was intended. Up to the morning of the 21st of March there was no change in the tactics of the enemy's artillery, though on two nights the right and centre divisions along the Corps front were subjected to severe bombardments with mustard-gas shells. These bombardments lasted for four hours and were particularly heavy in the neighbourhood of Trescault and Boar Copse Valley.

This gas was extremely virulent. Its action was insidious, for only after several hours did its victims begin to show signs of "gassing," first in the eyes and throat, then vomiting set in, and soon the man was in a terrible condition.

"We met a party of the 60th and R.A.M.C. coming down gassed. Those who were temporarily blinded (who were in the large majority) were being led by those who could see. Some of the men were in considerable pain in their eyes and lungs, others being sick and throwing themselves on the ground when there was a halt and clasping their heads."[1]

One battalion diary, after describing the frightful effects of this dastardly gas, said: "The most careful and thorough precautions had to be taken. For example, men who had been in the infected area and who, by wearing respirators were not affected at the time, were found to be subsequently made ill by sleeping in their clothes to which the gas had clung, consequently clothing had to be removed outside billets, and sleeping in close proximity to other men became unsafe."

Divisions in the line suffered most, though support companies and battalion headquarters suffered more than the actual front-line companies. In three days a brigade of the 2nd Division had nearly 1,000 officers and men "gassed."

Of the 19th Division only the gunners mention this heavy gas shelling, for they were nearer to the front line than the infantry

---

[1] G.O.C., 2nd Division. It is interesting to note that this incident was witnessed by that fine artist, the late John Sargent, and formed the subject of his picture, "Gassed," now in the Imperial War Museum.

of the Division. The Diary of the 87th Royal Field Artillery Brigade (near Trescault) records: "In action; the batteries experienced severe times, notably from the 11th to the 13th, when they were subjected to intense gas-shell bombardment. 'B' and 'D/87' were particularly heavily shelled." The 88th Brigade, R.F.A. (south of Metz and south-east of Vallulart Wood) also mention the gas bombardment, though no details of casualties are given.

THE BATTLE OF ST. QUENTIN: 21st–23rd MARCH

The night of the 20th/21st was quiet, with that ominous quietude which often heralds the coming of great events. The attack was expected on the 21st, for two German prisoners taken by the French further south had given definite information, but the hour was uncertain.

That night the 2nd Division was relieved by the 47th, but before command of the sector passed to the G.O.C. of the latter Division the great offensive had opened.

As the night advanced and midnight was passed, a thick mist gathered slowly over the battlefield-to-be.

At 4.40 a.m. the British guns opened fire in accordance with the usual counter-preparation programme. Ten minutes later hostile drum-fire of terrific violence was opened by the enemy's artillery. The forward trench systems and battery positions were wreathed in clouds of smoke from bursting shells of all calibres, which, added to the mist, shrouded everything in complete fog. Long-range hostile artillery shelled the back areas and all roads and communications for miles behind the front line. Trench-mortar fire on the front line and support trenches was very severe.

The nature of this bombardment left no doubt that the attack had started.

For five hours this savage hail of shell continued, and then the enemy's gun were concentrated in an intense barrage on the front-line and support trenches.

Between 9 a.m. and 9.30 a.m. his infantry advanced to the attack; they came across No Man's Land in thousands, in dense masses shoulder to shoulder, and they loomed up out of the fog and mist before ever the British outposts had time to realise that the attack had begun. S.O.S. signals sent up immediately were useless, as the fog hid the bursting lights, not only from the gunners who were on the watch for them, but also from observers actually in the front line. Nothing could be seen; only the sounds as of a great rustling and shuffling of feet and the hoarse, gutteral cries of the enemy's officers and N.C.Os. The outposts were overwhelmed and the grey avalanche swept on towards the trenches north and south of the Flesquières Salient; on the Salient itself no infantry attack was made, so, for the time being, the V Corps had little more to do than to man battle positions and watch developments, taking all possible precautions against attack.

At 5.30 a.m. V Corps Headquarters had ordered the 2nd and 19th Divisions to "stand to" and prepare to move to positions of assembly.

The Division immediately on the left of the 17th Division was the 51st belonging to the IV Corps, and the first news 19th Divisional Headquarters had from the front line was received from the liaison officer of the 51st, who at 10.25 a.m. reported that the enemy was attacking. At 10.55 a.m. the 51st Division reported that the enemy had occupied the front-line systems of their left and centre brigades and that it was their intention to hold the Beaumetz–Morchies system; on the right of the V Corps also the enemy was reported as advancing on the VIII Corps front.

At 11.10 a.m. orders were received at 19th Divisional Head-quarters from the V Corps to move to assembly positions, and by 11.30 a.m. all units had been informed.

The move of the 56th Brigade was completed by 3 p.m., at which hour the three battalions, i.e., 4th Shropshire Light Infantry, 8th North Staffords, and 9th Cheshires, were just west of Bertincourt with Brigade Headquarters at Sanders Camp, east of Haplincourt; the 57th Brigade moved to positions west of Velu Wood at 1 p.m., "B" Company of the 19th Machine-Gun Battalion being attached to the brigade. One company of the 10th Royal Warwicks was sent to form four platoon posts on the ridge north-east of Velu on a very wide front, i.e., a distance of over 1,500 yards, the left flank just east of Beaumetz.

As a result of the information received at 11.30 a.m. that the enemy was reported to have reached the second system between Louverval and Lagnicourt, one company of the 6th Wilts. (58th Brigade) was moved to the high ground between Beugny and Lebucquière to form a line of posts and keep Brigade Headquarters in touch with the situation on that flank. Orders to move to assembly positions in Gaika Copse had reached

58th Brigade Headquarters at 11.44 a.m. The brigade moved off, the 9th Welch sending one company to establish posts along the Hermies–Beaumetz Ridge from Hermies to the cross-roads west of that place, where they were to join up with the right of the company of 10th Warwicks (57th Brigade). By 12.35 p.m. the remainder of the 58th Brigade was concentrated in Gaika Copse and neighbourhood.

Meanwhile the situation as known at 19th Divisional Headquarters at 12.35 p.m. was as follows: north of the Bapaume–Cambrai road the Boche had captured the second system and Louverval, Louverval Wood and Boursies. We still held the third system (Beaumetz–Morchies line) intact. South of the Cambrai road we held the second system to Sturgeon Avenue, thence along the Sturgeon Support which was held south of Sturgeon Avenue only. South of Sturgeon Support and south of the Canal du Nord the front-line system remained intact.

But reports from several sources showed that the enemy was moving in large numbers in a southerly direction from the north and north-east; his attempt to "pinch off" the Salient was in progress.

At 2.15 p.m. the centre brigade of the 51st Division reported that Doignies had fallen, and that unless a counter-attack was made to capture that place they must withdraw from Sturgeon Avenue and Support.

At 3 p.m. the 19th Division was placed under orders of the IV Corps and instructed to insure the retention of the high ground between Hermies and Lebucquière. About 3.15 p.m. verbal orders over the telephone were received at Divisional Headquarters from the Corps Commander for the 19th Division, assisted by the 8th Battalion of Tanks, to counter-attack and re-take Doignies.

The G.O.C., 57th Brigade, and the O.C. 8th Battalion Tanks, were summoned to Divisional Headquarters and ordered to undertake the counter-attack with two battalions and twelve tanks, supported by "B" Company of the 19th Machine-Gun Battalion; two trench-mortars of the 57th Brigade Trench-Mortar Battery were also to co-operate.

Just before 5 p.m. the company of 6th Wilts.[1] was replaced

---

[1] It will be remembered that the 6th Wiltshires in 1917 had absorbed the Royal Wiltshire Yeomanry, their new designation being the 6th (Wiltshire Yeomanry) Battalion of the Wiltshire Regiment.

by the 4th King's Shropshire Light Infantry of the 56th Brigade.

As artillery to support the attack could not be got into position before, "Zero" hour was subsequently fixed for 7 p.m.

The 8th Gloucesters were attacking on the right, 10th Worcesters on the left, and the 10th Royal Warwicks were in reserve.

The objective was Doignies with a platoon thrown back along the Doignies–Beaumetz road.

Darkness had fallen when the attacking infantry, preceded by tanks, advanced on Doignies. Both the Gloucesters and Worcesters encountered the enemy in and beyond the third system. The Gloucesters, though under heavy machine-gun fire, penetrated as far as Doignies church; one company—"A" —was counter-attacked and surrounded. The Company Commander (Capt. James), however, succeeded in getting a runner through to "D" Company (Capt. Bowles) who immediately organised a counter-attack and gallantly extricated "A" Company. These two companies captured one officer and twenty-seven prisoners and two machine-guns. The 10th Worcesters reached the Doignies–Beaumetz road, their objective.

The Gloucesters were now in a desperate position; their right flank was "in the air" and artillery, machine-gun and rifle fire had been opened on them, their casualties being very heavy.

They were, therefore, compelled to withdraw. This withdrawal uncovered the right of the 10th Worcesters, and the latter, enfiladed also from Doignies and Louverval, were similarly forced to fall back, though two companies remained on the road some fifty yards from the enemy's most advanced line.

The two battalions (less the two companies mentioned) then reorganised in a sunken road running south-east from Beaumetz.

The attack was made with great gallantry and determination, and Brig.-General T. A. Cubitt (G.O.C., 57th Brigade) said in his report: "I am of opinion that if delivered at 6 p.m. with a simultaneous attack on Louverval it would have been completely successful."

From this time the 57th Brigade was involved in the fighting and was on the right of, and to some extent mixed up with, the 51st Division.

Meanwhile the 56th and 58th Brigades had been on the move. The former, at 6 p.m., had received orders to form the Divisional Reserve in the attack on Doignies, and move to the neighbourhood of Gaika Copse, south-west of Velu Wood. At 10.30 p.m. further orders were received to occupy the Green Line, from about 500 yards south-east of Delsaux Farm to the main Bapaume–Cambrai road. The Green Line was found to be strongly wired, but only partially dug, and at 3 a.m. work of strengthening the defences began, two companies of the South Wales Borderers (Pioneers), two Field Companies, R.E., and "A" Company, 19th Battalion, Machine-Gun Company, assisting in consolidating the line.

The 58th Brigade, at 4.45 p.m., was ordered to move to the ridge west of Hermies, battalions arriving on the ridge at about 6.45 p.m., when they at once began to dig in. The 9th Welch were on the right, 9th Royal Welch Fusiliers on the left, and 6th Wilts. in support. The 82nd Field Company, R.E., and one company Pioneers assisted in digging the line. Work was in progress when at 8.30 p.m. other orders arrived from the Division to occupy the Hermies Switch. Units were informed, but before the movement could be completed Divisional Headquarters stated that the brigade would probably have to move *en bloc* to west of Lebucquière. At 11.25 p.m. definite orders for the latter move were received, and by 4 a.m. on the 22nd the 58th Brigade was concentrated along the Lebucquière–Fremicourt road, with patrols pushed out to Mochies to keep touch with the situation on the Beaumetz–Morchies line.

The marching and counter-marching on the 21st caused great fatigue to all ranks.

Such were the movements of the three infantry brigades, with attached troops, on the 21st of March.[1]

Of the Divisional Artillery (87th and 88th Field Artillery Brigades) there is little information on the 21st of March. The gunners were in the line still, in the neighbourhood of Havrincourt and Trescault, shelled heavily but not having to move for the Flesquières Salient had "held" and orders had not been issued to withdraw.

---

[1]The Bearer Divisions of the 57th and 59th Field Ambulances did particularly good work during the 21st in clearing casualties suffered by the 57th Brigade in the counter-attack on Doignies, and by the 58th Brigade in front of Beugny on the 22nd and 23rd of March.

The diaries of the three Field Ambulances show the medical men doing their utmost to cope with the rush of wounded.

With gratitude those who served in the forward area during the March Retreat of 1918, well remember the devotion of the gunners and the doctors.

At nightfall on the 21st of March, as will be seen from the foregoing narrative, the 19th Division had not been attacked other than by shell-fire.

At dawn on the 22nd the Division held the following positions: Divisional Headquarters had moved to a position just south of Bancourt. From front to rear the three infantry brigades were disposed as follows: 57th Brigade in the third system, immediately east of Beaumetz facing north-east towards Doignies and Brigade Headquarters in Bancourt; 58th Brigade concentrated in readiness west of Lebucquière; 56th Brigade in the Green Line south and south-west of Beugny with its left on the Bapaume–Cambrai road.

Of the 19th Battalion Machine-Gun Company, "A" Company was with the 56th Brigade, "B" with the 57th Brigade, and "C" and "D" Companies in assembly positions just west of Velu Wood. The Pioneers (5th South Wales Borderers) had one company with the 57th Brigade and two working on the Green Line. Two of the Field Companies, R.E. (81st and 82nd) were also at work on the Green Line, while the 94th Field Company, R.E., was with the 58th Brigade.

Dawn of the 22nd broke with the ground again covered by a thick mist, under cover of which the enemy renewed his attacks in great strength all along the line. Fierce fighting was soon in progress.

At 4 a.m. the three front companies of the 8th Gloucesters again attacked Doignies, but without success, the battalion falling back on its original position after suffering heavy casualties.

At 6.15 a.m. (according to the Divisional Narrative) the 57th Brigade was placed under the orders of the 154th Brigade (51st Division), though the Gloucesters state that they were under the orders of the latter brigade at 12.1 a.m.

Between 9 a.m. and 1 p.m. the sunken road running south-east of Beaumetz and the positions held by the 10th Royal Warwicks were heavily shelled.

Three times during the morning and afternoon the enemy endeavoured to debouch from the outskirts of Doignies, but on each occasion was driven back by rifle and machine-gun fire by the Gloucesters,[1] 10th Worcesters, and "B" Company, 19th Battalion Machine-Gun Company. His losses were very heavy.

In the Doignies–Beaumetz road the Worcesters were under enfilade rifle and machine-gun fire from Doignies and suffered many casualties. Their left flank was still in the air, but though the enemy was only fifty yards away they kept him at bay and shot down his troops whenever they showed themselves. During the evening the Worcesters came under the orders of the G.O.C., 152nd Brigade (51st Division), though the remainder of the 57th Brigade remained attached to the 154th Brigade. At 11 p.m. the Worcesters were ordered to occupy a position in the open south and south-west of Beaumetz, the move being completed by 4 a.m. on the 23rd. The Gloucesters, however, remained in the Third System with elements of the 51st Division. The 10th Warwicks had remained in close support all day long.

The G.O.C., 58th Brigade (Brig.-General A. E. Glasgow) had received orders at about 1.30 a.m. that the brigade was to be prepared to counter-attack, assisted by tanks, if the enemy broke through the Beaumetz–Morchies lines. But no move of the brigade took place until between 10 and 11 a.m., and then under the following circumstances: shortly after 8 a.m. the enemy advanced against that portion of the Beaumetz–Morchies line north of the Cambrai road; he was at once engaged by machine-gun fire. At 9.30 a.m. a IV Corps message to 19th Divisional Headquarters reported that as the front of the 6th Division, east and north-east of Morchies, appeared insecure, the 58th Brigade was to be moved forward west of Lebucquière to the north-eastern side of Beugny, to protect that place and the spur running north and north-east from it.

The move took place and was completed by 11 a.m., at which hour three companies of the 6th Wilts. were dug in, in a line of posts east of the sunken road running from the Sugar Factory, on the Bapaume–Cambrai road, to Morchies. The left flank of the line was swung back to meet the 9th Royal Welch Fusiliers, who were on the left of the Wilts. and were dug in on a line crossing two ridges about 500 yards south-west of Morchies; they also had three companies in the line and one in support. The 9th Welch garrisoned and held

---

[1] The Gloucesters' casualties on the 22nd were 7 officers and 200 other ranks.

Beugny, three companies formed a semi-circle round the northern outskirts of the village, and one in the village in support. The Welch Fusiliers were unable to obtain touch with troops on their left, and two companies of the 9th Welch with a section of machine-guns were sent forward at 2 p.m. to endeavour to gain touch with troops on the left, failing that to form a defensive flank back to the Green Line. While the Welch were moving the enemy was observed massing in large numbers on the high ground between Vaulx and Morchies. Repeated requests for artillery fire met with no response, for there were no guns in the neighbourhood.

At 3.30 p.m. the Boche made a heavy attack along the front held by the 9th Royal Welch Fusiliers, though the Wilts were not attacked. The Welch Fusiliers, however, dealt with the situation in a most workmanlike manner—they shot down scores of the enemy and repulsed all his attempts to advance. The enemy had even brought up cavalry in readiness to support his attack, but thanks to the staunch defence by the Fusiliers the Boche found it unnecessary to call upon his mounted troops.

At about 5 p.m. a counter-attack by Tanks was launched, which drove the enemy helter-skelter back to the Morchies–Vaulx road and inflicted further severe casualties on him.

At about 8 p.m. the enemy attempted to raid a post of the 6th Wilts. nearest Morchies, but here again he had no luck and fell back, leaving one other rank dead in front of the post. This incident closed the fighting by the 58th Brigade on the 22nd.

In the Green Line, held by the 56th Brigade, the day had passed comparatively quietly. The 9th Cheshires held the southern half of the brigade front, the 8th North Staffords the northern half; the 4th King's Shropshire Light Infantry were in reserve just south of Fremicourt. Touch on the left had been obtained with the 7th Brigade, but not until later was touch on the right obtained with the 6th Brigade (2nd Division). Each battalion had three companies in the front line, distributed in depth, and one in support. There were also ten direct-fire Vickers guns and six guns to form a battery for barrage purposes. Six Stokes mortars were also in position. Without interruption the work of consolidation proceeded all day long.

At 9.10 p.m the K.S.L.I. were ordered to move to support

the right flank[1] of the 58th Brigade and prevent the enemy moving between the Cambrai road and Lebucquière. An hour later the Shropshires were ordered to dig in facing north on ground south-east of the Sugar Factory on the Cambrai road and thus cover Lebucquière. But the enemy had already frustrated the battalion and was, in point of fact, at that moment engaged in advancing on the village. The C.O. of the Shropshires, therefore, decided to take up a line just north-west of the village facing north-east, in touch with the 58th Brigade on his left and on the right with some Royal Engineers of the 51st Division who had been placed in position to defend Lebucquière.

But if the 21st and 22nd of March had not witnessed the heaviest fighting along the 19th Divisional front, the great struggle was close at hand when darkness fell on the latter date.

Final orders by 19th Divisional Headquarters, issued at 10 p.m. on the 22nd, gave instructions for adjustments in the line; the 58th Brigade was to effect a junction with the 51st Division on the Cambrai road in the neighbourhood of the Sugar Factory, and with the 123rd Brigade (41st Division) on the high ground about half-way between Beugny and Morchies, and was to hold the line from its junction with the 51st Division to the high ground previously mentioned, thus covering Beugny from the north-east. The 56th Brigade was to hold the Green Line from south of Delvaux Wood to the high ground north-west of Beugny, one battalion (the K.S.L.I. already mentioned) dug in to cover the ground between Lebucquière and Beaumetz. "D" Company of the 19th Battalion Machine-Gun Company was to concentrate just east of Fremicourt and so place its guns as to sweep the Cambrai road.

On the left of the 19th Division the 41st Division was holding the Green Line, and on the right the 2nd Division was in touch (also on the Green Line) with the right of the 56th Brigade.

It will have been observed that whatever attacks the 19th Division had made on the enemy, or had been made on the Division, were on the northern (or left) flank rather than frontally. The three divisions of the V Corps, i.e., 47th right, 63rd centre, and 17th left, had fallen back but a short distance

---

[1]All the records say "right flank," but from the map dispositions it seems the left flank is meant.

since the 21st, not under pressure from the enemy, but by orders from Corps Headquarters, in order that the flanks might not be unduly exposed. But the enemy, furious at being repulsed and unable to carry out his plan of "pinching off" the Flesquières Salient, now began to advance on the V Corps from the south-east and north.

During the night of the 22nd/23rd the V Corps had withdrawn to a line covering Equancourt and Metz-en-Couture, in touch with the Fifth Army about the former village.

The story of the fighting on the 23rd of March by the 19th Division is one of great gallantry, tenacity, and devotion to duty, but of a confused nature. It is impossible to follow the operations in any regular sequence, for at times the struggle was local, at others general. Movement was everywhere, some troops advancing, others retiring.

The narrative as contained in the documents of 19th Divisional Headquarters, is, therefore, followed, the story being enlarged as it proceeds with information from the diaries of all other units of the Division.

The situation at dawn on the 23rd was, as given in Divisional Orders, issued at 10.10 p.m. on the 22nd/23rd, and already described. At 2.30 a.m. on the latter date all units were notified that the 17th Division was withdrawing from Havrincourt during the night and occupying a line east of Havrincourt Wood to the Canal du Nord, west of the village.

As early as 4.33 a.m. instructions were issued for the withdrawal of all troops in front (east) of the Green Line, in conformity with a similar withdrawal on the V Corps front, on the night of the 23rd/24th. The 56th and 58th Brigades were then to hold the Green Line on the right and left respectively. The 57th Brigade was to withdraw to Fremicourt in Divisional Reserve, and come again under the orders of its own division.

In the Green Line the night of the 22nd/23rd passed quietly, which enabled rations to be brought up to units; they were lucky, for many battalions had no rations and little water. At about 6.20 a.m. the right company of the 9th Cheshires reported to Brigade Headquarters that S.O.S. signals had been seen on the IV and V Corps front near Lebucquière. The enemy was then seen advancing down the main road, making steady progress between Lebucquière and Velu. The right front of the Shropshires was exposed and the battalion then

L

withdrew to the Green Line, arriving at about 8 a.m. They assembled on the outskirts of Bancourt, where they were again in Brigade Reserve.

The 5th South Wales Borderers and 6th Gordons (51st Division) at this period came under the tactical orders of the G.O.C., 56th Brigade, and the O.C., 8th North Staffords, was placed in command of the forward area. The Brigade Commander (Brig.-General F. G. Willan) then moved his headquarters to the neighbourhood of the waterworks on the Bapaume–Bancourt road, where the O.C. Artillery Group, covering the Divisional front, also had his headquarters.

At 12.40 p.m. the Boche was seen coming on in large numbers towards the Green Line from the direction of Lebucquière. Reserves were moved further forward to meet this threatened attack, four machine-guns were brought into action in new positions to cover the threatened flank, and under their fire the enemy was forced to withdraw.

About 2.40 p.m. Brigade Headquarters received a report that troops in the Green Line, just north-west of Beugny, had fallen back, but they were sent back by the O.C., "A" Company, 19th Battalion Machine-Gun Company (Capt. Jones). This part of the line had been subjected to terrific shell-fire and the defences had been badly damaged. In the neighbourhood of Delsaux Farm also hostile shelling had considerably increased. But by 3 p.m. Brigade Headquarters received a report that all was quiet, and that the enemy had returned to Lebucquière. But it was only a lull in the struggle, for at 6.15 p.m. the Boche was seen coming on again in dense masses towards Beugny, though they were effectively dealt with by the guns.

At 10.35 p.m. a patrol came in contact with the enemy, who was observed massing south-east of Beugny. The artillery at once put down a heavy concentration on that area.

The 56th Brigade Narrative of the operations on the 23rd of March concludes with these words: "The night was quiet."

In the diaries of the three battalions of the brigade, *i.e.*, 9th Cheshires, 8th North Staffords and 4th K.S.L.I., there is nothing of importance which has not been related above.

But if the fury of the enemy's attacks had not yet fallen upon the 56th Brigade, the 23rd of March had witnessed fierce fighting along the fronts of the 57th and 58th Brigades. The confusion caused by troops moving quickly from place to place, and the intermixing of units, is responsible for the extraordinary, and at times contradictory, nature of the records. Each battalion was largely concerned with its own particular "show," though mentioning at times the positions of other battalions on the flanks, in front or in rear, *as they appeared to be.* It is, therefore, almost impossible to give a clear and coherent account of the fierce fighting and involved struggles, which, so far as the 57th and 58th Brigades were concerned, took place on the 23rd of March; and to add to the difficulty the Battalion Diary of the 10th Worcesters for March 1918 is missing.

The 57th Brigade Narrative states that in the early morning (it was about 2 a.m.) the 10th Warwicks were ordered to prolong their flank to the left and join up with the 10th Worcesters, which would have the effect of blocking the south-eastern exits of Beaumetz. So far as can be ascertained the Warwicks were then holding a roughly-dug line which faced a ridge immediately north of the railway between Velu and Hermies and south-east of Beaumetz. The order of companies from the right was "D," "A," and "B." "C" Company was in Battalion Reserve just south of the railway.

The blocking of Beaumetz was carried out by two platoons of "B" Company. The O.C., Warwicks, was then ordered by the G.O.C., 154th Brigade (51st Division) to hold the position to the east and not reinforce troops in the Third System[1] or counter-attack the enemy should the latter succeed in breaking into the Third System; these orders had also been given previously to the O.C., Warwicks, by the G.O.C., 57th Brigade. At 3 a.m. Headquarters, 154th Brigade, disappeared "into the blue" with the expressed intention of moving back to Fremicourt; but from that time no further communication whatever was received from the Brigadier of that brigade.

The 10th Worcesters, it will be remembered, had taken up position south and south-west of Beaumetz by 4 a.m. on the 23rd. The 8th Gloucesters, with elements of the 51st Division, were still in the Third System between Doignies and Beaumetz.

Thus the positions of the three brigades were fairly well defined when dawn broke on the 23rd.

The 57th Light Trench-Mortar Battery was behind the left flank of the 10th Warwicks.

[1]Approximately the Third System ran in a north and south line about half-way between the north-western corner of Havrincourt Wood and Velu Wood.

Dawn had already broken when the enemy's guns opened a terrific bombardment of the whole line, which continued until 9 a.m. At the latter hour his infantry came on in dense masses, utterly regardless of the loss of life. If the sight of those brave fellows (and no one will deny that when a man advances against troops whom he knows to be foes determined to hold their lines to the last, he is no coward) marching shoulder to shoulder in thickly-packed waves, was an inspiring sight—it was, nevertheless, sheer murder on the part of those who sent them forward in that formation. They provided targets such as rarely fall to the lot of the infantrymen, and of which the latter took full advantage. Machine-guns, Lewis-guns, and rifle bullets tore and shattered their ranks—they fell in hundreds. Yet still the mass poured on over the dead and wounded bodies of their comrades; it was a magnificent sight, yet terrible to behold.

Lieut.-Colonel Heath, commanding the 10th Warwicks, had assumed control of the operations on the 57th Brigade front, since he had been left without a brigadier to give him instructions.[1]

The 51st Division began to withdraw, which left the flanks of the 10th Warwicks and 8th Gloucesters in the air; they held their ground with grim determination until 11 a.m. and then began to withdraw, the 10th Warwicks to north of the railway between Velu and Velu Wood and facing Velu Wood.

Two incidents there were on the 23rd of March of outstanding gallantry, which will never be forgotten by the 19th Division and all who witnessed them.

The first was the withdrawal of the 8th Gloucesters. The battalion was very hard pressed, and that it was able to get away at all was due to the heroism of Capt. M. A. James and officers and other ranks of "A" Company who covered the withdrawal.

Ordered to "hold on to the last," with the enemy passing through on his right flank, he and his gallant little party stood their ground, inflicting heavy losses on the Germans and gaining valuable time also for the withdrawal of guns. On the 21st of March he had been wounded but continued to fight in the most gallant manner. As the bulk of his regiment was falling back, he led "A" Company forward on his own initiative in a local counter-attack, being wounded again. The

---

[1]The brigade was still under the G.O.C., 154th Brigade (51st Division).

company maintained its position until the last man fell. Capt. James was seen finally manning a machine-gun single-handed, having been wounded a third time; he and the remnants of his heroic little party were then overwhelmed, but not before they had successfully covered the retirement of the other companies. Capt. James was taken and later he was awarded the Victoria Cross, which he so richly deserved.[1]

There is, however, some doubt as to the position taken up by the Gloucesters on falling back. The 57th Brigade Narrative says: "8th Gloucesters were south of Velu Wood," while the 10th Warwicks say that "the Gloucesters apparently had fallen back either through, or to the west of, Velu Wood." The Battalion Diary of the Gloucesters has this entry: "Meantime collapse of the left allowed enemy to get into Velu Wood. The enemy was through Velu Wood very quickly and the brigade was saved from capture by rushing up a company of Gloucesters and Worcesters[2] in rear of Velu Wood, where they were able to stop the enemy on the edge and undoubtedly saved a battery of 18-pounders (2nd Division) which was in action in the open, firing with open sights on the enemy advancing over the ridge on the right."

With the Boche entering Velu Wood the 10th Warwicks threw back a defensive flank along the railway on the east side of the Wood. To form the flank Battalion Headquarters' personnel and any other men available were used, while some stragglers from the 51st Division were collected and formed up to hold a bank east of the railway and north-east of the Wood.

A major of the 51st Battalion Machine-Gun Company and Capt. Knox-Little, 19th Battalion Machine-Gun Company, reported to Colonel Heath and asked for instructions, and when told that the battalion was going "to hold on" they returned to their guns north-east of the Wood. The first-mentioned officer and his men appeared to be the only troops of the 51st Division in the neighbourhood.

---

[1] *London Gazette*, 28/6/18.

[2] The Narrative of the 57th Brigade has the following paragraph which apparently refers to the companies of Gloucesters and Worcesters mentioned:— "During the morning R.S.M. Hopcroft, 8th Gloucestershire Regiment, with seventy men 8th Gloucestershire Regiment and thirty men 10th Worcestershire Regiment, dug in in front of 104th Brigade, R.F.A., and by a most spirited resistance enabled all the guns to be withdrawn, though the enemy were only 500 yards away."

Velu Wood was occupied by the enemy at 12.30 p.m.

At about that time the O.C., "D" Company of the Warwicks (the right company of the battalion) reported that troops on his right were withdrawing, and shortly afterwards the battalion (all but "D" Company) was driven back from the ridge to a road running east to west, south of the ridge, which must have been the Hermies–Velu road.

The story of the gallant stand of "D" Company is almost a repetition of the heroism of "A" Company of the Gloucesters. The Company Commander—Capt. J. R. Gribble—might easily have withdrawn his men at one period, *i.e.*, when the rest of the battalion on his left was driven back to a secondary position. But he chose to interpret his orders to "hold on to the last" to the letter. His right flank was in the air owing to the withdrawal of all troops of another division on that flank. Sending a runner back to Battalion Headquarters he expressed his determination to hold on until he received other orders. And he and his gallant comrades *did* hold on to the bitter, but glorious end. They were last seen surrounded by the enemy at close range, Capt. Gribble emptying his revolver into the grey masses. He was wounded and taken prisoner, and later died as the result of his wounds. But he, too, was rightly awarded the Victoria Cross: "By his splendid example of grit he was materially instrumental in preventing the enemy obtaining a complete mastery of the crest of the ridge for some hours after the withdrawal of troops of other divisions, and by his magnificent self-sacrifice he enabled the remainder of his own brigade to be withdrawn, as well as the garrison of Hermies and three batteries of Field Artillery.[1]

It was about 2.30 p.m. by the time the 10th Worcesters had reached the Hermies–Velu road. Time and again the enemy attempted to debouch from Velu Wood, but on each occasion he was forced back again by rifle and machine-gun fire, the machine-guns of the 51st and 19th Battalions Machine-Gun Corps rendering the utmost assistance.

But hostile fire from Velu Wood and from towards Hermies was developing, while the enemy's infantry were leaving the southern end of the wood, actually in rear of the 57th Brigade.

Lieut.-Colonel Heath was in touch with the O.C., 2nd Oxford and Bucks. Light Infantry (2nd Division) at Bertincourt, who informed him that orders were that from 3 p.m. the Green

[1]For citation from *London Gazette* of 28th June, 1918, see Appendix.

Line (which ran east and north of Bertincourt, thence in a north-westerly direction west of Beugny) was to be the front line. Colonel Heath then withdrew his Battalion (10th Warwicks) in good order *via* the railway embankment east of the wood, thence round the eastern and southern sides of Bertincourt. Subsequently, orders were received to march to Bancourt, which was reached at about 7 p.m.

Of the action of the 10th Worcesters, nothing can be said but that which has already been written, owing to the loss of their diary.

By 12 midnight 23/24th the battalions of the 57th Brigade, once more under their own Brigadier and Division, were assembled south-west of Bancourt, with the exception of two companies of the 10th Worcesters, which were still detained by the 5th Brigade (2nd Division) in the Green Line; they did not reach Bancourt until 11 a.m. on the 24th.

The brigade had lost during the day 38 officers and 795 other ranks, but their losses must have been light compared with the casualties suffered by the enemy, whose superiority in numbers was estimated at not less than nine to one.

All our wounded, excepting walking cases, had to be left behind and fell into the hands of the enemy.

On the left of the 57th Brigade the 58th Brigade had also seen heavy fighting throughout the 23rd of March, for it will be remembered that the enemy's attacks were on the flanks rather than frontal.

Briefly the positions held by the three battalions of the 58th Brigade (although they have already been given) may be recapitulated as follows: 6th Wilts., with their right on the Bapaume–Cambrai road at the Beetroot Factory, the battalion facing east along a sunken road running north from the factory to south of Morchies; the 9th Royal Welch Fusiliers were on the left of the 6th Wilts., with their left thrown back as a defensive flank along the high ground south-west of Morchies; the 9th Welch held Beugny.

During the night two battalions of the 123rd Brigade (41st Division) came up on the left of the 9th Royal Welch Fusiliers.

One prisoner and a light machine-gun were captured by the 9th Royal Welch Fusiliers during the night of the 22nd/23rd, while consolidation of the position was being carried on.

Patrols sent out by the 6th Wilts. early on the 23rd found the enemy occupying a road which ran from the eastern side of

Morchies in a south-easterly direction to a crucifix on the Bapaume–Cambrai road.

The Wilts. discovered that the Shropshires, who, on the previous night had been in touch on their right, had disappeared. Two companies of a Cheshire battalion (25th Division), whose Battalion Headquarters were with Battalion Headquarters, 9th Royal Welch Fusiliers and 6th Wilts., were then sent to form a line from the Beetroot Factory in a south-westerly direction.

Between 7 a.m. and 8 a.m. the enemy's shells began to arrive and soon the line was under a very heavy bombardment, especially the 6th Wilts. Small parties of the enemy could be seen moving from north and north-east across the front of the Wilts. to the Bapaume road, about 1,200 yards away. At this time no frontal attack was attempted by the enemy. Battalion Headquarters of the Wilts. and Royal Welch Fusiliers were, however, getting a severe gruelling, while machine-gun fire swept all the slopes between Morchies and Beugny, making movement extremely difficult.

At about 9 a.m. orders similar to those issued to the two other brigades were received; the 58th Brigade was to withdraw to the Green Line at 9.30 p.m., the 9th Welch to fall back first and hold it, the Royal Welch Fusiliers and Wilts. sending parties to north and east of Beugny, the remainder retiring through them.

Brigade Headquarters moved to Bancourt at 11 a.m.

At 1 pm., in order to protect his flank and rear, the O.C., Wilts., placed one company of the 10th Cheshires facing the Bapaume road; later two platoons of the support company of Wilts. also joined the Cheshires.

Later in the morning Brigade Headquarters had discovered that the Shropshires, who on the previous night had been on the right of the 58th Brigade, had retired, and that the right of the Wilts. was uncovered, but, as already stated, the O.C. of the latter battalion had taken steps to protect his flank. The brigade, however, on discovering the withdrawal of the Shropshires, sent an order for the 6th Wilts. and 9th Royal Welch Fusiliers to withdraw to the outskirts of Beugny. This order did not reach the battalion until about 2.30 p.m., by which time the whole line was very heavily engaged and desperate fighting was in progress.

The Wilts. state in their diary that at 2 p.m. there was a

"general attack by enemy on all our positions." The order from Brigade Headquarters is stated to have reached the Battalion at 2.15 p.m., but a withdrawal at that period would probably have been more costly than to hang on, for the following words explain the dire straits in which the Battalion found itself: "Owing to nature of ground behind us—a glacis slope up to Beugny—and the fact that an attack on all our positions was in progress, it was considered impossible to withdraw, and it was decided to hold on until nightfall. It was not at that time recognised that we were left entirely unprotected from our right rear. It was also hoped that by holding on until nightfall, and keeping the enemy in check at this point, the defence of the next line of resistance might be organised and consolidated."

So, taking advantage of whatever cover their hastily-prepared position offered, and shooting carefully, the Wilts. and Royal Welch Fusiliers prepared to sell their lives dearly—if that was to be their heroic end. By 4 p.m. the enemy had begun to get round the flanks, *i.e.*, from the Sugar Factory on the right and from Morchies on the left. But his advance was measured in feet rather than in yards. He was held in check by the steadiness of all ranks, "who," as the records state, "refused to give way," and kept up a steady and well-directed fire on all approaches. "A stubborn resistance was made, and heavy casualties were inflicted on the enemy whenever he attempted to advance."

If ever a battlefield presented the appearance of a shambles it was on the 23rd of March, when out in front of our splendid fellows, who often were almost surrounded by their foes, the ground was littered with hundreds of dead and wounded Germans, the cries of the latter as insistent as the crackle of musketry and the barking of machine-guns. How many men the Boche lost that day it is impossible to say, but his casualty list must have been prodigious.[1]

At 4.30 p.m. the Wilts. record that "a general enveloping movement by the enemy, who had collected considerable forces south of the Bapaume road, made withdrawal necessary."

---

[1] Even General Ludendorff complained that the Seventeenth German Army "had lost too heavily on the 21st and 22nd, apparently because it had fought in too dense formation." On the 23rd the slaughter was terrible, and by the 25th the Seventeenth German Army, which had attacked the Third British Army, "was already exhausted."

Orders were accordingly issued to companies to fall back. At 5 p.m. Battalion Headquarters withdrew under a heavy barrage and severe cross-fire from machine-guns, to the Green Line east of Fremicourt, where reorganisation took place.

In all, "six officers (of whom two were wounded) and thirty-two men were present when the battalion was re-formed"; this remnant was supplemented later by a new draft of sixty-four men from the depot.[1]

Throughout the night of the 23rd/24th there was intermittent shell-fire and continual machine-gun fire on the Green Line, and towards dawn on the 24th the shelling was on the increase.

Turning now to the narrative of operations of the 9th Royal Welch Fusiliers on the 23rd, their story is practically the same as that told by the 6th Wilts., of flanks being turned, of violent shell and machine-gun fire, of runners sent back with messages who fell dead from bullet or shell ere they reached their destinations; but what the diary does not relate, and every word almost breathes it, is the splendid courage of all ranks.

Even when the order from Brigade Headquarters had been received "to withdraw in small groups to a line east and north-east of Beugny," the Welch Fusiliers would not do so for "the 41st Division (on the left) had received no orders to withdraw, and it was obvious that we could not withdraw without involving them."

Various attempts by Battalion Headquarters' staff to form a defensive flank were completely wiped out by the enemy's barrage; the remaining two companies of the Cheshires were also practically wiped out by the enemy's shell-fire.

Finally, at about 5 p.m., Battalion Headquarters and personnel, having burned all maps and papers, etc., prepared to get away as best they could.

With Battalion Headquarters of the 6th Wilts. and Cheshires, Battalion Headquarters, Royal Welch Fusiliers, "came away at 5 p.m. after it became obvious that companies were endeavouring to withdraw," but very few managed to get through the barrage, and undoubtedly many officers and N.C.O.s were captured in the Battalion Headquarters' dug-out. For by 5 p.m. the enemy had worked up the Bapaume–Cambrai road practically to Beugny.

---

[1] The C.O. of the 6th Wiltshires (Lord A. Thynne) was wounded, and the second in command, Major W. W. Awdry, was killed.

The remnants of the 9th Royal Welch Fusiliers reached the Green Line at about 6.30 p.m. They numbered about sixty other ranks with nine officers.

The 9th Welch Regiment (the remaining battalion of the 58th Brigade) were, early on the 23rd, disposed as follows:— "D" Company in Beugny, "A," "B," and "C" Companies occupying a line north-west, north, and north-east of the village.

During the morning troops south of the Bapaume–Cambrai road were observed to be falling back, and at 12.30 p.m. the enemy, having secured Lebucquière, was advancing in strength on Beugny. In the meantime "D" Company had taken up a position in a road running south-east from the latter village, and "C" also was ordered to strengthen this line on the right. The latter company thus connected with the Shropshires in the Green Line.

Again and again the enemy attacked these positions, but on each occasion he was repulsed. At 4.30 p.m., however, he attacked down the main road and penetrated the line on the north-eastern outskirts of Beugny, gaining a footing in the northern edge of the village at about 5 p.m. Under orders the Welch then withdrew in perfect order to the Green Line, and by 12 midnight were established in their new position.

The Welch, however, say nothing of the gallant stand they made in order to allow as many as possible of their comrades, the Wilts. and Welch Fusiliers, to escape from the enemy. But the story is told in the Brigade Narrative: "A message received from O.C., 9th Welch, timed 3.10 p.m. stating that evacuation of forward lines was proceeding and that he was holding enemy attack well. A later message stated that no considerable number of Wilts. or Royal Welch Fusiliers had come through and that he feared many must have been cut off." . . . A further message, timed 5.20 p.m., stated that he was very heavily engaged and that all other troops appeared to have retired to the Green Line, but that he would hang on till dusk to cover withdrawal of any more of Wilts. or Royal Welch Fusiliers who might possibly get back. The 9th Welch held the village (Beugny) till dusk, when they withdrew in good order to the Green Line. They had, however, suffered very heavy casualties. "I am of opinion," said the Brigadier, "that had it not been for the fine defence of the village by the 9th Welch, none of the Wilts. or Royal Welch Fusiliers would have got away at all."

It is gratifying to note that Sir Douglas Haig mentioned this fine feat of gallantry by the 9th Welch Regiment by recording the incident in his official despatches. The latter state: " On the Third Army front, where our resources were greater, the enemy was held in check though he gained possession of Lebucquière and Beugny after a prolonged struggle. In this fighting the 9th Battalion, Welch Regiment, 19th Division, greatly distinguished itself in the defence of Beugny, which was held till dusk, thereby enabling the other battalions of the brigade, in position to the north of the village, to retreat themselves successfully from what would otherwise have been a hopeless situation."

Thus, the infantry of the 19th Division on the 23rd of March. But of those units whose efforts and devotion to duty were not less constant than those of the gallant fellows in the front line of the battle, there are, alas! few details.

No one worked harder than the 81st, 82nd, and 94th Field Companies, Royal Engineers, and the 5th South Wales Borderers (Pioneers). They dug trenches, constructed strong points, put out wire, demolished buildings, and even manned the defences; their work was invaluable. Their records contain nothing in the nature of a personal narrative, but from the hard facts stated therein it is possible to deduce something of the terrible strain upon these devoted units of the Division.

The 57th, 58th, and 59th Field Ambulances were similarly untiring in their efforts to collect, dress, and evacuate the wounded. Their casualties were heavy also, especially among the stretcher bearers. The 58th lost fourteen men, captured by the enemy in the Regimental Aid Post of the 6th Wilts. and the Royal 9th Welch Fusiliers.

The gunners were much too busy to give any more information in their diary than moves of the batteries; both the 87th and 88th Brigades, Royal Field Artillery, were continually on the move. There is, however, available a small private diary, kept by the O.C., Wagon Lines (Capt. S. F. F. Rees), and something of the situation, as viewed by a gunner, may be gathered from the following extracts which begin from the first day of the Boche offensive:—

"*Thursday, 21st March* 1918: I was at the Wagon Lines on this date, having been here since the 19th, *viz.*, at Ytres. This place has been shelled now with high-velocity guns for the last week. I woke up at 4.30 a.m. with a very heavy bombardment by the enemy. This Wagon Line was shelled the whole day. The enemy continued this heavy firing along the whole front for eight hours, sending over 1,000 gas shells. Received an order at 10 p.m. to go up with limbers to remove guns as the enemy was advancing in large number. Got them out and into a new position by midnight, and returned with the limbers to Wagon Line; got there at 4 a.m.

"*Friday, 22nd March*: Got to bed at 4.15 a.m. Just got down with boots and clothes on. Got up at 6 a.m. ready for another order to move guns, and we expect this to be the enemy's great offensive.[1] Did not get an order until 8.30 p.m. to remove guns. Got them back into another position by midnight. The enemy very quiet just here but was putting a very heavy barrage on the right and left. Got back to Wagon Line at 3 a.m. Got to bed, or rather put a couple of rugs around me and slept until 6.30 a.m.

Saturday, 23rd March: Up at 6.30 a.m. to remove Wagon Line or we should soon have all the horses killed. We had one large 9-inch shell on the saddlers' place, burying one man, but by some good luck he was got out with only a small wound on the lip. Another got the Gun Park Store and it all 'went up' together with six battery 'bikes.' Another hit the harness room about half an hour after we had got harnessed up to move. We cleared out of the place (Ytres) at a trot and went to a village called Haplincourt. The Town Major I found was packing up, and told me everybody else was and I could have the whole village. On our way we passed a large Expeditionary Force Canteen which was full of soldiers taking anything they liked, as the enemy was expected in before dark. My servant kept the mess cart back for half an hour, and with another servant they got two cases of good cigarettes, *viz.*, 5,000 in each case. Every man in the battery had a box of 100. We also got away amount of other stuff. Two officers were in there smashing up dozens of bottles of whiskey . . . . The limbers had gone off before we moved, under one of the sergeants, to bring the guns back. The guns came back as far as the Wagon Line. Got into action for a few hours. We kept the horses and limbers only fifty yards behind the guns so as to be ready to move out at a moment's notice, so did not get any sleep."

---

[1] It should be remembered that owing to the Germans attacking north and south of the Flesquières Salient the troops holding that Salient, and especially the gunners holding the front line, had little knowledge of the true situation.

Thus a gunner's story of the operations.

The trench-mortar batteries also had a strenuous time. On the 23rd the 57th Light Trench-Mortar Battery, whose guns were on the ridge south-east of Beaumetz, put up a gallant fight. They clung to their positions as long as possible, and at last, when their gun emplacements had been blown in by the enemy's shell-fire, they disabled their guns and took to the rifle and engaged the enemy with rifle-fire.

At nightfall on the 23rd the Third Army front ran approximately from west of Manancourt, thence north until it turned north-east, passing round the eastern outskirts of Bertincourt,[1] then turning west on the northern side of the village, north-west again just west of Beugny, Vaulx-Vraucourt, east of Mory to just west of St. Leger.

During the night of the 23rd/24th, the 19th Division prepared for further attacks by the enemy on the following morning.

THE FIRST BATTLE OF BAPAUME, 1918: 24TH-25TH MARCH

Dawn on the 24th of March found the 19th Division disposed as follows:—The Green Line was held by the 56th Brigade on the right from 1.28 Central[2] as far as the Bapaume–Cambrai road just west of Beugny; the 58th Brigade was on the left of the 56th, north of the Bapaume–Cambrai road. The 56th Brigade was as yet fairly strong, but the three battalions of the 58th Brigade were very weak in numbers. Two companies of the 5th South Wales Borderers were with the 58th Brigade. The 57th Brigade was still engaged in reorganising west of Fremicourt prior to moving into the Red Line, which ran approximately north and south, east of Bancourt, thence in a north-westerly direction to Monument Wood, to a point north-east of Achiet-le-Grand; all three Field Companies of Royal Engineers were at work on this line. The third company of Pioneers was working in the Green Line under the 56th Brigade. Headquarters of the 56th and 58th Brigades were just south-east of Bapaume, while 57th

---

[1]Note that the map with Colonel Boraston's edition of Lord Haig's Despatches is incorrect. The map shows Ytres, Lechelle, and Bus in our hands, whereas they were held by the enemy on the night of the 23/24th March.

[2]1.28 Central was just south of the Lebucquière-Fremicourt road and about half-way between the two villages.

Brigade Headquarters were south-west of Bancourt. Of the 19th Battalion Machine-Gun Company, "A" Company (complete) was with the 56th Brigade, "B" Company (seven guns) with the 57th Brigade, "C" Company (number of guns unknown) with the 58th Brigade, while "D" Company (eight guns) covered the front of the latter brigade.

Divisional Headquarters were at Grevillers.

The night of the 23rd/24th had by no means passed quietly. Desultory firing went on all round, and as soon as it was light our guns put a heavy barrage down in front of the Green Line. The enemy's artillery replied vigorously, and soon the battle-field was again like a seething cauldron with smoke from bursting shells.

The story turns first to the right of the line, *i.e.*, of the 56th Brigade. Here, during the early hours of the morning, the right company of the 9th Cheshires, which was at Delsaux Farm and somewhat in advance of the general line, formed a defensive flank to the 9th Welch, who were on the left front on the eastern edge of Beugny. Our guns opened with counter-preparation fire at 5 a.m. and 6.15 a.m., but the troops holding Beugny and the ground in front were, however, compelled to withdraw. This withdrawal had been anticipated and was in accordance with definite orders.

At 9 a.m. the enemy put down a heavy barrage on the front held by the 9th Cheshires, which lasted until 10.45 a.m. when his infantry advanced to the attack in massed formation. Again and again the sheer recklessness of the enemy in advancing in close order had been demonstrated by his enormous losses; but he continued to waste gallant lives in this manner. By weight of numbers, however, he forced the right of the Cheshires out of their front line, but in the support line they were reorganised and led forward immediately to counter-attack.

This counter-attack was the most brilliant piece of fighting carried out on the 24th. It was led by Capts. A. D. Milner and F. A. Palmer.

The following is the narrative (written by Capt. Palmer) of the part taken by "A" Company of the 9th Cheshires in this counter-attack:

"Following a heavy preliminary bombardment of the Green Line lasting two hours, Delsaux Farm, which I was holding with 'A' Company, was attacked. The S.O.S. which was sent up brought no artillery fire from our own guns beyond the usual shelling of the Boche assembly positions.

"At the same time my left flank was in the air through the withdrawal of 'B' Company's advanced post, and likewise the remainder of 'B' Company. My right flank was threatened in the same way by the withdrawal of the South Staffords (?) on my right.[1] Consequently we were being heavily enfiladed by machine-gun fire from both flanks.

"The thickness of the wire, and its close proximity to the trenches which we held, proved an obstacle to ourselves in dealing with the Boche, and afforded him a certain amount of cover from view. I therefore decided to withdraw to a point a little further back still in the alignment of the Green Line, cutting the cross-roads, where the men could have a fair show and a good target.

"By this means we were able to inflict many casualties on the enemy. It was proved by subsequent events after we successfully launched our counter-attack against him according to plan, by finding many killed lying in and around the trenches. The counter-attack was delivered within half-an-hour of my withdrawal. During this time my three other officers were casualties, Owen killed, Mallalieu and Carruthers wounded, and after the completion of the counter-attack I was hit myself."

The following is a narrative of "D" Company's action in the counter-attack: "On the morning of the 24th of March, 1918, Capt. A. D. Milner was in command of 'D' Company, which held a part of the support line near Beugny. After a very heavy bombardment which lasted for about one hour and twenty minutes, the enemy attacked our position and broke through on the right flank and came within fifty yards of our support trench. Under very heavy rifle and machine-gun fire Capt. Milner left the support line and went over to the reserve trenches, which were about eighty yards in rear, and led the reserves up to counter-attack, in which he was very successful, and drove the enemy back to his original positions. In leading the men up he was killed."

The counter-attack, which was splendidly carried out, resulted in the recapture of all the lost trench; heavy losses were inflicted on the enemy by rifle, Lewis-gun, and machine-gun fire.

[1] The 2nd South Staffords were 2nd Division Troops.

At 12 noon the Cheshires received preparatory orders to withdraw in the event of the brigade on the right of the 56th giving ground; these orders were passed on to companies.

At 2 p.m. definite instructions came to hand that the right brigade was under orders to withdraw and that the Cheshires were to conform. Almost simultaneously with the receipt of these orders the troops on the right of the Cheshires began to withdraw and companies could not be warned. The companies, therefore, hung on until forced to fall back by superior numbers of the enemy attacking on the now exposed right flank.

Fighting practically all the way the Cheshires then fell back to a line in front of (East) Bapaume. At 5.30 p.m. a further retirement took place (under orders) to the old German trench system, south-west of Bapaume, where positions were taken up covering the line from attack up the Le Transloy–Bapaume road. Yet another move took place during the night, the Cheshires moving back to positions south of Grevillers in support of the King's Shropshire Light Infantry. This move was completed by 2 a.m. on the 31st.

On the left of the Cheshires the North Staffords had, all the morning, seen no enemy on their immediate front or left, but at 2 p.m., when the Cheshires had withdrawn, the right of the battalion was uncovered. With the enemy almost on top of them the battalion received orders to fall back on Bapaume, but the Germans were so close that the Diary records "some of our men were not able to get away." Here again the withdrawal was carried out in good order, though not without considerable fighting; "Some very gallant rearguard actions were fought," records the Battalion Diary.

The North Staffords also had withdrawn to the line east of Bapaume, but were later compelled to fall back through the town to positions in support at Grevillers.

The final entry in their diary gives an excellent idea of the confused nature of affairs in the front line during the 24th: "The situation during the day had been most indefinite, and at times the commanding officers became brigade commanders to control affairs on the spot."

The King's Shropshire Light Infantry had reached the south-eastern outskirts of Bapaume at about 5 p.m., and started digging in, but at 10 p.m. were ordered to take up a line on the Bapaume–Albert road. The Diary of the Shropshires, however, does not mention that a company of the battalion

M

made a spirited counter-attack on the enemy, who, at one period of the night 24th/25th, made an attempt to cross the main Bapaume–Albert road. The Shropshires then held an outpost line south-east of Grevillers with patrols and sentries pushed out well forward.

The action of the 56th Light Trench-Mortar Battery on the 24th is well worth recording. The diary of this unit states: "Enemy attacked right flank of the brigade at Delsaux Farm (Cheshires) and captured the front line. No. 1 gun fired several rounds at the advancing enemy and then the N.C.O. in charge destroyed the barrel by inserting a Mills bomb, and the team fell back with the infantry. No. 2 gun fired twenty-five rounds at the advancing enemy, then the N.C.O. in charge removed the lock-cap, and, along with his team, fell back with the infantry. He reported to the nearest infantry officer (Capt. Palmer of the Cheshires) and took his team forward as infantry in the counter-attack delivered under that officer's orders. On arrival at his gun position he found the mortar and bombs intact, and he immediately replaced the base cap and fired his remaining rounds at the retiring enemy. Having no more ammunition he brought his gun down to Battery Headquarters."

A little further back, again owing to pressure, three mortars had to be destroyed, and finally, at the end of the day, only two were left with no ammunition for them. The Battery Commander then placed himself and his battery (two officers and nineteen other ranks) at the disposal of the 9th Cheshires as infantry.

Meanwhile, on the left of the 56th Brigade, the 58th, not being attacked during the morning of the 24th, were, nevertheless, bound to conform to the movements of the 56th Brigade on their right. Under orders, the Wilts., Welch, and Royal Welch Fusiliers fell back to the Red Line. The withdrawal was covered by the 9th Royal Welch Fusiliers to a position east of Fremicourt, where a stand was made and (so the Brigade narrative states) several local counter-attacks delivered to relieve the pressure. The withdrawal was then continued to a line east of Bapaume, but at 9.30 p.m. the 58th Brigade was ordered to fall back to, and on the left of, the line held by the 56th Brigade.

This was carried out, though before the three battalions of the brigade reached their destination all available men that could be collected from the transport and about headquarters, bandsmen, cooks, etc., were sent out to occupy the line pending the arrival of the battalions. Finally, the 58th Brigade re-organised on their new line, 9th Welch on the right, 9th Royal Welch Fusiliers in the centre, and 6th Wilts. on the left.

The three battalions of the 57th Brigade, however, during the night of the 23rd/24th, each received reinforcements of about 100 men, and reorganisation was hastily carried out. At 6 a.m. on the 24th the brigade held a line between the Bapaume–Cambrai and the Bapaume–Fremicourt roads, facing north-east, 10th Royal Warwicks on the right, 8th Gloucesters in the centre, and 10th Worcesters on the left. All battalions had been disposed in depth. The 57th Brigade was in touch with troops of the 51st Division on the right and 41st Division on the left.

Little happened until 2.30 p.m., when the 56th and 58th Brigades began to withdraw through the 10th Warwicks and 10th Worcesters. Simultaneously masses of the enemy were observed north of Fremicourt, but fire from the Vickers-guns and motor machine-guns held them up. The brigade now came again under the orders of the 51st Division, and General Cubitt was ordered to transfer his headquarters from the Brickyard just east of Bapaume to a brickyard just north of Thilloy.

Between 5.30 and 6 p.m. the troops on the right of the Warwicks began to withdraw, leaving the right flank of the latter completely in the air. A defensive flank was then formed along the Bapaume–Cambrai road. But it was obvious that Bancourt was held by the enemy in strength, while towards Beaulencourt Very lights frequently soared up into the air.

The brigade then fell back; the 10th Worcesters, with their flank turned from the direction of Sapignies, withdrew at about 6.30 p.m., the Warwicks following at 7 p.m. The 8th Gloucesters held out in the eastern outskirts of Bapaume until 8 p.m.[1] Eventually the 57th Brigade was ordered to take up positions between the Bapaume–Albert road and Grevillers, on the left of the 58th Brigade, 8th Gloucesters on the right, 10th Worcesters on the left, and 10th Warwicks in reserve; two companies of South Wales Borderers (the Pioneers) prolonged the left of the Warwicks. By 10 p.m. the 51st Division appears to have withdrawn south-west of Thilloy.

[1] General Jeffreys states that the enemy did not occupy Bapaume until the early hours of the 25th March.

Thus Corps orders had been carried out, and by 2 a.m. on the 25th the 19th Division (56th Brigade on the right, 58th in the centre, and 57th on the left) held from Le Barque to Avesnes-les-Bapaume (east of Grevillers) with 2nd Division troops on the right and the 41st Division on the left.

Divisional Headquarters were now at Achiet-le-Petit.

The total strength of the Division in rifles was now about 2,200.

About Sapignies and Behagnies (just north of the 19th Division) the night of the 24th/25th of March passed with constant fighting, but dawn on the 25th broke on lines of tired troops determined still to hold up the Boche.

No sooner was it light than again the field-grey masses were in motion, advancing westwards, though still persevering in their outflanking tactics, which had been their only means of penetrating our lines held by much weaker forces. It was only the vastly superior numbers of the enemy which enabled him to pour troops through gaps thus created, otherwise his frontal attacks were rarely successful.

On the 56th Brigade front hostile cavalry were observed on the Bapaume–Albert road, while German infantry could be seen collecting in Thilloy-le-Barque. The Shropshires, holding the brigade front, fell back to the ridge north of the Bapaume–Albert road at about 8.30 a.m. Their right flank had been turned. For three hours they put up a protracted fight and prevented the enemy crossing the main road, though in doing so the battalion suffered severe casualties. Their ammunition began to run out, and their right flank being still threatened, they fell back through Grevillers and by 3 p.m. were established on the high ground west of Irles. From this position, however, the battalion was again forced to retire and take up a new line west of Miraumont.

The 9th Cheshires, who in the early morning had been supporting the Shropshires, had taken up a new position on the left of the 51st Division where they could the better protect the right flank. The Shropshires had already been forced to retire, when at 12 noon the Cheshires observed the enemy preparing an attack on their position. Shrapnel and machine-gun bullets began to fall on the position, under cover of which the Boche was gradually working his way forward until contact was made on the road between Grevillers and Thilloy. The enemy then gained possession of the high ground south of

Grevillers. Three sections of the 19th Battalion Machine-Gun Company had taken up positions in the support lines of the Cheshires, and these, with machine-guns established in Loupart Wood, west of the ground upon which the Boche had established himself, gave him a terrible time. In vain he tried to force large numbers of men over the high ground—they were shot down in dozens. Nevertheless he was able to establish a number of machine-guns with which he proceeded to enfilade the positions held by the Cheshires. By 1.30 p.m. masses of the enemy were able to approach the trenches and prepare for a heavy assault. The front companies of the Cheshires withdrew through the supports under cover of rifle-fire and the machine-gun fire from Loupart Wood. The latter fire was most effective, large numbers of the enemy being shot down. But still others took their places—the supply seemed inexhaustible. Soon swarms of Germans were heading for the support positions held by the battalion, and the remaining companies, weak in numbers, withdrew under cover of small rearguards and formed up on the rise west of Loupart Wood. From this position the Cheshires, in conjunction with the remainder of the brigade, withdrew to high ground at Irles, commanding the slopes down from Loupart Wood to the village. As the enemy advanced from the Wood he was kept under heavy fire. But there was low ground on the battalion's right and the enemy was able to get along without being brought to a standstill, and finally occupied positions near Miraumont, from which he enfiladed the 56th Brigade, which thereupon withdrew through the 62nd Division to the support line of the latter, south-east of Achiet-le-Petit, which was reached at about 7 p.m.

The North Staffords, being in Brigade Reserve, fell back early in the morning and formed a line from west of Grevillers to Loupart Wood, but this line was untenable for long, and later the battalion withdrew to the Achiet-le-Petit–Irles line, east of the railway.

The Diary of the North Staffords records that: "Continually, owing to the great numerical superiority of the enemy, and the turning of our flanks, we were again compelled to fall back across the railway." The battalion now became split up, headquarters and several elements of companies taking up positions along the Achiet-le-Petit road with troops of the 51st and 62nd Divisions on the left, while the major portion of the battalion took up a line with the 57th Brigade and 62nd Division east of the railway at Achiet-le-Petit.

By nightfall all units of the 56th Brigade were very much disorganised, but later orders were issued to withdraw and concentrate in Hébuterne.

"This concentration," states the narrative of the 56th Brigade, "was carried out under most difficult circumstances, as it was not known where units of the brigade had halted for the night. As many men as possible were collected and two weak battalions were formed: practically the whole of the 9th Cheshire Regiment was unaccounted for." The brigade was billeted in Hébuterne and Brigade Headquarters at Sailly-au-Bois.

Turned flanks, huge numbers of hostile infantry pouring into the gaps, and then enfilade machine-gun fire—almost every unit fought under such conditions.

The narratives of the 58th and 57th Brigades do not differ in a general sense from that of the 56th Brigade.

It was about 7 a.m. when an attack developed south of the Bapaume–Albert road against the 58th Brigade, and by 9 a.m. it was general along the whole line, though mainly south of the road.

The 9th Welch, from 9 a.m. till 12 noon, were engaged in a fierce contest, during which every attempt on the part of the enemy to advance broke down under the Welshmen's rifle-fire. But hostile machine-guns had worked their way round in rear of the left flank of the battalion, and there was only one course to adopt in order to prevent being cut off, and that was to fall back. Skilful rearguard actions, covered by well-controlled fire, enabled the Welch to withdraw to the ridge west of Grevillers, the next main line of defence. But again the right flank had to give way, and by this time the battalion, very scattered, numbered hardly more than twenty-five. Some strong points in Loupart Wood were then held until another retirement was necessary to the high ground south-east of Irles. At 11 p.m. the Welch (all that was left of them) were withdrawn to a position in front of Puisieux-au-Mont, and finally to Hébuterne.

The 9th Welch Fusiliers, on the left of the Welch, tell much the same story. They began that most trying of all days with a strength of eighty rifles.

Heavy machine-gun fire and sniping from the south-east warned the Fusiliers at 7 a.m. that the enemy was approaching

from that direction. By 10.30 a.m. the 57th Brigade had been
forced back on Grevillers, which left the 58th, in the centre,
forming a dangerous salient. The latter brigade then withdrew
to a line running along the edge of Loupart Wood. The Loupart Wood line was apparently threatened at 1.30 p.m., but
only (as previously stated) after the enemy had again and
again been beaten off, and the right and left flanks had gone.

There is little information in the Diary of the Welch Fusiliers
which does not state what has already been written, but the
paragraph in their narrative which follows the statement concerning the retirement from Loupart Wood is of distinct
interest as showing the state to which units had been reduced:
"The brigade then retired through the 51st Division and took
up a position in G.26.C (at Irles) on a line running north-east
from the Quarry in that square. This line was reached by
4 p.m. *The brigade at this juncture was thirty strong with four
officers. The 9th Royal Welch Fusiliers were eight strong with
one officer.*"

At 5 p.m. the 51st Division was again forced out of its position
and with the Welch Fusiliers fell back on Puisieux. Eventually
the latter reached Hébuterne at about 2 a.m. on the 26th.

Probably the best story of the operations, from the battalion
point of view, is that told in the Diary of the 6th Wilts., who
were on the left of the 9th Royal Welch Fusiliers, and for that
reason it is given in full. The narrative is headed: "Battle of
Grevillers," and continues:

"8 a.m. Strong attacks supported by machine-gun fire on our
right flank along Bapaume road, necessitating our rear two
line of posts being moved across to reinforce right flank along
Bapaume road. No frontal attack from enemy attempted.
Enemy adopted outflanking tactics entirely, and at 11 a.m.
we commenced rearguard and flankguard actions, our front
posts covering the retirement by steady Lewis-gun and rifle-
fire supplemented by machine-guns. All our positions heavily
shelled and rifle-grenaded at this time. Enemy employing gas
shells. We also came under fire from our own field guns.
Organised retirement was difficult. 1 p.m. Withdrawal to
system of trenches on high ground west of Grevillers, where
we continued to suffer heavily from shell and machine-gun fire
from enemy from ridge to south of Bapaume road. This
system of trenches was an impossible position owing to dead
ground and close country around it, of which the enemy took

full advantage in assembling his troops, and eventually (2 p.m.) withdrew to west and north-west of Loupart Wood. S.A.A. at this time was short.

"An excellent opportunity now occurred for making a good stand as we could hold approaches to this position, but owing to action of troops on right of 19th Division in retiring towards Irles, practically in mass, this opportunity was lost.[1]

"A good stand was made by part of 19th Division on north-west of Loupart Wood, chiefly by Royal Warwicks, held up enemy advance for about forty minutes; steady and controlled fire by these troops on edge of Wood held enemy entirely in check, and, had their flanks been supported, a position might have been consolidated here; as it was the enemy advance was delayed by this resolute stand and the retiring troops were enabled to withdraw in safety.

"Eventually the enemy at this point, by means of a fold in the ground, were able to creep round and assemble for an assault on the position, and these troops withdrew in an orderly rearguard action after inflicting heavy casualties on enemy and suffering very slightly themselves.

"At 3.15 p.m. withdrawal, covered by harassing fire from aeroplanes, a further stand was made in trenches in front of Irles by our troops (19th Division). There was a subsequent withdrawal through Miraumont to ground east of Puisieux where a line of outposts was established.

"Our troops finally withdrew to line of posts at Hébuterne."

The final entry in the 58th Brigade Diary states (on reaching Hébuterne): "*The brigade was reorganised as a battalion, each battalion one company with from one to three platoons.*"

It was 8.45 a.m. when the 10th Warwicks (57th Brigade) observed contact between the 58th Brigade and the enemy, and saw the former withdrawing across the Bapaume–Albert road towards Grevillers. Simultaneously the Boche advanced against the line of the Brigade from the east. The two companies of 5th South Wales Borderers, which for the time being had abandoned pick and shovel for the rifle, after putting up a good show, were driven out of Biefvillers and retired on the railway. From this position they made a still further retirement shortly afterwards. This retirement uncovered the left of the Warwicks, and "C" Company of the latter was moved

---

[1]It should be remembered that the Wiltshires could only judge *by appearances*: the actual reason for the retreat of the troops they mention was unknown to them.

to a position on the Grevillers–Thilloy road about 150 yards back.

At about 9 a.m. the Gloucesters, on the right of the Warwicks, with the 58th Brigade, had withdrawn. The Warwicks were now isolated, holding a position on the high ground (so the records state) just south of Grevillers.[1]

The enemy had by this time reached the belt of wire in front of the battalion and was making frantic efforts to get through it. Again and again his troops were shot down by Lewis-gun and rifle fire until he abandoned the attempt and turned his attention to the left flank, where he succeeded in getting into the village. Major Wingrove then ordered all excepting "B" Company and a platoon of "C," to withdraw through Grevillers to a position near Loupart Wood. But even here the Warwicks were outflanked. They held up the enemy until 11 a.m., then as the Boche had penetrated Grevillers and appeared on the right rear over the Bapaume road, the battalion retired to a ridge north of Loupart Wood.

At 2 p.m. the position of the 57th Brigade appears to have been as follows: the 10th Royal Warwicks held the right of the Blue Line, which was north of Loupart Wood and west of Grevillers; the 10th Worcesters were in the centre, and the 8th Gloucesters, on the left, had formed a defensive flank north of the Grevillers–Irles road.

The enemy began to debouch from Grevillers, but was counter-attacked by the Warwicks and Worcesters and driven back into the village, nevertheless the right of the 57th Brigade was very much in the air. All attempts by the Boche to emerge from Loupart Wood were smothered by Lewis-gun and rifle fire, until 4.30 p.m. when he was seen advancing round the southern edges of the Wood; his guns put down some smoke shells, obviously in order that his infantry might rush the Warwicks' post. The latter battalion and the Worcesters then withdrew fighting, each party covering the other. By 5.30 p.m. the two battalions had successfully joined the rest of the battalions of the brigade on the ridge east of the railway near Achiet-le-Petit. At 7 p.m. a further short retirement took place to a ridge south-east of the latter village. The enemy was kept off successfully, but as the flanks were in danger the brigade was again withdrawn and at 11 p.m. held a line facing south-east from south-west of Achiet-le-Petit.

---

[1] This surely should be Biefvillers.

One of the outstanding features of the fighting on the 25th was the fine leadership of Lieut.-Colonel Sole of the 10th Worcesters: "The rearguard action at Grevillers and Loupart Wood," narrates the 57th Brigade Diary, "reflects the greatest credit on all ranks, notably Majors Wingrove and Butler, but especially Lieut.-Colonel Sole, who displayed the highest qualities of courage and leadership, and by his skilful dispositions and masterly tactics extricated the brigade from a most difficult situation, and when the enemy was 4,000 yards (Puisieux) in rear of his right flank. Very many casualties were inflicted on the enemy, while our own were comparatively light."

During the evening of the 25th of March, Brigade Headquarters moved to Puisieux. Lieut.-Colonel Heath, assisted by Divisional and Brigade staffs, collected some 200 men of the 57th Brigade and took up a position covering Puisieux. This party, together with two companies South Wales Borderers, marched back to Hébuterne during the night and was reorganised by 4 a.m. Brigade Headquarters were at Hébuterne.

The staff had had a busy day. All officers on the staff or attached to Divisional Headquarters were summoned to a conference and were divided into parties (with orderlies and police attached) and were sent to different cross-roads and likely lines of retreat between the Sugar Factory, south-east of Colincamps, and Gommecourt, with orders to stop all stragglers of any units, collect them into parties and march them to a position of assembly west of the Sailly-au-Bois– Fonquevillers road.

Arrangements were made for rations to be collected at the position of assembly so that all men collected might be given a meal. Upwards of 4,000 of all ranks of various divisions were collected by this means by dawn on the 26th, including about 500 men of the 19th Division.

At 2.15 a.m. on the 26th the 19th Division was ordered to concentrate in Hébuterne. "This concentration," states the Divisional narrative, "was carried out under most difficult circumstances—darkness, new reinforcements arriving, some without their proper badges, and all without distinguishing marks," but by 4 a.m. it was complete and Hébuterne was occupied with posts east and south-east of the village.

Brigadiers were informed at 3.45 a.m. that they must not

expect the New Zealand Division (ordered to relieve the 19th Division) to arrive before 12 noon. They were, therefore, to keep a vigilant watch on the right flank by means of patrols.

The strength of brigades at this period was approximately:— 56th Brigade, 800 rifles; 57th Brigade, 600 rifles; and 58th Brigade, 400 rifles; the Machine-Gun Battalion had only seven guns.

At 6.15 a.m. 19th Divisional Headquarters moved to Souastre, but finding no accommodation there moved to Pommier, with advanced headquarters at Fonquevillers.

The C.R.A. of the Division had, in the meantime, formed three patrols of artillery officers and mounted gunners. These were despatched to Hébuterne and placed under the orders of the 56th Brigade. They were sent out immediately to reconnoitre the roads leading to Sailly-au-Bois, Beaumont Hamel, Serre, and Puisieux.

At about 10 a.m. one of these patrols was fired on by a German patrol and saw large numbers of the enemy advancing west and south from the direction of Serre; simultaneously outposts on the eastern outskirts of Hébuterne reported that the enemy was within 500 yards of the village. The alarm was at once given and circulated to the G.O.sC., 41st, 25th, and 51st Divisions.

The attack was not as serious as at first contemplated, and was easily checked. Some parties of the enemy penetrated into Hébuterne, but, after fighting amidst the ruins, were killed or driven out. A fresh outpost line was at once organised; 57th Brigade holding the eastern outskirts of the village, 56th Brigade continuing the line along the southern outskirts, linking up with the 58th Brigade which occupied the high ground north of Sailly-au-Bois. The right of the latter Brigade was continued by Field Companies, R.E., 19th Division, and by other units found in the neighbourhood of Fonquevillers who were moved into positions under the orders of the G.O.C., 19th Division.

By 1 p.m. there was almost a continuous line of troops from Gommecourt to Souastre, and until the relief by the 4th Anzac Brigade all was quiet. No further attempt to advance was made by the enemy, nor was he seen in the neighbourhood of Sailly-au-Bois.

Some excitement was caused during the afternoon by the sight of a battalion of whippet Tanks covering the advance of the Anzacs, who were moving up to relieve the Division. This was the first appearance in the field of these new steel engines of war; they were of much lighter build than the ordinary tank and more mobile. As no notification had been received warning the troops of these new tanks some guns were moved forward to deal with them should they prove hostile; one R.A. patrol definitely reported them as German tanks.

On the arrival of the 4th Australian Brigade the 56th and 57th Brigades withdrew to the Sailly-au-Bois–Fonquevillers road, on the right and left respectively, and the 58th Brigade, with the 5th South Wales Borderers, Machine-Gun Company and Field Companies, R.E., to reserve positions about Bayen-court, all Brigade Headquarters to the latter village.

Divisional Headquarters were at La Cauchie.

So far as the 19th Division was concerned the Boche offensive of March, 1918, on the Somme, was over, for although the enemy attacked Hébuterne again on the afternoon of the 27th the Division was not involved and the Australians dealt adequately with the attack.

It is impossible to read the records from the beginning of the offensive on the 21st to the close of the 26th of March without feeling that the 19th Division carried out the tasks which fell to its lot in a splendid manner. The results of careful training when out of the line were almost immediately evident when the Division became first involved with the enemy; all units fought grandly, their fire discipline was splendid, their rear-guard and flank actions were carried out with grit and tenacity, and indeed they often hung on long after it was necessary for them to do so.

The dangerous position occasioned by the gap between the inner flanks of the Third and Fifth Armies was responsible for the constant retirements and the continual turning of flanks. But if ever a Divisional Commander had reason to be proud of his men, General Jeffreys must have felt pride in having under him officers and men who so willingly and gallantly responded to every call made upon them.

Disorganisation was unavoidable, the intermixing of units impossible to prevent, and a great retrograde movement was bound to lead to congestion and confusion; but there was never at any time a debacle.

The 19th Division proved its worth in the greatest trial to which it had been subjected.

The total casualties suffered by the infantry brigades were as follows:—

       56th Brigade; 32 officers, 938 other ranks.

       57th   ,,   53   ,,   1,090   ,,   ,,

       58th   ,,   52   ,,   1,382   ,,   ,,

       19th Bn. M.G.C.; 17 officers, 309 other ranks

A total of 154 officers and 3,719 other ranks.

The German Offensive on the Somme, March, 19
Positions held by 19th Division.

Scale of miles

Infantry Brigades & date
Machine-Gun Companies
Brigade Headquarters

200 of 57th Bde. & elements
of other Brigades & of
41st & 25th Divisions.

BAPAUME

Favreuil

Beugnatre

Vaulx Vraucourt

Railing Points of 57th Bde on 24th

DIVISIONAL BOUNDARY

V CORPS BOUNDARY

Riencourt

Villers au Flos

Fremicourt

22nd

23rd

2 Cos. S.W.B.
B1 & B2 F.C.R.E.S.

22nd

H.Q.
19 Div
21st

1 Bn.
23rd

3 Fd. Coy. R.E.
& Pioneers
21st

22nd

19

V.

Haplincourt

Bertincourt

21st

21st

A C & D 22nd

19

Velu

1 Bn.
23rd

Lebucquiere

Beaumetz

22nd
1 Coy. S.W.B.
22nd

1 Bn.
23rd

A & C
F.C.R.E.

RAILWAY

Doignies

Beugny
1 Bn.
23rd (less 1 Coy)

1 Coy
23rd

1 Bn.
23rd

Sugar
Factory

Chauffours
Wood

1 Bn.
23rd

Morchies

Lagnicourt

IV.

Louverval

Boursies

Mœuvres

CANAL

51

FRONT LINE 21-III-18

17

Graincourt

CAMBRAI 6 m.

CANAL DU NORD

DIVISIONAL BOUNDARY

Ruyaulcourt

2

HAVRINCOURT WOOD

Hermies

Havrincourt

Flesquieres

63

Trescault

TO PERONNE 10 m.

CHAPTER XVII
THE GREY AVALANCHE
THE GERMAN OFFENSIVES OF 1918

II. IN FLANDERS, 9TH-29TH APRIL

ON the 29th of March the 19th Division entrained at Doullens and Candas for the Second Army area (Dranoutre), and the following day orders were received to take over the Messines sector from the 2nd Australian Division on the night of the 31st of March/1st of April. The 19th Divisional Artillery was to relieve the 6th Heavy Brigade, R.F.A., and place one additional brigade in position in the Messines sector on the night of the 3rd/4th of April.

The line to be taken over by the Division, east of Messines and Wytschaete, extended from the River Douve on the south to Charity Farm (due east of Ravine Wood) on the north, a frontage of just under six thousand yards, the inter-brigade boundary being the River Wambeke.

The 57th Brigade (Brigadier-General T. A. Cubitt) went first into the line, taking over the right sub-sector: the 58th Brigade (Brigadier-General A. E. Glasgow) followed, relieving Australian troops on the left: the 56th Brigade (Brigadier-General R. M. Heath) was in reserve.

On the morning of the 9th of April the 57th Brigade had been in the line eight days and the 58th two days. The 57th disposed all three battalions in the front line, i.e., 8th Gloucesters on the right, 10th Worcesters in the centre and the 10th Royal Warwicks on the left: the 58th Brigade held the front with two battalions, i.e., 6th Wilts. on the right, 9th Royal Welch Fusiliers on the left, and the 9th Welch in support. The 25th Division was on the right and the 9th Division on the left of the 19th Division.

Headquarters of the 19th Division (Major-General G. D. Jeffreys) were at Westhof Farm, south-west of Neuve Eglise.

The defence of the Divisional front was organised in three lines of posts—Front, support and reserve—the latter in course of being made a continuous trench line. Behind these three lines of posts was a Corps Line running nearly parallel with the reserve line and five hundred yards or so east of Messines and Wytschaete.

The 57th Brigade was due to be relieved and arrangements had already been made with the 9th and 25th Divisions each to take over a part of the Brigade sector, thus leaving the 56th Brigade available for Corps Reserve. Headquarters of the 56th Brigade were at Gibraltar Camp on the Kemmel-Lindenhoek road, 57th Brigade Headquarters were at North Midland Farm on the Wulverghem-Messines road and 58th Brigade Head-quarters were at Regents Street Dug-Outs.

The Divisional front was covered by the 19th Divisional Artillery.

Although indications that preparations for a hostile attack north of the La Bassée Canal had been observed and were nearing completion early in April, the extent and force of it could not be gauged: nor was it possible to judge the date upon which it would be launched. No intimation had been received up to the morning of the 9th of April. On the 7th of April the enemy opened an unusually heavy and prolonged bombardment with gas shell along practically the whole front from Lens to Armentières. At about 4 a.m. on the 9th the bombardment recommenced with the greatest intensity, gas and high explosive being used in great profusion.

A thick fog lay over the battlefield-to-be when dawn broke on the 9th, and at about 7 a.m. the Boche made a heavy attack on the left brigade of the 2nd Portuguese Division hold-ing the front line in the neighbourhood of Neuve Chapelle. Having broken through the Portuguese front the enemy turned right and left and rolled up the flanks, attacking the right of the 40th Division and the left of the 55th Division. When dusk had fallen on the 9th the enemy had penetrated as far as the eastern, and in several places to the western, banks of the Lys River from north-west of Festubert to north-west of Bois Grenier.

An attack against the front held by the 19th Division was more than likely and the relief of the 57th Brigade by portions of the 9th and 25th Divisions was cancelled. Special vigilance was ordered from 6 p.m. on the 9th, but the night passed quietly with the exception of gas shelling of the gun positions of the field batteries west of Messines.

From 5.50 p.m. on the 9th the 56th Brigade was placed in Corps Reserve and warned to be ready to move at short notice to support either the 25th or 34th Divisions. At 1 a.m. on the 10th the 9th Cheshires were ordered to move by bus to Nieppe under the 34th Division: the battalion completed this move by 6 a.m. the following morning.

THE BATTLE OF MESSINES, 1918: 10–11TH APRIL

When dawn broke on the 10th of April thick mist again prevailed, offering ideal conditions under which to make an attack. At about 5.30 a.m. a heavy hostile barrage was falling all along the line. At Messines the front and support lines and battery areas behind Frelinghien and Hill 60 were swept by violent shell-fire: also the crossings over the River Lys at Lestrem and Estaires.

At about 6 a.m. the enemy's infantry, in great numbers, attacked the front held by the 25th (right) and 19th (left) Divisions east of Ploegsteert Wood and Messines, and Wytschaete respectively. Against the front held by the 57th Brigade as many as eleven battalions and two "storm" battalions were estimated to have attacked the 8th Gloucesters, 10th Worcesters, and 10th Warwicks (right to left), all three battalions (as previously described) holding the front line of their Brigade. The enemy's numerical superiority was roughly five or six to one.

At 6.15 a.m. both the Gloucesters and Worcesters reported that the left and right posts respectively had been lost. By 6.30 a.m. it became evident that the left brigade of the 25th Division had been driven out and had lost its front line and that the enemy was advancing against the Gapard Spur (held by the Gloucesters) along Hirondelle road.

The enemy's rapid attack through the mist could not be properly observed and the front and support line of posts of the 57th Brigade were completely overrun. Practically none of the garrison were seen again. In one instance the enemy was observed all round a British post, killing off the garrison who were greatly hampered in their defence by the large camouflage screens which at daybreak were pulled over the posts to conceal them from observation by hostile aircraft. By 6.40 a.m. the enemy was attacking the reserve line of the centre battalion and S.O.S. signals were reported from the left battalion's front.

At this point the Brigadier of the 57th ordered the 81st Field Company, R.E., and "B" Company of the South Wales Borderers (Pioneers), who had been placed under his command, to occupy the posts of the Corps Reserve Line which had been allotted to them on the 8th of April.

By 7.30 a.m. the position was that the 8th Gloucesters were holding the support and reserve lines, the 10th Worcesters their reserve line, but the situation of the 10th Warwicks was obscure, though it was known that the right of the battalion front had been penetrated.

So serious was the situation that General Jeffreys obtained permission from Corps Headquarters for the 8th North Staffords (56th Brigade) to be released from Corps Reserve. Two companies of this battalion were then placed at the disposal of the 57th Brigade for counter-attack and were ordered to advance from Wulverghem to the Corps front and support lines in front of Messines.

The enemy had, however, by this time (about 8.30 a.m.) occupied the eastern edge of Messines, and the two companies, after gallant though fruitless efforts to get through the village, were obliged to occupy a line running north through the Hospice. The remaining two companies of the 8th North Staffords, who had also by now been placed at the disposal of the 57th Brigade, then occupied a reserve line two hundred yards east of North Midland Park.

On the left front of the 57th Brigade the situation remained obscure, but at 9.30 a.m. elements of the 10th Royal Warwicks were reported by the G.O.C., 58th Brigade, to be at Pick House. The G.O.C. of that Brigade also stated that he had thrown back a defensive flank from his front line (which had not yet been attacked) along Manchester Street facing south to Torreken Corner Cutting and south-east of Wytschaete.

Corps Headquarters then placed the 56th Brigade Headquarters with the 1/4th K.S.L.I. under the command of the 25th Division, the 9th Cheshires passing from the 34th Division to the 25th Division and coming under the command of the G.O.C., 56th Brigade. The latter, with the Shropshires, moved off at 10.15 a.m. to the Hill 63 area.

Meanwhile B Company of the South Wales Borderers and the 81st Field Company, R.E., in the face of strong opposition had occupied portions of the Corps Line as ordered; elements of the 10th Royal Warwicks were also in the Corps Line and

N

around Pick House and the two companies of North Staffords were making good headway towards Messines. All these units were having a hard struggle, and the gallant Pioneers and Sappers were putting up a splendid fight. The G.O.C., 57th Brigade, despatched an officer to the Royal Warwicks to assist in reorganising them, with orders to hold on to the Pick House position and connect up with "B" Company of the South Wales Borderers in the northern portion of the Corps Line in the Brigade sector. By 11.15 a.m. this had been done.

A new reserve line was now being established which ran from Maedelstede Farm—east of Spanbroekmolen—west of In de Kruisstraat Camp—Bristol Castle. This line had already been occupied by the two remaining companies of the 8th North Staffords and was also filled by 700 surplus personnel composed of recently arrived drafts for the 57th Brigade, under the command of Lieut.-Colonel R. B. Umfreville, 8th Gloucesters.

These drafts consisted mainly of young and untried troops who had come out to France for the first time: many of them were mere boys—the last reinforcements possible from England. It was a rough introduction to warfare, to be thrust without any previous knowledge or experience into the very thick of a terrific battle, but they were stout-hearted and on the whole did splendid service.

As a result of their counter-attack the 8th North Staffords reported that they reached the western edge of Messines Village and had captured two machine-guns and a few prisoners. The 8th Gloucesters were then ordered to gain touch with the right flank of the North Staffords and the latter were reinforced by two platoons of the former regiment.

Twelve machine-guns were sent forward under Divisional orders and placed astride the Wulverghem-Messines road, four on each side and four in reserve close to North Midland Farm.

This somewhat bald narrative of events is unavoidable, for C.O.s were too hard pressed to record individual acts amid the involved nature of the operations; units being continually moved here and there precluded a clear vision of the heavy fighting and gallant stand made by our troops.

During the afternoon the two forward companies of the 8th North Staffords pushed forward from their left and turned the enemy out of Swaynes Farm, just north of Messines: the two remaining companies, under Major Martin, were ordered to advance and prolong the left from the Farm and endeavour to join up with the 10th Royal Warwicks at Pick House, while the latter, with "B" Company, 5th South Wales Borderers (right) who had held on to their original position in the Corps Line with great tenacity and gallantry in the face of repeated attacks, were ordered to work to their right towards the 8th North Staffords. In this way something in the nature of a continuous line was formed, though (be it understood) the pressure of the enemy was very great and our troops were continually harried by heavy shell and machine-gun fire.

Shortly after noon the South African Brigade of the 9th Division then at Neuve Eglise, was placed under the 19th Division. This brigade, although numerically weak, totalling in all about 1500, was placed at the disposal of the 57th Brigade for the purpose of a counter-attack on Messines and to regain generally the lost positions of the Corps Line east of that village.

The counter-attack, carried out towards dusk, succeeded on the left in reaching Bay Farm, Derry House and Lumm Farm, all well east of the Messines-Wytschaete road, but on the right was held up by violent machine-gun fire from the Messines Ridge and made little progress, resulting only in reinforcement of the existing line then held by the 8th North Staffords.[1]

This closed the fighting on the 57th Brigade front.

At 2 p.m. the 59th Brigade was attacked and the 9th Royal Welch Fusiliers reported that 9th Division troops, at and north of Charity Farm, were falling back. With both of his flanks in the air the G.O.C., Brigade, then ordered the Wilts. and Welch Fusiliers (the two front-line battalions), to withdraw to their support line. At this period the whole line was under violent shell-fire and heavy casualties were sustained.

At 4 p.m. the 58th Brigade passed to the command of the 9th Division.

By the early evening the enemy was attacking the reserve line of the 58th Brigade, having broken through between the support and reserve lines from the direction of Torreken Farm cutting off the 6th Wilts., of whom few ever got back.

During the night of the 10th/11th 19th Divisional Headquarters moved from Westhof Farm to Dranoutre.

---

[1] The official despatches state that: "Messines was retaken early in the afternoon by the South African Brigade of the 9th Division," but this must be an error.

At 1.20 a.m. on the 11th, the 108th Brigade (36th Division) was placed under the G.O.C., 19th Division, and attached to the 57th Brigade, under Brigadier-General Cubitt who then assumed command of all troops on the west of the Messines Ridge south of Pick House. By dawn the 108th Brigade was disposed from Pick House southwards in support of the South African Brigade and the troops immediately west of Messines which was now definitely in the hands of the enemy.

The night of the 10th/11th of April passed quietly.

By noon on the 11th the enemy had launched a heavy attack against the 25th Division in the direction of Ploegsteert, and Hill 63 (southwest of Messines), from which the Messines Ridge could be taken in reverse, was seriously threatened. At 2.15 p.m. General Jeffreys issued orders for a defensive flank to be thrown back along the Wulverghem-Messines road, and No. 6 Motor Machine-Gun Battery was posted on the high ground south of Wulverghem to guard the Division's right flank. No improvement took place in the Hill 63 area, and late in the afternoon the G.O.C., 19th Division, decided that if the Hill fell all troops in front of the Wulverghem Line were to be withdrawn and that line held as the front line. During the evening Hill 63 was definitely reported lost and at 1 a.m. on the 12th the withdrawal began, outposts covering the withdrawal were to fall back at 2 a.m.

As previously mentioned, the Wulverghem Line was held by elements of the 57th Brigade, including "C" Company, 5th South Wales Borderers (Pioneers) and 94th Field Company, R.E. The 108th Brigade and South African Brigade withdrew through the above and then reorganised behind them. Reorganisation was hurriedly carried out and during the night of the 11th/12th the 108th Brigade, on the right, and the South African Brigade, on the left, took over the Wulverghem Line (which now became the front line) from the 57th Brigade. This line extended from the cross-roads 700 yards south of Wulverghem, then round the eastern side of the village in a north-easterly direction to Bogeart Farm.

These movements were successfully carried out and all but the 10th Royal Warwicks and "C" Company of the 5th South Wales Borderers were relieved; these two units, in consequence of heavy losses sustained by the South African Brigade in their counter-attack against Messines, could not be relieved. Both the Warwicks and the South Wales Borderers

were ordered to remain in their positions in the Wulverghem
Line until arrangements for their relief could be made. This
they did until the night of the 13th/14th when they were
relieved by the 58th Brigade.

Of the gallant Pioneers the Divisional Narrative relates: "The
conduct of 'B' Company, 5th South Wales Borderers
(Pioneers), during this trying period, reflected the greatest
credit on its commander, Capt. Evans, and all ranks. This
company, though repeatedly attacked and heavily bombarded,
never moved from the position originally taken up in the Corps
Line east and north of Messines in the neighbourhood of Pick
House, and after the South African counter-attack on the
afternoon of the 10th remained in the front line on the left of
the South African Brigade connecting up with the 58th Brigade
on the left."

So far as the 19th Division was concerned the Battle of
Messines, 1918, was over, but two outstanding acts of gallantry during the first phase of the fighting must be recorded.

The first is that of Capt. E. S. Dougall, M.C., R.F.A., who
was in command of "A" Battery, 88th Brigade, R.F.A. This
officer maintained his guns in action near Messines on the
10th of April throughout the heavy concentration of hostile
shell-fire. When, finding he could not clear the crest of the
ridge, owing to the withdrawal of our line, Capt. Dougall ran
his gun on to the top of the ridge to fire over open sights. By this
time our infantry had been pressed back in line with the guns.
Capt. Dougall at once assumed command of the situation,
rallied and organised the infantry, supplied them with Lewis-
guns and armed as many gunners as he could spare with rifles.
With these he formed a line in front of his battery which,
during this period, was harassing the advancing Germans with
rapid fire. When one gun was turned over by a direct hit and
the detachment knocked out, casualties were replaced and the
gun brought into action again. Although exposed to both rifle
and machine-gun fire, Capt. Dougall fearlessly walked about as
though on parade, calmly giving orders and encouraging everybody. His remark to the infantry at this juncture: "So long as
you stick to your trenches I will keep my guns here," had a
most inspiring effect on all ranks. This line was maintained
throughout the day, thereby delaying the enemy's entry into
Messines for over twelve hours. In the evening, having expended all their ammunition, the battery received orders to

withdraw. This was done by man-handling the guns over a distance of about 800 yards of shell-cratered country, an almost impossible feat considering the ground and the intense machine-gun fire.

Owing to Capt. Dougall's personality and skilful leadership throughout this trying day there is no doubt that a serious breach in our lines was averted.

This gallant officer was unfortunately killed four days later, but the Victoria Cross was posthumously awarded him for his invaluable work and outstanding bravery.[1]

The second very gallant action concerned a nest of four machine-guns and twenty-five other ranks, under Second-Lieut. Hodgson, M.G.C., of "B" Company, 19th Division, Machine-Gun Battalion, dug in just off the Wulverghem–Messines road about 1,000 yards east of Wulverghem Village.

During the 10th and 11th this section rendered great support to the infantry, and during the 12th they still remained in their position, although, in consequence of the withdrawal on the night of the 11th/12th, they were some 600 yards in front of the front line. The fact that no attack developed against the brigade on the 12th was (so it was believed) due to the determination and gallantry of this machine-gun section which made the Wulverghem-Messines road impassable to any German, and killed, without exaggeration, hundreds of the enemy who attempted to debouch from Messines or cross the Messines Ridge. This section never retired and hung on to the last, and, with the exception of two men who were wounded and got back, never shifted and were killed or taken prisoner at their posts, fighting to the last.

Along the front of the 19th Division the day of the 12th of April passed without event. A certain amount of reorganisation was carried out and by the evening the following troops (all under the command of the G.O.C., 19th Division) held the positions given:

Of the 57th Brigade the 10th Royal Warwicks, with "C" Company, South Wales Borderers, were in the Wulverghem Line; the 8th North Staffords (of the 56th Brigade) were in the Army Line near Spy Farm; the 10th Worcesters, "B" Company, 5th South Wales Borderers (Pioneers) and 8th Gloucesters were also in the Army Line, *i.e.*, the Worcesters south of

[1]For citation from *London Gazette* of 4th June, 1918, see Appendix.

the North Staffords, the Pioneers south of the Worcesters, and the Gloucesters south of the Pioneers; the 81st and 94th Field Companies, Royal Engineers, were in reserve to the Army Line. The South African Brigade was in the front line on the left in touch with "B" Company, 5th South Wales Borderers, elements of the 10th Royal Warwicks, and the 58th Brigade; the 108th Brigade was on the right in touch with the 25th Division. The 178th Brigade of the 59th Division was on its way up to reinforce the 19th Division, while in the Kemmel Hill defences the 19th Lancashire Fusiliers, one company Machine-Gun Battalion, one company Royal Engineers, and one Trench-Mortar Battery were also under the G.O.C., 19th Division. The 58th Brigade (including 82nd Field Company, Royal Engineers, and "D" Company, 5th South Wales Borderers) were under the 9th Division on the left of the 57th Brigade, while the 56th Brigade (less 8th North Staffords) was still attached to the 25th Division. The 1/4th King's Shropshire Light Infantry were on the right of the 8th Gloucesters.

Divisional Headquarters were still at Dranoutre.

At nightfall, however, fighting began again on the Divisional front. At about 7.30 p.m. the 108th Brigade reported that they had been attacked and their right battalion driven in. An immediate counter-attack restored the position on the left of the brigade's front, but on the right the situation was at first obscure though restored later. Next, at 10.20 p.m., reports were received that the enemy had broken through the 25th Division front in the direction of Neuve Eglise and was advancing north up the Neuve Eglise–Lindenhoek road. The 94th Field Company, R.E., was immediately rushed up to the railway north of Neuve Eglise, machine-guns were placed on the road threatened, and a battalion of the 178th Brigade moved forward to the railway in support. But patrols from the 8th Gloucesters and 1/4th K.S.L.I. reported Neuve Eglise still in our hands; the right of the 108th Brigade had been broken but was being rallied in the Army Line by the Gloucesters.

At 10.30 p.m. the 94th Field Company, R.E., plus one company of the 10th Worcesters, was ordered to fill the gap and this was done by 5 a.m. on the 13th despite great difficulties. It was mainly due to the skill, initiative, and energy shown by Capt. Mackintosh, O.C., 94th Field Company, R.E., that this movement was so successfully carried out.

Other determined attacks by the enemy during the night of the 12th/13th, east and south-east of Spanbroekmolen, were broken up.

THE BATTLE OF BAILLEUL: 13TH–15TH APRIL

The day of the 13th was one of alarms rather than of heavy fighting, the situation at Neuve Eglise being the chief cause. The possession of this place, standing as it does on high ground, was necessary to the enemy in the development of his turning movements.

By daylight on the 13th a gap of something like 1,200 yards existed on the 108th Brigade front south-west of Wulverghem and between that place and Neuve Eglise. The gap was then filled by troops of the 178th Brigade.

But at 9.30 a.m. the 25th Division again reported that the situation in Neuve Eglise was acute; fighting was in progress on the southern outskirts of the village. The 8th Gloucesters then formed a defensive flank on the right. Next, at 10.20 a.m., the 1/4th K.S.L.I. (now under the 148th Brigade, 25th Division) reported that the enemy had been driven out of the village and that the line was 500 yards in front (*i.e.*, south) of Neuve Eglise.

At 11 a.m. the 3rd Worcesters (148th Brigade) reported that they were still at Petit Pont (some 2,000 yards as the crow flies south-east of Neuve Eglise) and were being shelled by their own artillery. In vain 19th Divisional Headquarters endeavoured to gain touch with 148th Brigade Headquarters in order to acquaint them of the serious position at Neuve Eglise, which was considered to be the key position to the whole of the 19th Divisional line. Eventually the G.O.C., 57th Brigade, sent out his Intelligence Officer with instructions to search for the missing brigade's headquarters. He found them and explained the situation.

The remainder of the 13th passed without attack. Shell-fire on the Army Line in the Douve Valley was continuous, and the enemy was seen massing east of North Midland Farm, which presaged further attacks. Two new German divisions had been identified opposite the Divisional front.

Further reorganisation took place during the day; the 58th Brigade, having returned to the 19th Division at 11 a.m., was ordered to relieve the South African Brigade, "B" Company, 5th South Wales Borderers, and elements of the 10th

Royal Warwicks in the Maedelstere–Spanbroekmolen sector, and for a battalion of the 178th Brigade to take over support positions in the valley of the Douve.

In view, however, of the extremely unsatisfactory position round Neuve Eglise and of the advent of the two fresh German divisions on the Divisional front (mentioned above), the G.O.C., 57th Brigade (under orders from G.O.C., Division) arranged with other brigadiers to establish the Meteran–Kemmel–Spy Farm–Spanbroekmolen Line, which would be held as a front line if (and when), on account of the fate of Neuve Eglise, the Army Line became untenable.

This line was allotted as follows: 58th Brigade on the left, 57th Brigade in the centre, 178th on the right to gain touch with Bousfield's Force in the Kemmel Defences. In case of need this line was manned (so that a defensive line should be available) by the 9th Welch in Regent Street joining up on their left with the 6th Wilts. south-east of Spanbroekmolen, 10th Warwicks in Regent Street west of the Welch from Spy Farm to Lindenhoek cross-roads, whence the 8th North Staffords continued the line to the 178th Brigade.

Divisional Headquarters were now at Mont Noir where they remained until the night of the 15th/16th.

During the night of the 13th/14th the 19th Division was not attacked, but the position on the right again appeared extremely precarious. Not once, but many times, Neuve Eglise was reported in the hands of the enemy, though patrols from the 19th Division reported British troops still holding out and certainly the village was *not* in possession of the enemy.

The 25th Division reported that they had lost touch on their right and that the enemy was in Nordhoek (about 1,250 yards west of Neuve Eglise) from which place he was advancing north. In spite of the fact that at a conference the G.O.C., 25th Division, was urged to re-occupy Neuve Eglise immediately in the event of its being lost, and that water, ammunition, and food were sent up to the 1/4th King's Shropshire Light Infantry (who were, however, still under the 25th Division), the 25th Division during the night abandoned the intention of retaking or re-occupying the village.

Till after mid-day, excepting for snipers in the southern outskirts of Neuve Eglise, the village was unoccupied by the enemy; elements of the 25th Division, though unsupported, still held on in the village. The position of the 1/4th K.S.L.I., south of the Neuve Eglise–Wulverghem road, had now become impossible, for the enemy was bombing up the Army Line west of L'Allouette and trench-mortaring and shooting into the 1/4th K.S.L.I. from the rear. The gallant O.C. of the Shropshires (Major Wingrove), however, stuck to his position till mid-day, rallying retiring troops on his right as long as possible. One company of the 8th Gloucesters was immediately sent up to support him and two companies from the 178th Brigade manned the railway west of Neuve Eglise to prevent the enemy debouching from the village, surrounding the Shropshires and attacking the Army Line from the south-west.

At about 2 p.m. the enemy attacked at Neuve Eglise, and it was inevitable that the Shropshires were forced back, though they still clung to a line north of and parallel with the Neuve Eglise–Wulverghem road. East by north-east of the village the enemy's attack was driven off by the 178th Brigade.

The 1/4th K.S.L.I. reverted again to the command of the 19th Division at 4 p.m. and were attached to the 57th Brigade. The Staff of the latter, having made a general reconnaissance of Major Wingrove's position, came to the conclusion that with the right flank of the Division exposed the Shropshire line and the Army Line, just north-east of Neuve Eglise, could no longer be held. It was decided, therefore, to withdraw the line during the night to the railway line north of Neuve Eglise, thence eastwards north of Wulverghem and along Durham road to the front line to about 500 yards east of Shell Farm; in other words, the right of the Division would be facing south. But before the withdrawal could be effected the situation became acute. At about 7 p.m. troops of the 25th Division on the right of the Shropshires were again forced to retire. Major Wingrove partially succeeded in rallying them, but by 8.15 p.m. reports were received of further straggling and it was certain that the line north of Neuve Eglise was definitely broken. It subsequently transpired that Major Wingrove, whose tenacity, gallantry, and determination had held the much-tried and isolated line up to this time, was wounded and the line, therefore, broke.

The G.O.C., 57th Brigade, then ordered Major Parkes (acting O.C., 8th Gloucesters) and Capt. Pearson (acting O.C., 10th Worcesters) who were at their battalion headquarters at Daylight Corner (north of the railway siding) to

stop and rally all troops retiring north up the Neuve Eglise–
Lindenhoek road and establish a line along the railway, using
the 8th Gloucesters and 10th Worcesters respectively to gain
touch on the left with the 178th Brigade and to rest the right
on the railway at a point 400 yards west of the point where the
railway crossed the Neuve Église–Lindenhoek road; here a
defensive flank was to be formed facing west.

The Divisional Narrative then states: "These instructions
were ably carried out to the letter in spite of difficulties as
obvious as they were great, and it is considered that these two
officers, coupled with Lieut.-Colonel D. M. A. Sole, O.C.,
10th Worcestershire Regiment, who had been immediately
despatched from Brigade Headquarters to take charge of the
new line, deserve the highest credit for rallying the men,
leading them to their new position, and so preventing what
might have been a serious penetration."

This new line (known as the Wulverghem–Bailleul line) was,
however, only an expedient, for it was at the bottom of a valley
completely commanded from the Neuve Eglise Ridge. During
the night of the 14th/15th this line was organised and manned
by the 178th Brigade on the right, 108th Brigade in the
centre, and 58th Brigade on the left, which merely had to
swing back its right and stand fast on the left. All moves were
completed by the morning of the 15th.

On the 15th the enemy shelled all positions held by the 19th
Division accurately, and his infantry attacked the 58th
Brigade whose front was slightly driven in, though Spanbroekmolen was still held; the remaining elements of the
108th Brigade between Wulverghem and Durham road were
also attacked.

In the evening it was reported that the enemy had taken
Crucifix Corner and was working westwards. Brigades were,
therefore, ordered to make preparations for a withdrawal to the
Meteren–Kemmel line (already mentioned) should it become
necessary.

At 10.45 p.m. Divisional Headquarters received orders for
the withdrawal; the only movement required in the 57th
Brigade was the withdrawal of the 10th Worcesters and one
company of the 10th Royal Warwicks from their position in
support of the 58th Brigade, the Worcesters to Rossignol
Camp, and the Company of Warwicks to rejoin its unit. The
10th Royal Warwicks and 8th North Staffords were ordered

to put out and dig in outposts in front of their positions, now the front line. The 9th Cheshires extended to the north in the Kemmel Defences, east of the Hill, the 108th Brigade being relieved and sent to the La Clytte area. The 9th Division had taken over the 58th Brigade front as far south as Stanbroek-molen inclusive, otherwise the dispositions of the brigade remained unchanged. Of the 178th Brigade one battalion was in posts in front of the Kemmel Defences and two in reserve south-west of Mont Kemmel, though one subsequently re-inforced the line of posts.

During the night of the 15th/16th Divisional Headquarters moved to Westoutre.

The Battle of Bailleul was over. The 19th Division had added another Battle Honour to its already distinguished roll. Of the hundred-and-one deeds of gallantry which occurred every day, of the fine tenacity and courage of our troops, the records contain little. No one had time to "write up" the official diaries—they were indeed mostly written when the Division was out of the line "at rest," and the sharp edge of the mighty struggle was somewhat blunted. All that can be done is to follow closely the moves of the fighting troops during that tense period, though in many instances even to do *that* is impossible. Of the dramatic fighting of some units, of the glorious end of parties of men (even whole companies) who went down resisting to the end, nothing will ever be known.

THE FIRST BATTLE OF KEMMEL: 17TH–19TH APRIL

Kemmel Hill was now the objective of the enemy. On the 16th he made a number of strong local attacks on the Meteren–Wytschaete front. The 19th Division on this date, however, was not seriously involved.

At 5 a.m. all Brigade Headquarters moved to Fairy House in rear of Kemmel Hill. The withdrawal to the Meteren-Kemmel line was not followed up by the enemy with much energy, for patrols and outposts, aided by a heavy mist were able to operate freely.

At about 6 a.m. a heavy barrage fell on the 9th Divisional front and by 7.15 a.m. the enemy had launched a vigorous attack, during which he gained Spanbroekmolen and the line thence to Maedelstere Farm; he was also reported in Wyt-schaete. The 58th Brigade, however, regained touch with the

62nd Brigade (21st Division, attached 9th Division) at Lagachie Farm.

For the time being no other hostile attack developed but it was considered advisable to man the Kemmel–Vierstraat line as a reserve line. Accordingly orders were issued to brigades and positions were taken up as follows: 8th North Staffords on the right, 10th Worcesters on the left east of Kemmel Village, with the 9th Cheshires supporting the North Staffords, and the 8th Gloucesters the Worcesters behind Kemmel.

All Brigade Headquarters were moved to dug-outs at Scherpenberg Hill and farm houses in the neighbourhood.

Later, the French were to attack on the general line, Wulverghem–Wytschaete, but the attack did not materialise.

The night of the 16th/17th was without incident.

On the 17th the enemy made a determined attempt to capture Kemmel Hill. After a preliminary bombardment of great intensity he attacked the Meteren and Menin sectors as well as the Kemmel sector.

On the 19th Divisional front the attack was launched at about 10.50 a.m., after a very heavy barrage put down at 10 a.m. on the front of the 178th Brigade (south of Kemmel Hill) and on the front of the 8th North Staffords and 10th Royal Warwicks of the 57th Brigade. The front-line troops, however, held firm, and what with fine shooting by the Divisional Artillery, Lewis-gun and rifle fire, as well as a most effective overhead machine-gun barrage by the Kemmel Defence Force, dug in on the crest of the Hill, the enemy's attack was broken up and he again suffered with heavy losses. The only gain accruing to him was the temporary occupation of Donegal Farm, just on the boundary between the 19th and 49th Divisions. By 12.30 p.m. all was quiet again.

The official despatches thus record the part taken by the 19th Division and other divisions: "The enemy's attack in the Kemmel sector was pressed with great determination, but ended in his complete repulse at all points by troops of the 34th, 49th, and 19th Divisions, his infantry being driven out by counter-attack wherever they had gained a temporary footing in our line."

At 3 p.m. Divisional Headquarters moved to a farm south-west of Westoutre, as that place was under heavy shell-fire.

At 6 p.m. the enemy made another attack against the front

held by the 10th Royal Warwicks, but again he was repulsed with heavy losses.

Later in the evening the French made an unsuccessful attack on Spanbroekmolen.

About this time also Divisional Headquarters were informed by Corps Headquarters that the 19th Division would be relieved on the night of the 18th/19th by the 28th French Division, though from 12 noon on the 18th the latter would assume responsibility for the defence of Kemmel Hill.

During the night of the 17th/18th the French twice raided Donegal Farm, killing several Germans and taking eight prisoners. Active patrolling along the Divisional front during the night revealed the fact that north of the railway line north of Neuve Eglise the enemy held no well-defined line. The Intelligence Officer (Second-Lieut. C. E. Duruty) of the 10th Royal Warwicks is specially mentioned as having done valuable work in this respect.

At 9.22 a.m. on the 18th the French reported large numbers of the enemy advancing against Donegal Farm, but they were driven off, the Divisional line remaining absolutely intact. During the afternoon also the 10th Royal Warwicks reported another attack on their front.

Apart from the above incidents the day of the 18th was passed in comparative quietude. The relief of the 19th Division was carried out without incident during the night of the 18th/19th, only the gallant and hard-worked artillery remained in the line assisting the French, as well as the medical personnel of the Division, the latter by special request of the G.O.C., 28th French Division, until relieved by a French medical unit on the 20th. All other troops of the Division were clear of their position by 8.30 a.m. on the 19th, and at 10 a.m. 19th Divisional Headquarters moved to Abeele Aerodrome.

Very tired and much reduced in numbers, the troops rested during the remainder of the 19th and 20th April, then moved to the Proven area for a further rest and to refit.

The losses incurred by the 19th Division (excepting the 19th Divisional Artillery), from the time they were in action until relief on the 19th, were heavy, the total casualties, *i.e.*, killed, wounded, and missing, of the three Infantry Brigades, the R.E. Companies and 5th South Wales Borderers, being 3,774. The artillery were in the line until the 27th of April and had a total casualty list of 259.

On the 25th of April the enemy attacked heavily on the Wytschaete–Kemmel front, and the 19th Division took up positions of assembly in support of the 21st and 49th Divisions, *i.e.*, 56th and 57th Brigades in the Ouderdom area and 58th Brigade in the Busseboom area in Divisional Reserve.

By noon on the 26th Kemmel Hill and village had been taken by the enemy from the French, the 25th Division being heavily engaged in the Werstraat–Cheapside area. The 19th Division continued to man and strengthen by digging the Poperinghe and the Vlamertinghe–Hallebast Lines. The Division carried on with this work up to the night of the 30th;[1] the 58th Brigade, on the right, and 56th Brigade, on the left, then relieved the 21st Division in the Dickebusch sector from French Farm (1,000 yards south-west of Zillebeke Lake) to about 1,300 yards due west of Vierstraat; the 57th Brigade was in reserve about Ouderdom.

An intended attack by the enemy on the 4th of May was broken up by counter-artillery measures.

The 56th Brigade was relieved by the 98th Brigade (33rd Division) on the 4th of May, and the 58th Brigade, which by minor enterprises skilfully carried out, had advanced their line some 500 yards, were relieved during the night of the 10th/11th by the 56th Brigade. On the 11th/12th the 56th Brigade was relieved.

The 19th Division, on relief, was withdrawn to the Wormhoust–Zeggers–Cappel area, and ordered to entrain on the 15th of May to join the VIII Corps near Chalons.[2]

---

[1] On the 30th of April the following Order of the Day was issued to all units of the 19th Division:—

"The Divisional Commander has much pleasure in forwarding the following wire which has been received from the Commander-in-Chief, and which he wished to be conveyed to all ranks of the Division:—

'Begins: I wish to thank General Jeffreys and all officers and men under his command for the very gallant service rendered by them both on the battle front south of Arras and in the recent fighting south of Ypres. The great effort which the enemy is making to break down the resistance of the British Army will undoubtedly fail if all ranks of our Army continue to show the same resolute and determined courage which has characterised the action of the 19th Division. Ends.' "

[2] Brig.-General R. M. Heath had succeeded Brig.-General Willan (evacuated ill) in command of the 56th Brigade a few days before the Lys Battles began, and just before the 19th Division entrained for the Champagne country Brig.-General T. A. Cubitt was appointed to command the 38th Welch Division. General Cubitt was succeeded in command of the 57th Brigade by Brig.-General A. J. F. Eden on the 24th of May.

Although never actually attacked during this period of reconnaissance, work on new lines of defence, manning support and assembly positions (26th–30th April) and in holding the line from the 30th of April to the 13th of May, considerable casualties had been incurred and the strength of the Division still further reduced. On the 4th of May, when the threatened attack did not materialise, the enemy's shell-fire was heavy; also on the 8th of May when heavy attacks (successful at first but afterwards neutralised by French and British counter-attacks) were launched by the enemy against Ridge Wood and the French line south of it. On the 12th the enemy heavily barraged the Ridge Wood front, including the 19th Divisional sector. These bombardments, during which no infantry action resulted, were responsible for a further appreciable reduction in the already attenuated infantry battalions.

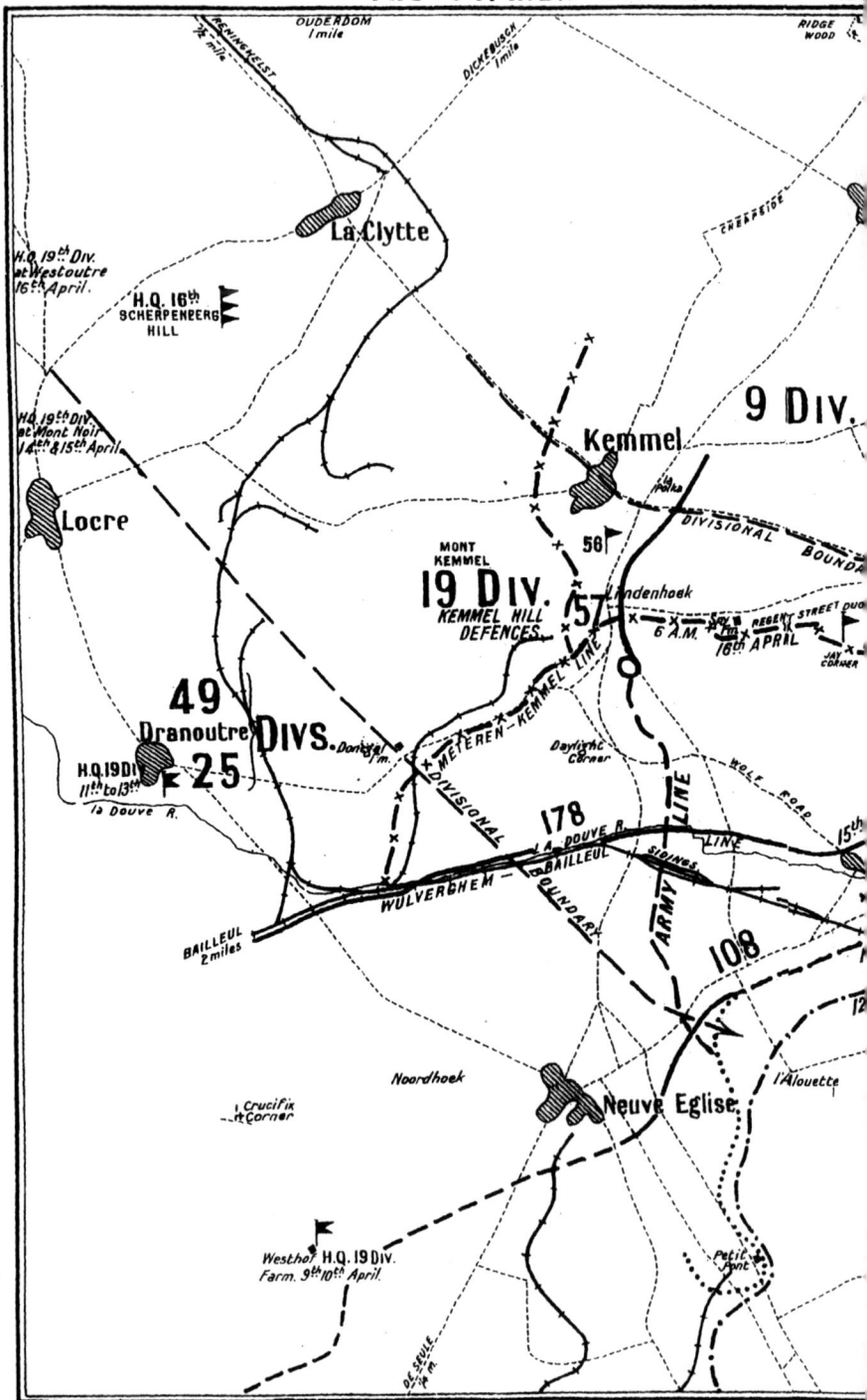

OUDERDOM
1 mile

TRENINGHELST
¾ mile

DICKEBUSCH
1 mile

RIDGE
WOOD

CHEAPSIDE

La Clytte

H.Q. 19th DIV.
at Westoutre
16th April.

H.Q. 16th
SCHERPENBERG
HILL

H.Q. 19th DIV.
at Mont Noir
14th & 15th April.

9 DIV.

Kemmel

The Polka

DIVISIONAL BOUNDA

Locre

58

MONT
KEMMEL

Lindenhoek

19 DIV.
KEMMEL HILL
DEFENCES

57

6 A.M.
16th APRIL

SPUR

REGENT STREET DUG

JAY
CORNER

49
Dranoutre DIVS.
25

H.Q. 19 DIV
11th to 13th

la Douve R.

Donkel fm.

METEREN-KEMMEL LINE

DIVISIONAL

Daylight
Corner

WOLF ROAD

ARMY

LINE

LINE

178
LA DOUVE R.
BAILLEUL

WULVERGHEM — BOUNDARY

SIDINGS

15th

BAILLEUL
2 miles

108

12

Noordhoek

l'Alouette

Crucifix
Corner

Neuve Eglise

Petit
Pont

Westhof H.Q. 19 DIV.
Farm. 9th 10th April.

DE SEULE

1000   0

9th to 29th April, 1918.

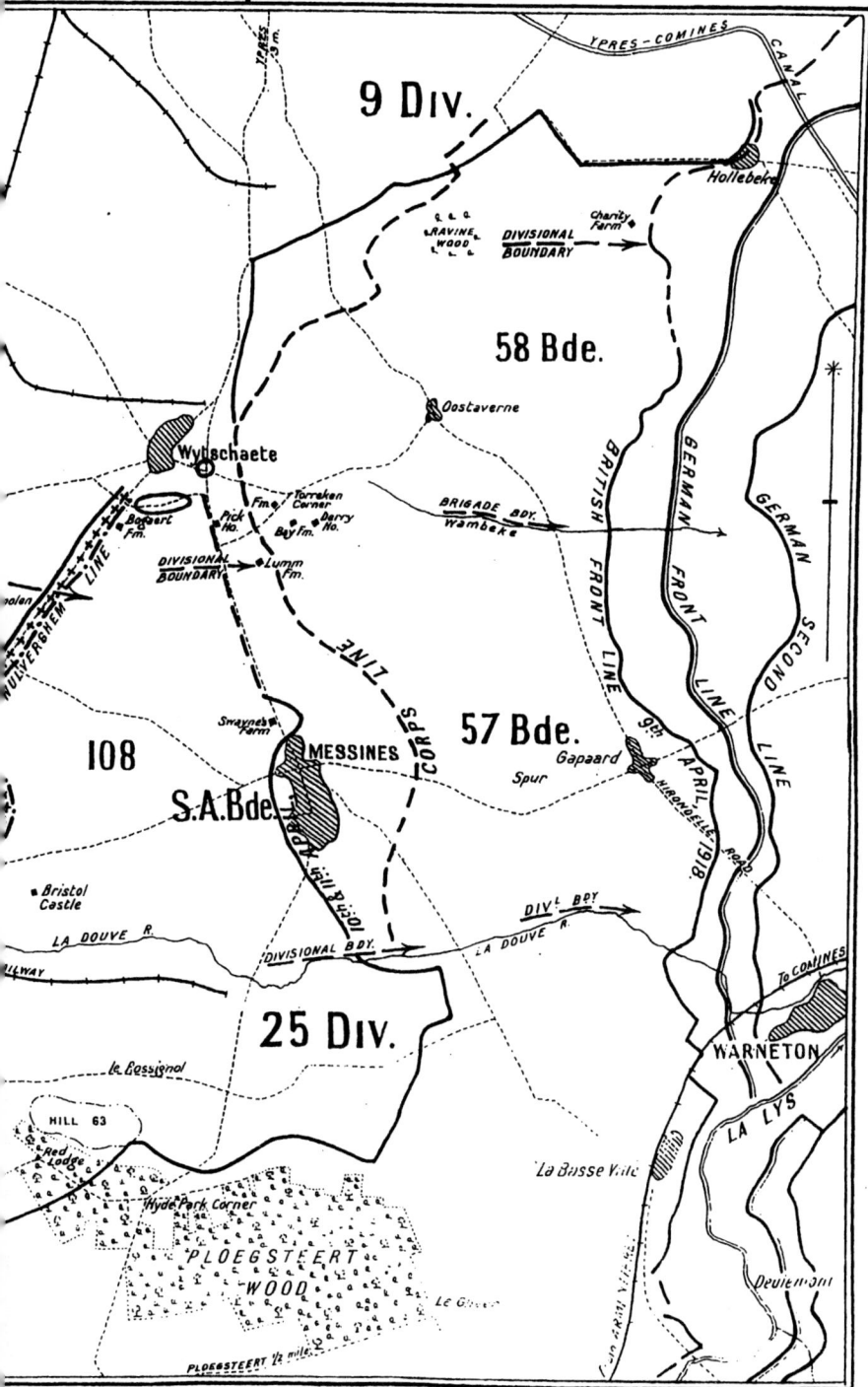

9 Div.

Ypres—Comines

Canal

Hollebeke

Ravine Wood

Divisional Boundary

Charity Farm

58 Bde.

Oostaverne

British Front Line

German Front Line

German Second Line

Wytschaete

Torreken Corner

Pick Ho.

Bay Fm.

Derry Ho.

Fm.

Bogaert Fm.

Brigade Bdy.

Wambeke

Divisional Boundary

Lumm Fm.

Wulverghem Line

Corps Line

57 Bde.

Gapaard

Spur

9th April 1918

Wulverghem Road

Swayne's Farm

Messines

S.A. Bde.

108th April Line

108

Bristol Castle

La Douve R.

Div'l Bdy.

La Douve R.

Railway

Divisional Bdy.

To Comines

Warneton

La Lys

25 Div.

le Rossignol

Hill 63

Red Lodge

Hyde Park Corner

La Basse Ville

Deulemont

Ploegsteert Wood

Le Gheer

Ploegsteert ½ mile.

Army Line

3000   4000

Phil, 1918

CHAPTER XVIII

THE GREY AVALANCHE
THE GERMAN OFFENSIVES OF 1918

III. IN CHAMPAGNE: 27TH MAY–6TH JUNE

THE entrainment of the 19th Division for the Chalons-sur-Marne area began on the 16th of May: all units had reached their destinations and detrainment was completed by the 19th. The Division formed part of the IX British Corps, under the command of the Fourth French Army.[1]

The Division was now billeted in the pleasant villages of St. Germaine Chalons, with Divisional Headquarters at St. Germaine-la-Ville.

The heavy fighting through which the 19th Division had already passed on the Somme and the Lys necessitated a prolonged period of rest, training, and reorganisation, for the Division was now composed almost entirely of new drafts, many of whom were totally inexperienced and others not fully trained; the number of fully-trained men was relatively small.

After training it was intended that the Division should take over a quiet sector of the line in the Tahure area on the Rheims–Verdun front.

The Division settled down in the training area and all units were benefitting greatly from the changed conditions under which they were living when, on the 27th, there came a rude awakening.

THE BATTLE OF THE AISNE, 1918: 27TH MAY–6TH JUNE

At 4 p.m. on that date Divisional Headquarters received information that early that morning the enemy had launched a

---

[1]The other divisions of the IX Corps were the 8th, 21st, 25th, and 50th, and when the 19th Division arrived at Chalons the 21st, 8th, and 50th Divisions were holding a front of about fifteen miles between Bermicourt and Bouconville, north-west of Rheims.

o

very heavy attack on a wide front between Rheims and Soissons, and had penetrated the Allied positions to a considerable depth. This attack involved the whole of the IX Corps front as well as the French corps holding the Chemin des Dames on the left of the British sector. By nightfall the enemy had forced the line of the Aisne on a wide front, crossed the Vesle west of Fismes, and in the British sector had compelled the left and centre of the IX Corps (now reinforced by the 25th Division) to swing back to a position facing west and north-west between the Aisne and the Vesle.

The dismounted personnel of the 19th Division was then ordered to be held in readiness to proceed by 'bus, while the Divisional Artillery, all mounted personnel and transport were to proceed by road under the C.R.A., to the Joncherry-sur-Vesle area.

On the 28th the enemy again attacked in great force on the whole battle-front, pressing the French back to west of Soissons and south of Fere-en-Tardenois, and the IX Corps across the Vesle thence in a south-easterly direction between the Vesle and the Ardre.

At 7.15 p.m. that night orders were received for the dismounted personel of the 19th Division to "embus"; this was completed during the night of the 28th/29th of May, and in the early hours of the 29th units arrived in the following areas; the 57th Brigade reached Chambrecy at 3.30 a.m. and bivouacked in and around the village, the 8th Gloucesters taking up an outpost line on the high ground north of the village; the 58th Brigade arrived in the neighbourhood of Chambrecy, and, having "debussed," marched to the Bligny area, the 2nd Wilts (as outposts) taking up a position on the high ground north and north-west of Bligny village.

Divisional Headquarters opened at Chaumuzy at 6.30 a.m.

General Jeffreys then went off to IX Corps Headquarters at Romigny. The situation, as ascertained from Corps Headquarters and from the G.O.C., 154th French Division, was that the enemy, after his initial successes, had continued to gain ground rapidly and had reached an approximate line Branscourt–Crugny–Wood north-west of Brouillet–Bois des 5 Piles. British and French units were much intermixed and all were tired and had lost heavily. The G.O.C., 154th French Division, also stated that the situation on his front was distinctly critical and that a gap existed from Broillet to Serzy le

Prin. The G.O.C., IX Corps, then ordered General Jeffreys to push forward troops to occupy this gap.

At this period only the 57th and 58th Brigades had arrived, though the 56th Brigade with the 19th Machine-Gun Battalion was expected in from two to three hours' time. The Divisional Artillery was, however, still far away on the road, and owing to loss of guns there was very little other artillery to cover the Allied Line.

At 8.25 a.m. on the 29th orders were issued to the G.Os.C., 57th and 58th Brigades, to move forward one battalion each to take up and hold a line from Faverolles, through Coemy to Lhery, i.e., 58th Brigade on the right, 57th Brigade on the left. The latter brigade was to get into touch with the 13th French Division at Lhery, and the 58th Brigade with the 154th French Division on the high ground north of Faverolles. Both Brigade Headquarters moved to Sarcy to be in close touch with 21st Divisional Headquarters, also in the village.

By 9.30 a.m. the troops were moving forward in accordance with the above orders.

The remaining two battalions of the 57th and 58th Brigades were disposed in support of the two holding the forward line. The two brigades were instructed, however, that as soon as the Faverolles–Coemy–Lhery line had been established, every effort was to be made to push forward and occupy the line Savigny–Prin–Brouillett, providing Savigny and Brouillett were held by Allied troops.

The dispositions of the two brigades when the Faverolles–Lhery line had been established was 58th Brigade (right)— 9th Royal Welch Fusiliers from a quarter-of-a-mile south of Coemy to Faverolles, 9th Welch Regiment in support about Tramery, and 2nd Wilts in reserve in the eastern outskirts of Sarcy; 57th Brigade (left)—8th Gloucesters on the right, 10th Worcesters on the left, holding from Lhery to a quarter-of-a-mile south of Coemy, 10th Royal Warwicks in reserve.

But patrols sent out to ascertain who held Savigny and Brouillett reported that, although there were certain disorganised elements of French and British troops north-west of the Faverolles-Lhery line, Savigny and Brouillett were held by the enemy in considerable strength; consequently the line Savigny–Prin–Brouillett was not established.

Although the 57th and 58th Brigades were in close touch with one another the flanks were far from secure. Elements of the 13th French Division were some 800 to 1,000 yards away on the left of the 57th Brigade and touch was obtained with them by means of patrols; the 58th Brigade similarly endeavoured to gain touch on the right with elements of the 8th and 25th British and 154th French Divisions. The latter, however, proved unsatisfactory and the 2nd Wilts were, at 2 p.m., ordered to move *via* Sarcy and Poilly and take up a position protecting the right flank of the brigade on the high ground north of Boulouse. This move was carried out, the Wilts digging in on a front of 1,500 yards.

The above was the situation at 2 p.m. on the 29th of May.

Several hours later (during the morning) the remaining units of the 19th Division (other than artillery) had arrived and "debussed" in the neighbourhood of Chambrecy and Chaumuzy. The 19th Machine-Gun Battalion arrived at 9.15 and one company each was allotted to the 57th and 58th Brigades. The other two companies, coupled with the 56th Brigade (which reached Chambrecy at about 9.30 a.m.) were placed in reserve in that village. The 5th South Wales Borderers (Pioneers) and the three Field Companies, R.E., were concentrated around Chaumuzy. The Divisional Artillery had not yet arrived.

Between 3 p.m. and 4 p.m. it became evident that the situation in front and on both flanks of the 19th Division was rapidly changing, and that soon the Division must be engaged in heavy fighting.

Early in the afternoon the enemy was in possession of the high ground north-west of Savigny, and at 3 p.m. he was reported as having reached Faverolles, with the result that French and British troops were retiring in that neighbourhood. The 57th and 58th Brigades were then ordered to consolidate and stand fast on their front line, the 58th to ensure that the enemy made no further progress up the Ardre Valley. The 57th Brigade assumed responsibility for the front held by the 74th Brigade[1] (between Lhery and Coemy). The 56th Brigade, plus one company Machine-Gun Battalion, was ordered to move to positions of readiness near Sarcy. Four machine-guns of the last remaining company of the Machine-Gun Battalion were sent to assist the 2nd Wilts, holding the high ground

[1] The 74th Brigade was not the 74th Brigade proper, but a composite force of elements from the 25th, 8th, and 50th Divisions—all very much intermixed.

north of Bouleuse. The three Field Companies, R.E., and the 5th South Wales Borderers were also concentrated in and around Chambrecy.

During the afternoon heavy fighting appeared to be taking place on the ridge immediately north of the Bouleuse Spur and in the neighbourhood of Treslon and Germigny.

Later, troops of the 8th and 25th British and 154th French Divisions were driven back to the line held by the 2nd Wilts; they were reformed and placed in immediate support positions, as the line held by the Wilts, owing to the enemy having gained the Spur north-east of Faverolles, had become the front line.

On the left of the Divisional front, at 3.30 p.m., all French and British troops in front of the Faverolles–Lhery road were being driven in, and shortly those units of the Division holding forward positions observed that they also were now the front line.

About an hour later the enemy was seen steadily advancing from Prin Château, and at least a battalion began to form up in the woods near Point 186 north of Lhery. From the southern slopes of the high ground north of Treslon also Germans were advancing in extended order in a south-easterly direction.

During the evening several temporary changes in commands of units took place; the 2nd Wilts and 56th Brigade (less the 9th Cheshires) were placed under the 8th Division (by order of IX Corps), the Cheshires under the command of the 58th Brigade. The two battalions of the 56th Brigade (1/4th Shropshires and 8th North Staffords) were to have advanced to occupy the ridge north of Mery Premecy, but the movement was not carried out and the two battalions finally prolonged the right of the Wilts on the Bouleuse ridge, North Staffords on the right in touch with the 154th French Division, Shropshires on the left.

Meanwhile the 19th Divisional Artillery had arrived and by 8 p.m. were in action covering the infantry.

Hitherto the 19th Division had been engaged in moving into positions of defence ready to respond to whatever calls were made upon it. Early, positions taken up had been in close support of units belonging to the four divisions which had borne the terrific onslaughts of the enemy on the 27th, 28th, and 29th. But when, towards the close of the latter date, the remnants of the 8th, 21st, 25th, and 50th Divisions had been driven in and the infantry of the 19th Division became the front line, it was obvious that ere many hours passed the Division would be engaged in heavy fighting.

The night of the 29th/30th of May was without incident. Dawn on the latter date broke on the infantry of the Division holding the following positions, *i.e.*, from right to left: 8th North Staffords, 1/4th Shropshires, 2nd Wilts on the Bouleuse Ridge; then came a line of French Senegalese Tirailleurs who were in touch with the Wilts on the right and the 9th Royal Welch Fusiliers on the left at Faverolles; on the left of the Welch Fusiliers were the 8th Gloucesters, whose right was a quarter-of-a-mile south of Coemy and left in touch with the right of the 10th Worcesters at a point about 1,400 yards south-west of Coemy and north of the Coemy–Lhery road; the left of the 10th Worcesters was at a point a quarter-of-a-mile south-west of Lhery, thence round the northern outskirts of that village. The 9th Welch were in support from Coemy to Tramery, while the 9th Cheshires were in Brigade Reserve in the neighbourhood of Sarcy. On the left the 10th Royal Warwicks were in reserve about the Lhery–Ville-en-Tardenois road at a point a quarter-of-a-mile south-west of Bois D'Aulnay. The Warwicks were echeloned back towards the west in touch with the 13th French Division, as the left was very precarious, being maintained only by patrols. The 74th Composite Brigade, very weak in numbers, held the high ground about the Bois des Limons and just north of it.

The front-line battalions of the 19th Division had temporarily absorbed various small parties of troops belonging to the 8th, 25th, and 50th Divisions—some 500 all ranks.

Liaison had been established with the 154th and 13th French Divisional Headquarters (right and left respectively) and Lieut.-Colonel Lord A. Thynne, commanding the 2nd Wilts, was with the latter division as Liaison Officer.

Such were the dispositions of the 19th Division in the front line, when very early on the morning of the 30th the enemy began to continue his advance by means of "infiltrating patrols," one of which was captured by the 9th Royal Welch Fusiliers.

As early as 3.30 a.m. it became apparent that the enemy was on the point of delivering another strong attack. His troops were massing on the forward edges of the woods around Point 186 and his patrols were advancing in the neighbourhood of Lagery (west of Lhery). On the right of the 58th

Brigade he had driven back the French and the 9th Royal Welch Fusiliers were already engaged on the south-eastern outskirts of Faverolles. By 6 a.m. he had worked round the left flank of the 57th Brigade, completely outflanking the 10th Worcesters, and was entering Lhery from the south-west.

The enemy's main attack against the whole of the Divisional front was launched at 6 a.m. Preceded by violent artillery and trench-mortar fire eight lines of Germans successively advanced against our front line. The French troops and 74th Composite Brigade, on the left of the 10th Worcesters, were driven in, leaving the left of that battalion completely exposed. Severe fighting ensued. The Worcesters, faced with a hopeless task against superior forces, were in an untenable position and the only way to hold up the enemy was to make a short withdrawal; the left company of the battalion had already lost all its officers and 60 per cent of its men.

On the 58th Brigade front and beyond the right of that brigade the enemy succeeded in driving back the Senegalese troops holding the line between the Wilts and 9th Royal Welch Fusiliers. By this penetration the enemy was enabled to envelop the right flank and capture a platoon of the 9th Royal Welch Fusiliers, as well as driving in the flank of the Wilts. Both the Welch Fusiliers and Wilts suffered heavy casualties in the severe fighting resulting from the enemy's penetration of the line.

The result of the attack on the left of the Divisional front was that the left of the 57th Brigade was forced back to the high ground south of Lhery where, with the reserve company of the Worcesters, another desperate attempt was made to stem the advance of the enemy.

All along the line heavy fighting, with here and there enforced withdrawals, took place until, at 7.30 a.m., another line had been formed from Tramery to a farm south-west of that village, thence to Point 225 west of Bois D'Aulnay, thence again to the Lhery–Romigny road, about a mile north of the latter place.

Away on the right, where the French had fallen back[1] creating a gap between the 9th Royal Welch Fusiliers and the 9th Welch, practically the whole of the former battalion and three companies of the 9th Welch were surrounded and killed or captured.

---

[1] They retired without informing the two British battalions.

As the morning wore on the line held (described above) at
7.30 a.m. had also to give way under repeated heavy attacks.
Every available man had to be used. On the extreme flank of
the Divisional front the 2nd Wilts most gallantly maintained
their position on the high ground north of Bouleuse until
2 p.m. On the left the 5th South Wales Borderers, who had
established themselves on the high ground south of Romigny,
covering the Romigny–St. Gemme and Romigny–Chatillon
roads, maintained their position in the face of strong attack,
rendering possible the reorganisation of the 57th and 58th
Brigades after they had fallen back from the line held at
7.30 a.m.

By 1 p.m. the situation on the Divisional front (from left to
right–that is the order given in the official records) was as
follows: 5th South Wales Borderers on the high ground south
of Romigny; elements of the 74th Composite Brigade astride
the Romigny–Ville-en-Tardenois road, west of the latter
village; 10th Royal Warwicks from right of the 74th Composite Brigade to a point on the track leading from Fm.D'Aulnay to Chambrecy, about 1,000 yards south of the farm; 8th
Gloucesters from this point to high ground immediately west
of Sarcy; 9th Cheshires and remnants of 9th Royal Welch
Fusiliers, and 9th Welch, and the 58th Trench-Mortar
Battery (acting as infantry) to the Sarcy–Bouleuse road; 1/4th
Shropshires and 8th North Staffords from the Sarcy–Bouleuse
road to the ridge north-west of Aubilly where touch was
obtained with troops of the 28th French Division, arriving in
relief of the 154th French Division. The 13th French Division,
on the left, had completely disappeared, all touch having been
lost with it. But the 40th French Division was coming up to
relieve it. Meanwhile, in order to attempt to close the gap,
the South Wales Borderers and the 74th Composite Brigade
extended the line far over the left Divisional boundary.

By this reorganisation the 10th Worcesters were in Brigade
Reserve in the valley between Chambrecy and Ville-en-
Tardenois, while the 2nd Wilts, when they were finally forced
to abandon their position on the Bouleuse Spur, were located
in reserve east of Sarcy.

During the afternoon General Jeffreys was placed in charge
of all British troops in the line. Headquarters of IX Corps
and of other British divisions were withdrawn, and to the 19th
Division were attached British troops coming under the

command of General Pellé, commanding V French Corps. All Brigade Headquarters were moved to the neighbourhood of the cross-roads near Chambrecy, and later to the western outskirts of that village.

At 9.20 p.m. 19th Divisional Headquarters moved to Pourcy, having been severely shelled in their former headquarters, the Mess and personal kit having been destroyed.

During the afternoon Brig.-General B. E. Glasgow, 58th Brigade was wounded and Brig.-General R. M. Heath, commanding 56th Brigade, assumed command of the remnants of the 58th Brigade as well as of his own brigade.

The hours between 1 p.m. and early evening had not passed without excitement. During the afternoon the enemy was reported massing in the Bois D'Aulnay Valley, indicating a renewal of the attack. The Divisional Artillery, therefore, concentrated their fire on that neighbourhood. At about 5 p.m. an attack by from one to two battalions was made from south of Hill 191. The 8th Gloucesters, aided by some guns of "B" Company, 19th Machine-Gun Battalion, firing from a copse south of Sarcy, dealt effectively with this attack. It then appeared that an attack on a large scale had been broken up by the Divisional Artillery before it could develop.

Meanwhile, on the left of the Divisional front, the enemy had attacked south of Romigny on a line Villers Argon—Berthenay—Romigny, and was reported to have crossed the Romigny—St. Gemme road. The 74th Composite Brigade, therefore, formed a defensive flank on the western edge of the Bois de Bonval, touch being maintained with the 10th Royal Warwicks just west of Ville-en-Tardenois.

Throughout the night of the 30th/31st of May, the situation remained unchanged along the Divisional front, and no further attacks were made by the enemy.

Certain changes, however, took place during the night which must be referred to briefly: During the morning of the 30th the 19th Division had been ordered to pass forthwith to the command of the V French Corps, as Headquarters, IX British Corps, were to be withdrawn from the line. The corps front was to be held by the 28th French Division on the right, 19th British Division in the centre, and 40th French Division on the left. The boundaries of the 19th Division were—northern (or eastern) boundary from the south-western edge of Bois de Rheims to Aubilly (exclusive) Bouleuse (exclusive); southern (or western) boundary—a road from La Neuville to Ville-en-Tardenois (inclusive) then the road to Lhery (inclusive).

The above boundaries placed the defence of the Ardre Valley still in the hands of the 19th Division.

At midnight 30th/31st, therefore, the G.O.C., Division, took command of all troops within this sector irrespective of whatever division they belonged to or what nationality they were.

The V French Corps was commanded by General Pellé, a courteous and considerate officer, whose kindness the 19th Division, during the time it took part in the operations, very greatly appreciated.

At 7.45 p.m. the G.O.C., 19th Division, urged strongly to the V French Corps that all British troops outside the Divisional sector should be relieved as they were holding a considerable extent of line none of which was, or had been, within the Divisional sector. The 40th French Division was at that period holding support positions so that the relief could easily have been arranged. Through the kind efforts of General Pellé (though the 40th Division was not under him) the relief *was* eventually carried out; the General also agreed to relieve British troops holding positions in his own corps area. Two battalions of the 28th French Division took over the line held by the 1/4th Shropshires and the 8th North Staffords, the former battalion remaining in support of the French, and the latter in reserve about the road running west from Bligny; the 58th Trench-Mortar Battery and elements of the 8th and 25th Divisions who had become intermixed with units of the 19th Division, were withdrawn to reserve to the bend of the Chambrecy–Bligny road. A portion of the 74th Composite Brigade and the 5th South Wales Borderers on relief were withdrawn, the former to an area around Nappes, while the latter (having again reverted to the direct command of the G.O.C., 19th Division) concentrated on the Chaumuzy–La Neuville road.

Heavy hostile shell-fire (causing considerable casualties) characterised the morning of the 31st of May. Posts in the neighbourhood of Sarcy had to be withdrawn and a line was established from west of Ville-en-Tardenois (as before), thence north-east to a small bridge about 1,000 yards south of Sarcy, over the stream running parallel with the Sarcy-Chambrecy road and thence to the *A* of *A*ubilly.

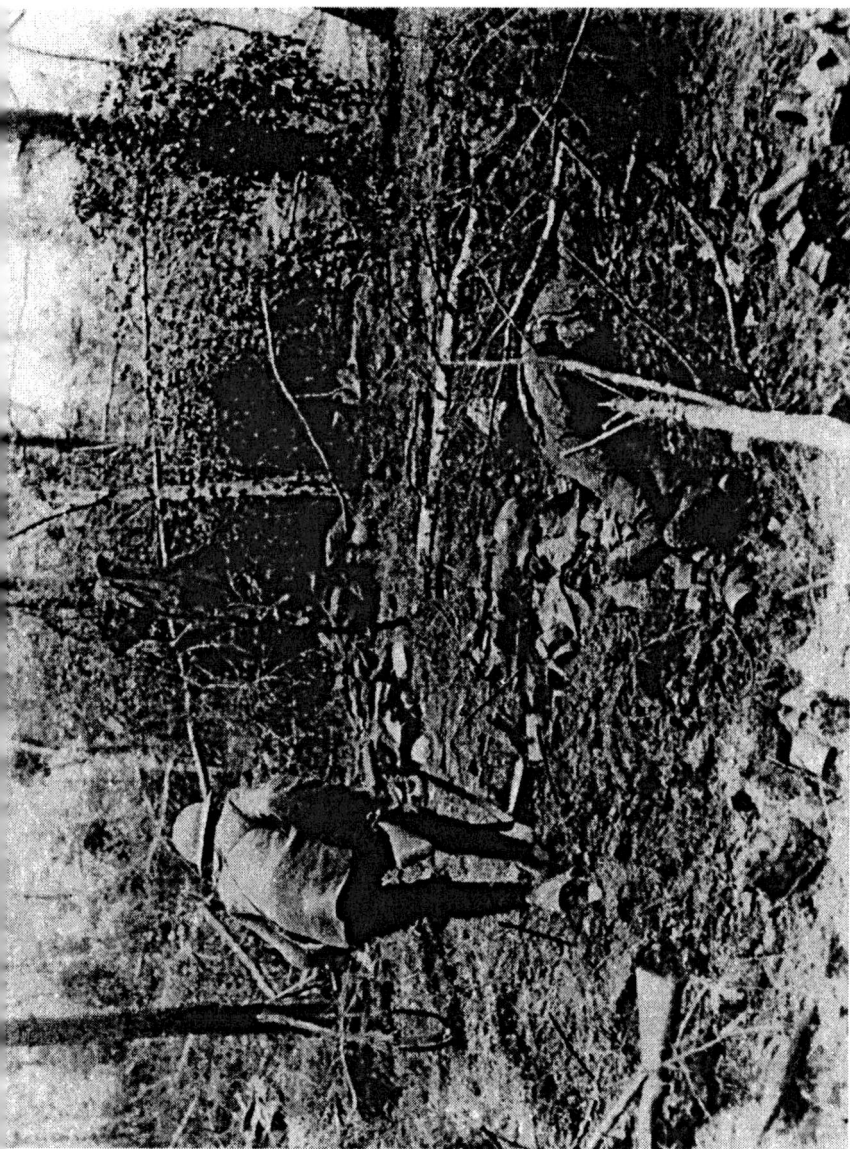

IN THE WOODS IN CHAMPAGNE: THE BOIS DU PETIT CHAMP

During the morning also the remnants of the 9th Royal Welch Fusiliers and 9th Welch were organised into a composite company and placed under the command of the 9th Cheshires and put into the line as a company of that battalion.

At 1 p.m. the enemy was observed massing in the valley south-west of Ville-en-Tardenois, but every available gun was turned on to his troops, who were dispersed with heavy loss. A little later, however, a heavy attack developed from the direction of Romigny and from a small wood north-west of Ville-en-Tardenois. The remnants of the 74th Composite Brigade (who had not been relieved by the French on the previous night) were driven in and the 10th Royal Warwicks were heavily engaged. Ville-en-Tardenois was entered by the enemy from the south-west and the position of the Warwicks becoming untenable, they fell back to the high ground south-east of the village, maintaining touch with the 8th Gloucesters on their right. The Warwicks were, however, holding a too greatly extended front and the 10th Worcesters, were, there-for, put in between them and the Gloucesters.

By 3 p.m. the attack had been taken up by the enemy opposite the right of the 19th Division and the French were being driven off the Aubilly Ridge. Heavy fighting was in progress on the front held by the 9th Cheshires and on the right of the 8th Gloucesters. Both of these battalions were having to give ground before the enemy's vastly superior forces.

At 4.45 p.m. General Jeffreys, who was at Brigade Headquarters, personally ordered a counter-attack to be undertaken by the 2nd Wilts to regain the high ground 1,000 yards north-west of the first C in Chambrecy.[1] The Wilts were to assemble behind the ridge west of the Sarcy–Chaumuzy road and attack due west. At 5 p.m., however, it was reported that the French on the right were advancing again towards their old position on the Aubilly Ridge. This report was confirmed by the 1/4th Shropshires, who were advancing with the French; the Shropshires also reported that a local counter-attack was in progress.

This counter-attack was made by the 9th Cheshires, led in person by the C.O.—Lieut.-Colonel W. W. S. Cunninghame[2] (2nd Life Guards). This gallant officer, immediately realising

---

[1] The high ground north of the Chambrecy-Ville-en-Tardenois road.

[2] He was wounded and subsequently awarded the D.S.O. for his gallantry.

the gravity of the situation, had ridden on horseback into the valley, into the midst of heavy artillery, machine-gun and rifle-fire, rallied the troops, formed them up and led them forward to the assault. His horse was shot under him, but he continued to direct the counter-attack on foot. The counter-attack was successful and restored the situation, greatly assisting the counter-attack by the 2nd Wilts at 7.15 p.m.

The 2nd Wilts, in face of heavy fire, advanced to the Montagne de Bligny, east of the farm just north of Chambrecy. Severe fighting ensued but the position was gained and held by the Wilts who then came into line between the Gloucesters and Cheshires.

Meanwhile, attempts by the enemy to push along the Ville-en-Tardenois–Chambrecy road were repulsed by artillery, machine-gun and rifle-fire. The covering fire of the artillery was splendid.

The night of the 31st May/1st June passed quietly.

By dawn on the 1st the line of the Division was still unbroken, but the rifle strength of brigades was very weak; the 56th Brigade numbered 900, the 57th Brigade 750, while the 58th Brigade could only muster 350. The Pioneers were at a strength of 500. Out of 64 guns the 19th Battalion Machine-Gun Corps had only 35 in action.

The line held by the Division ran (right to left) from the left of the 28th French Division, just south-west of Aubilly and east of the River Ardre, thence in a south-westerly direction to first bend in the Ville-en-Tardenois–Champlet road, the order of units being (right to left) 56th Brigade—1/4th Shropshires, 8th North Staffords, 9th Cheshires; 57th Brigade—2nd Wilts, 8th Gloucesters, 10th Worcesters, and 10th Warwicks. On the left of the 19th Division the 40th French Division from the left of the 10th Worcesters to the north-west corner of Bois de Bonval.

Up to 7 a.m. there was no change in the Divisional front. At 8 a.m., however, heavy and accurate enfilade machine-gun fire was opened on the left of the 57th Brigade from Ville-en-Tardenois; at 3 p.m. the enemy was seen massing at various points south of Bois D'Aulnay.

At 4 p.m. a heavy attack was launched against the 40th French Division, which was driven back through the Bois de Bonval and Bois de la Cohette, but the enemy was prevented from debouching from these two woods. Simultaneously a

heavy frontal attack was made on the 57th Brigade, particularly against the right of the Gloucesters and left of the Wilts.
The enemy continued to press the French on the left and the
latter formed a line on the western edge of Boujacourt Village.
The left of the Warwicks was, therefore, swung back to conform to the line. The high ground south of Chambrecy was
firmly held.

Meanwhile the situation in the centre of the 57th Brigade
front was critical. The enemy had succeeded in penetrating the
line at the junction of the Wilts and Gloucesters and had
proceeded to roll up the right and centre companies of the
latter battalion. The left company had stood firm, also the 10th
Worcesters. The enemy at once attempted to follow up his
advantage and pressed the right and centre companies of the
Gloucesters down the hill towards Chambrecy. Capt. E. B.
Pope ("B" Company), 8th Gloucesters, however, rallied the
company in the valley and with great determination and
gallantry led them back up the slope in a counter-attack,
driving the enemy back to his original line and taking twenty
prisoners from him, as well as inflicting heavy casualties.[1]

The 2/22nd French Regiment which was in support at the
time also joined in the counter-attack (on their own initiative)
led by their gallant C.O. (Commandant A. de Lasbourde)[2]
and eventually took the place of the 8th Gloucesters in the
line, thus freeing the latter to fall back to support positions
and reorganise.

But the line of the 19th Division, owing to the enemy's
success against the 40th French Division on the left (where
the Germans were in possession of the Bois de Courmont), was
now untenable and at a conference the Divisional Commander
decided to take up a new line running from just north of
Chantereine, thence northwards along the western edges of the
Bois d'Eclisse—round the northern slope of the Montagne
de Bligny (to include the Montagne) thence north-east to the
cross-roads a mile north of Bligny Village; 56th Brigade on
the right, 57th on the left. The 40th French Division, on the
left, would hold the line Cuisles, thence north-east along the
southern edge of the Bois de la Cochette–Boujacourt to

---

[1]Captain Pope was awarded the D.S.O. for his gallantry in this action.

[2]This gallant French officer was also awarded the D.S.O., while the 2/23rd
French Battalion was cité in French Corps Orders.

Chantereine. At 7 p.m. the withdrawal began and by 11 p.m. had been successfully carried out.

"This line," records the Narrative of the 19th Division, "included the hill north of Bois d'Eclisse known as the Montagne de Bligny, which was shortly to become the scene of heavy fighting. This hill was a feature of the greatest tactical importance as, once in possession of it, the enemy would gain direct observation and command of the Ardre Valley and so all our battery positions in the valley would become untenable and communication (especially the Nanteuil–Chambrecy road) extremely precarious."

The night of the 1st/2nd of June was uneventful and many minor reorganisations were effected, principally the formation of the 9th Cheshires, the remnants of the 9th Royal Welch Fusiliers, 9th Welch, and 56th Trench-Mortar Battery into one composite battalion known as the 9th Cheshire Regiment under the orders of the G.O.C., 56th Brigade.

Throughout the 2nd, 3rd, 4th, and 5th of June no further attacks were made by the enemy on the 19th Division, though his shell-fire was heavy, and on the latter date showed a marked increase as he had brought up his huge 15 and 21 cm. howitzers.

At midnight 5th/6th of June the line as previously given remained unchanged, with the exception that during the night of the 4th/5th the 28th French Division had taken over from the 19th Division a part of the line east of the Ardre extending from the cross-roads half-a-mile north of Bligny to a wood a quarter-of-a-mile south-west of these cross-roads.

Units holding the line, from left to right, were as follows:— "161st Regiment of 40th French Division, 8th Division Composite Battalion (with a composite battalion from 25th Division in close support), 57th Brigade comprising 10th Royal Warwicks, 10th Worcesters, 8th Gloucesters (with 50th Division Composite Battalion) and 1/6th Cheshires (of 25th Division) and 5th South Wales Borderers (Pioneers) in support; 56th Brigade comprising 58th Brigade Composite Battalion, 9th Cheshires, 8th North Staffords, 1/4th King's Shropshire Light Infantry in support; 28th French Division. Elements of the 134th French Division (about 1,200 all ranks) were in Divisional Reserve."[1]

[1] Divisional Narrative.

From 2 to 3 a.m. on the 6th the 19th Divisional and attached artillery opened counter-preparatory fire. At 3 a.m. the enemy's guns put down a heavy bombardment along the whole of the Divisional front and along the front of the 28th French Division. With great violence and intensity this bombardment continued until 4 a.m.

The enemy then launched a big infantry attack against the right of the 57th Brigade, the 58th Brigade Composite Battalion, and the 56th Brigade, i.e., against the north-western edge of the Bois d'Eclisse and the Montagne de Bligny.

The 58th Composite Battalion (formed from the remnants of the 2nd Wilts, 9th Royal Welch Fusiliers, and 9th Welch) got out of their trenches and met the enemy in the open. Using their bayonets with great effect these gallant troops fell upon the enemy and, after inflicting heavy casualties on him, completely repulsed his attack.

He had also attacked (though less heavily) the remainder of the 57th Brigade line along the western edge of the Bois d'Eclisse. Two bodies of Germans advanced towards the 10th Worcesters and 8th Gloucesters. These two battalions allowed the enemy to advance to within a short distance of the line and then opened heavy machine-gun and Lewis-gun fire. Many Germans were killed and the remainder scattered and took cover in the long grass where they lay under fire all day.

The 9th Cheshires, on the left of the 56th Brigade, and the 8th North Staffords on the extreme right of the Divisional front, similarly repulsed the enemy, causing him heavy losses.

By 8 a.m. the fighting had died down on the 19th Divisional front; the line of the Division had remained firm and intact.

On the right, however, the 28th French Division had also been heavily attacked and driven back past the village of Bligny on to the line of the track running in a north-easterly direction between Bouilly and the Ardre. The 8th North Staffords, therefore, reinforced their right flank, gaining touch with the French at Chaumuzy Hill.

Meanwhile, General Jeffreys had issued orders that the Montagne de Bligny was to be held "at all costs."

At about 11 a.m., preceded by an intense bombardment, the enemy launched a further determined attack against positions on the Montagne, and this time succeeded in gaining the summit of the Hill. An immediate counter-attack, made by the

9th Cheshires, though pressed with great gallantry, failed to restore the situation.

Another counter-attack was immediately organised and the 1/4th King's Shropshire Light Infantry were brought up for the purpose.

This counter-attack was a very brilliant affair.

Though hurriedly planned and organised, the Shropshires went forward with great dash, the remnants of the 9th Cheshires being carried forward (for the second time) by the magnificent dash and spirit of their comrades. The enemy, who, having warded off one counter-attack, apparently considered himself immune for some hours from further attacks, was completely taken by surprise. The Shropshires charged the enemy and drove him well down the forward slopes of the hill, taking one officer and thirty-three other rank prisoners as well as killing many Germans.

By 12.15 p.m. the Montagne de Bligny was again in our hands and the gallant Shropshires had added another brilliant incident to the fine history of the Regiment.

For this action the 56th Brigade was cité in French Corps Orders, and, as a brigade, was decorated with the Croix de Guerre (with star), while the 1/4th King's Shropshire Light Infantry were also cité in French Army Orders, and, as a battalion, were awarded the Croix de Guerre (with palm). Decorations to officers and men for individual acts of gallantry were also awarded by the French authorities.[1]

The successful defence of, and counter-attack on, the Montagne de Bligny, enabled the 28th French Division on the right to deliver a counter-attack late on the afternoon of the 6th. They retook the village of Bligny and one company with the 8th North Staffords restored their original line.

Thus, after a day of hard fighting, the original line of the early morning along the Divisional front was successfully maintained and heavy losses had been inflicted on the enemy.

---

[1]The wording of the citation was as follows: "On June 6th, 1918, when the right flank of an English brigade, which had been heavily engaged, was threatened by the enemy's advance, the battalion in reserve, the 1/4th Battalion of the King's Shropshire Light Infantry, was ordered to deliver a counter-attack against an important position from which the garrison had been driven. With magnificent dash and after heavy fighting the position was recovered and with it the key to the whole line of defence, which made it possible to re-establish the line and maintain it intact."

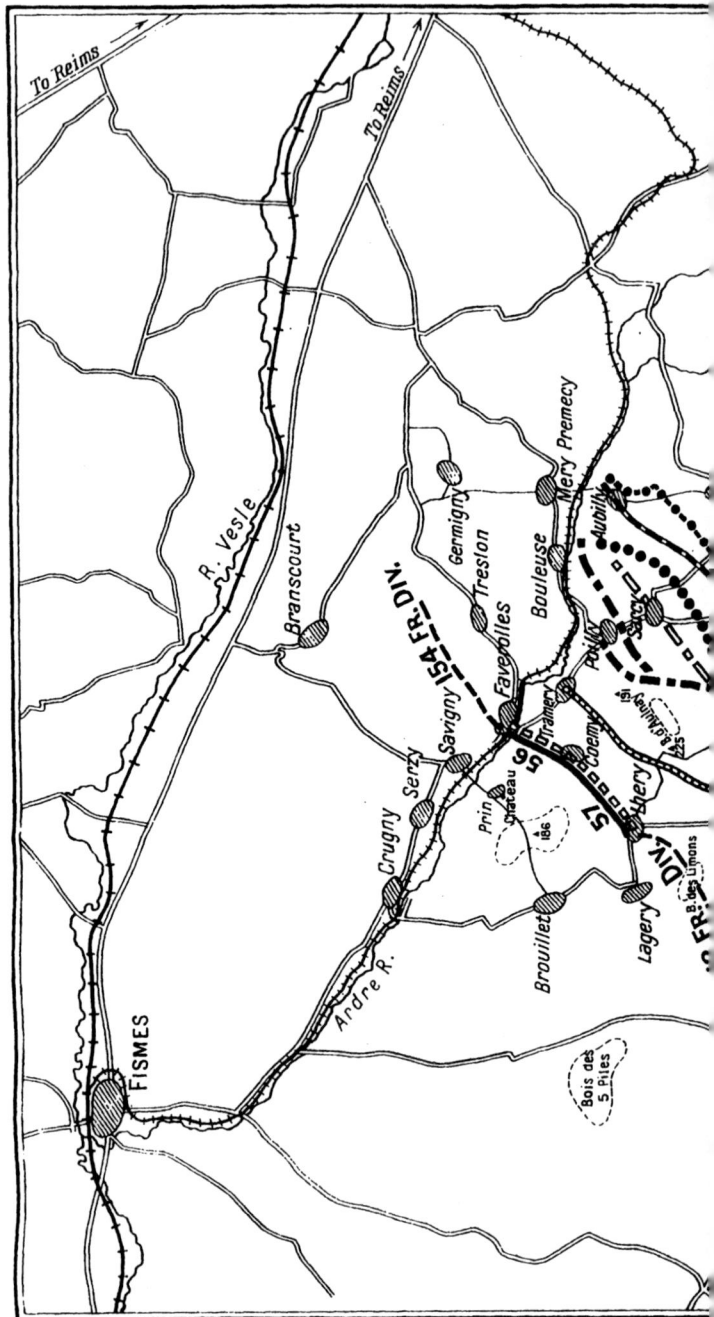

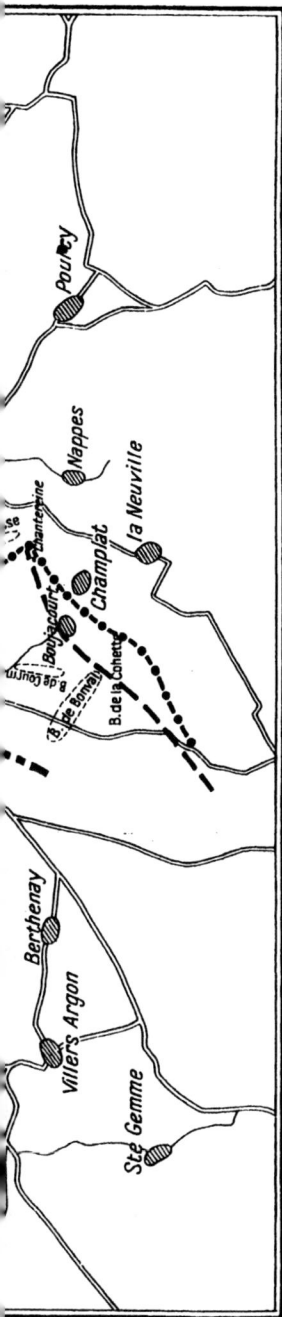

Poulcy

Nappes

Chantereine

la Neuville

Champlat

B.de Bonnay

B.de la Cohette

B.de la Cour

Berthenay

Villers Argon

Sté Gemme

Scale of Miles

0   ½   1   2   3   4   5

The Battle of the Aisne, 1918.
27th May – 6th June.

Line....11 a.m....29th..May......
....,,.....Dawn...30th......,,......
....,,......9.30 a.m.........,,......
....,,.........1 p.m.........,,......
....,,.......11 a.m....31st......,,......
....,,........Dawn.....1st...June......
....,,.......11 p.m......1st......,,......}
                   and onwards
Small French Adv. 2nd. June......

THE GERMAN OFFENSIVE IN CHAMPAGNE, MAY–JUNE, 1918.

Face p. 208.

All units of the Division were, however, worn out with incessant fighting and sadly reduced in numbers.

During the night of the 6th/7th various reliefs were carried out and all troops in the front line relieved.

Between the 7th and 19th of June no further operations on a large scale were undertaken by the enemy or by the 19th Division. Shelling, in which a large proportion of gas was used, was persistent and heavy.

By its fine resistance the 19th Division had completely frustrated the enemy's plans to advance up the Ardre Valley and envelop Rheims from the south-west. Had he succeeded the consequences to the Allies must have been very serious.

On the 19th June the 19th Division was relieved by the 8th Italian Division and withdrawn to an area south of Epernay and later further south to the Mondiment area, to rest and refit. In this area the troops from other divisions, temporarily attached to the 19th, were sorted out and returned to their own divisions. New drafts were incorporated. On the 22nd of June the remnants of the 10th Worcesters were reduced to Training Cadre and transferred to the 25th Division, the remainder being absorbed and replaced in the 19th Division by the 3rd Worcesters.

On the 30th of June and 1st of July the Division moved by train northwards, back to the British Zone, and on its arrival was billeted in the Fauquembergues area.

P

CHAPTER XIX

THE ADVANCE TO VICTORY

ON the 11th of July the 19th Division was transferred to the XIII Corps and moved to the Bomy-Auchel area where training was continued. The very heavy fighting through which the Division had passed had robbed it of many experienced officers and men, and the majority of the new drafts were young, inexperienced soldiers, only partially trained.

The Division relieved the 3rd Division in the line in front of Locon and Hinges on the night of the 6th/7th of August, but early the next morning the enemy began to withdraw his line from south of Locon and patrols were at once pushed out to keep touch with him. Orders were also received by the brigades holding the front line to continually harass the enemy, while the Divisional Artillery kept the opposing lines of trenches and back areas under constant and heavy bombardment. This was the nature of warfare in the front line (so far as the 19th Division and divisions on left and right were concerned) for the next few weeks.

The Advance to Victory had begun. While the Division was out of the line, in training, the Allies had counter-attacked in Champagne and had thrust the enemy back. Then on the 8th of August the Battle of Amiens opened and ended in disastrous defeat for the enemy. "The Black Day of the German Army" General Ludendorff called it, for he lost thousands of prisoners and guns and miles of territory, a great dent being made in his line east of Amiens. Thereafter, attack followed attack, the enemy being kept in a state of uncertainty as to where the next blow would fall.

Reference to the despatches and a map, however, will show that the early stages of the great Advance to Victory took place along the fronts of the Fourth, Third and First British Armies, *i.e.*, between the Amiens-Roye road and Lens, and that the advance along the front of the Fifth and Second Armies (from Lens to just north of Ypres) was much slower, the enemy holding on to his positions until forced to abandon them by the advance farther south. He had, however, evidently

determined to evacuate the costly Lys Salient (between the
La Bassée Canal and Ypres) formed by his advance in April.
His retirement coincided with the relief of the 3rd Division
by the 19th Division on the 6th/7th of August.

So far as actual Battle Honours are concerned the 19th
Division did not take part in a major operation until the
Battle of the Selle in the middle of October. Nevertheless,
between the 7th of August and the 17th of October the life
of the Division was of a very strenuous nature, and more than
one small attack of importance was carried out successfully,
while patrol encounters were frequent which finally ended in
the Division gaining complete control of No Man's Land.

All three infantry brigades of the Division (56th, 57th and
58th, in that order from right to left) were in the front line
on the 7th of August, which ran approximately from Pont
Tournant, on the right, to La Panneme, on the left. But the
line was on the move and the southern end of Locon was
cleared that day: on the left Vertbois Farm held up the
advance. On the 8th the advance was continued, though at the
Farm already mentioned strong opposition was again encountered. Vertbois Farm was reached on the 9th, but it
could not be held owing to shell-fire: it was, nevertheless,
denied to the enemy. On the 10th the 2nd Wilts. carried out
a successful operation against a post near the Farm, killing ten
Germans and capturing two.[1]

For several days no further advance took place. On the 13th
a patrol of the 1/4th Shropshires rushed a hostile post,
killing several Germans and capturing four. Two days later a
fighting patrol of the 10th Royal Warwicks raided the enemy's
posts, killing eight of the enemy and capturing two machine-
guns. On the 19th patrols, pushed out to maintain close touch
with the enemy, took a further twenty-three prisoners. The
Germans were still withdrawing at various points, and on the
21st progress was made in the Locon sector.

Our line in the Lys Salient then ran from just east of Locon
in the south, northwards east of Merville to just west of
Bailleul. On the 21st of August also the Second Battle of the
Somme, 1918, opened with the Battle of Albert, 1918, in
which action the Fourth, Third and extreme right of the

---

[1]On the 10th, Brig.-General A. J. F. Eden (G.O.C., 57th Brigade) was
wounded and temporary command of the Brigade was taken over by Lieut.-
Colonel C. Umfreville.

First Armies made a further big advance between Chaulnes and Neuville St. Waast (south of Arras).

Along the front of the 19th Division the enemy was now very much on the alert, checking any attempt of fighting patrols to advance. But the Air Force reported numerous fires and explosions at Laventie, Armentières, La Bassée, Aubers and Fromelles—signs of another withdrawal.

Divisional Headquarters were at this period at Labeuvrière and on the 27th were shelled by high-velocity guns and bombed by aeroplanes.

On the 28th there were indications of another enemy retirement. At 7 a.m. an officer's patrol from the 9th Royal Welch Fusiliers reached the Lestrem road without interference. A general advance, to take place during the night of the 28th/29th, was then ordered. At 6 a.m. on the 29th the Divisional line had been pushed forward to just west of Vieille Chapelle, and Zelobes had been occupied. Patrols were constantly out towards the former village. That night the enemy fired Estaires, and the skies were illuminated by the glare from burning dumps, etc., behind his front line.

During the night of the 29th/30th the line of the Chapel Road was gained by the right brigade, and by 8 a.m. on the 30th along the whole Divisional front. During the afternoon the Outpost Line of Resistance was established on the western bank of the Lawe Canal, while patrols had pushed across the latter with orders to make good, if possible, the line of the Marais Road as a picquet line with patrols in front. No signs of the enemy were seen.

On the 31st at midday patrols located the enemy in posts about Les Huit Maisons.

Meanwhile, along other parts of the front in the Lys Salient, the enemy had begun extensive retirements on the night of the 29th/30th of August. Early on the latter date our patrols found Bailleul unoccupied: by the evening of that day we had reached the general line Lacouture-Lestrem-Noote Boom, east of Bailleul.

On the 3rd of September the · 19th Division attacked the enemy with the Richebourg-St. Vaast-Croix Barbée line as the objective. The attack began at 5.30 a.m. when, under cover of an intense artillery and machine-gun barrage, the 57th and 58th Brigades advanced and gained all their objectives. Fighting patrols were at once pushed forward to the

La Bassée road. The final line gained by the Division at nightfall ran from Landsdowne Post (on the south) thence to
Pont Logy-Euston Post (on the La Bassée road)-Tilleloy
South, all these positions being well beyond the objectives
originally ordered. About 170 prisoners and 15 machine-guns
had been captured.

Brigades in the front line were now ordered to adopt a policy
of deliberately establishing themselves in salients in the
enemy's outpost screen, and thus compel him to fall back
from the remainder of his line in order to avoid being cut off.

By the evening of the 6th of September the Lys Salient had
disappeared: Kemmel Hill had been recaptured from the
enemy and we had reached the general line Givenchy-Neuve
Chapelle-Nieppe-Ploegsteert-Voormezeele.

Until the 20th of September[1] "nibbling" tactics were
adopted, but on that date the 57th Brigade attacked the
Distillery, south of La Tourelle, Nora Trench and a defended
locality known as Shepherd's Redoubt immediately west of
La Tourelle.

The 10th Royal Warwicks (in conjunction with the left
brigade of the 55th Division) made the attack and, in spite
of a stout resistance, by 8 a.m. had captured all objectives,
i.e., Shepherd's Redoubt, Nora Trench and the Distillery:
they also took prisoner one officer and seventy-eight other
ranks. But at 9.30 a.m. the enemy put down a very heavy
barrage and counter-attacked in considerable strength. A hard
struggle now took place and finally, at about 3 p.m., the
Germans had forced their way back into the Distillery and
Shepherd's Redoubt, which they continued to hold at nightfall.

The "19th Divisional Intelligence Summary," records that
"From about 10 a.m. to 12 noon . . . . the enemy, making
excellent use of his knowledge of the ground and cover
(bushes, crops and drains) was infiltrating forward, and it
appears had worked up Biczer Trench up the various drains
east of the Distillery leading into our positions and also
northwards up the ditches alongside the La Bassée road from
the direction of Pioneer Dump."

---

[1]On the 16th of September Lieut.-Colonel Lord A. Thynne, commanding
2nd Wilts., was killed by a chance shell when going forward to Battalion
Headquarters.

The next morning, at 3.30 a.m., he also recaptured Nora Trench.

After two or three days, during which the Divisional guns kept the above positions under very heavy fire, cutting the wire also, the 3rd Worcesters (57th Brigade) attacked the Nora Trench–Shepherd's Redoubt–Distillery line, and captured all objectives. At 6 p.m. the 10th Warwicks attempted to establish themselves on the eastern side of the La Bassée road. This attack apparently coincided with a general counter-attack by the enemy to retake the Redoubt and Distillery, but he was completely repulsed and lost just over eighty prisoners.

The Division made a final attack in this area on the 30th of September, when the 1/4th King's Shropshire Light Infantry and the 9th Cheshires of the 56th Brigade, with the 58th Brigade co-operating on the right and 59th Division on the left, advanced the line farther east and took more prisoners and machine-guns.

On the 1st and 2nd of October the 19th Division was relieved by the 74th Division, but during the relief the enemy again retired and the 56th Brigade (which, on the 2nd, was still in the line) pushed forward and occupied Aubers and the high ground south-east of it (the famous Aubers Ridge, which the British Army had gazed at for four years and had experienced many a bloody repulse in attempting to capture it), where a halt was made so that a defensive line could be handed over to the 74th Division that night.[1]

In this advance the newly-formed Divisional Mounted Detachment, under Lieut. Siddons, went out on patrol and encountered a strong German mounted patrol south-west of Fournes. A skirmish took place, the Mounted Detachment withdrawing as the enemy was in superior force. Nevertheless, valuable information as to the extent of the enemy's withdrawal had been obtained and the Fifth Army Commander sent his congratulations to General Jeffreys.

On completion of the relief the 19th Division moved to the

---

[1]During September Brig.-General W. P. Monkhouse (the C.R.A.) was appointed G.O.C., R.A., X Corps, and was succeeded in command of the 19th Divisional Artillery by Brig.-General E. J. R. Peel. Also, Colonel C. V. Trower, who had been in command of the 5th South Wales Borderers (Pioneers) since their formation in 1914 and was regarded by all ranks as "The Father of the Division," resigned and proceeded to England for a well-earned rest, handing over command of the Battalion to Lieut.-Colonel R. R. Raymer.

TANKS AND INFANTRY MOVING UP DURING THE ADVANCE TO VICTORY

Auchel area, and on the 3rd orders were received transferring the Division to the XVII Corps, Third Army. On the 4th, the Division began to move south, and by the 5th was concentrated round Henu. On the 7th the Division moved to Graincourt, coming under the orders of its new Corps Commander, Lieut.-General Sir C. Fergusson.

CHAPTER XX

THE LAST PHASE

ON the 8th of October the second and concluding phase of the British Offensive opened with the Battle of Cambrai,[1] but the 19th Division was in Corps Reserve,[2] and it was the 10th before a move forward was made to the outskirts of Cambrai, the troops being billeted in houses. By this date the British front line had been pushed far beyond Cambrai and on the Third Army front had reached the line Neuvilly-St. Hilaire-Avesnes. The enemy evidently intended making a stand on the eastern bank of the Selle River, but on the 12th continued his retirement on the left of the Third Army front, and the 24th Division pushed on to the western bank of the Selle River.

On the evening of the 14th of October the 19th Division was ordered to take over the front held by the 24th Division on the night of the 17th/18th of October, and the G.O.C., 57th Brigade, was warned that his Brigade would take over the whole of the 24th Divisional front. On the 15th further orders from Corps Headquarters ordered the 19th Division to be prepared to attack and capture the high ground east of the Selle River, extending from the cross-roads south of Maison Bleue, thence north-west to the cross-roads at Fme. Canonne, *i.e.*, the Blue Line.

Two brigades were detailed to make the attack, 57th on the right and 58th on the left; the 56th Brigade was in reserve.

In order to obtain a good "jumping-off" line for the infantry on the eastern bank of the Selle, the 24th Division carried out an attack on Haussy on the morning of the 16th of October. This attack was at first successful, but in a heavy counter-attack the 24th Division was driven back across the river. On this date also, preparatory to the attack on the 20th, the 57th Brigade (less one battalion) moved to St.

---

[1] The official despatches designate this Battle as "The Second Battle of Le Cateau."

[2] The XVII Corps on the 8th of October consisted of the 19th, 24th, 57th, 61st and 63rd Divisions.

Aubert, with the one battalion at Couroir, and the 58th Brigade to Rieux.

THE BATTLE OF THE SELLE, 17TH-25TH OCTOBER

Between the 8th and 17th of October much had been done to improve communications which, as the result of our rapid advance, had become dislocated. On the morning of the latter date, therefore, operations for the forcing of the Selle positions and attainment of a general line from the Sambre et Oise Canal-western edge of the Foret de Mormal-Valenciennes were begun. The first stage of the operations was opened by the Fourth Army which attacked on a front of about ten miles from Le Cateau southwards.

The crossings over the river presented formidable obstacles. "The enemy was holding the difficult country east of Bohain and the line of the Selle north of it in great strength, his infantry being well supported by artillery."[1]

The situation on the 17th, so far as was known at 19th Divisional Headquarters, was as follows: The 24th Division held the high ground west of the Selle from south-west of Haussy to just north of Montrecourt with two platoon posts some sixty yards south of the river bank. The enemy was established on the high ground east of the river and also held machine-gun posts in Haussy, through which the Selle flowed in a north to south direction. Temporary bridges, erected by the 24th Division, had been destroyed, and it was believed that there might possibly be some of the enemy in Haussy west of the river. It was decided, therefore, that the Royal Engineers should place infantry bridges across the river during the opening barrage, which was arranged to rest on its opening line for fifteen minutes. Ten bridges were allotted to each attacking brigade. The 57th Brigade was to establish posts in Haussy on the western bank of the river and, if possible, cross and establish bridge heads east of it.

On the night of the 17th/18th of October the 57th Brigade relieved the 73rd Brigade (24th Division), taking over the whole divisional front; the 3rd Worcesters were on the right and the 10th Royal Warwicks on the left: the 8th Gloucesters were in reserve in St. Aubert. During the night the Worcesters

---

[1] Official despatches.

advanced their line to the railway on the western outskirts, and immediately south-west of Haussy without meeting with opposition.

On the 18th, at 10 a.m., General Jeffreys assumed command of the line, and Divisional Headquarters were established at Avesnes-les-Aubert. Daylight patrols were pushed out towards the Selle by the Worcesters, who located hostile machine-gun posts north of Haussy. After dusk posts were established east of the railway. On the night of the 18th/19th the 58th Brigade took over the left portion of the front which included Montrecourt, 2nd Wilts. on the right and 9th Welch on the left; the 9th Royal Welch Fusiliers were in reserve.

The enemy's guns were busy during the night and also continued active throughout the 19th. At about 3 p.m. the 4th Division, on the left of the 19th, reported that the enemy was again retiring and that patrols had reached Saulzoir. Patrols from the 19th Division then went out along the whole divisional front and, although posts were established in the north-western suburbs of Haussy, the river could not be crossed, as the bridges had been destroyed.

As soon as it was dark bridges, prepared for the attack, were brought up, and the river was bridged and bridge heads established on the eastern bank before "Zero."

Too much praise cannot be given to the splendid work of the Sappers at this period: they, with the Pioneers, were having a strenuous period, but they did their work with great devotion and skill.

Patrols from the 58th Brigade (on the left) met with heavy machine-gun fire from the railway embankment east of the river, south-east of Montrecourt and the high ground behind the embankment; they suffered a considerable number of casualties. Eventually, however, followed by platoons in support, they succeeded in crossing the river and getting to the embankment, and by nightfall the line of the railway was made good along the whole brigade front. Bridges were at once brought forward and were in position by 11.30 p.m. The 58th Brigade, having thus advanced, the "jumping-off" line of that Brigade was put forward to the railway embankment. Just south of Montrecourt an artillery bridge was also constructed and completed by 1.30 a.m. on the 20th.

During the night the 8th Gloucesters (right) and the 10th Warwicks (left) took over the line from the 3rd Worcesters, the latter becoming Brigade Reserve and moving into cellars on the western outskirts of Haussy.

At "Zero" hour on the 20th, *i.e.*, 2 a.m., the situation was as follows: the 57th Brigade had crossed the Selle and Gloucesters and Warwicks were formed up on the eastern side of the river. The 58th Brigade was formed up with its leading troops on the railway embankment. All infantry and artillery bridges had been placed across the river.

The weather was abominable, heavy rain was falling and fell continuously until after dawn had broken.

As the barrage fell the troops moved forward to the attack. But the enemy's resistance was not severe, though his machine-gun and shell-fire caused many casualties. A pocket of Germans held out for a while in some practice trenches north-east of Haussy and delayed the advance of the Warwicks, but two platoons dealt with this opposition and took nineteen prisoners. By 5.30 a.m. all objectives had been captured.

The 58th Brigade, on the left, was for a short space held up also by machine-gun fire, the 2nd Wilts. particularly, in front of a road junction in their line of advance; but they overcame the opposition.

During the morning the 9th Royal Welch Fusiliers (the left of the 58th Brigade) advanced their line further north-east to include some practice trenches astride the Chaussée Brunehaut.

Patrols later obtained touch with the enemy who held Sommaing and Vendegies. No further change took place during the day, and Brigade Headquarters of the 57th and 58th Brigades moved into Haussy.

Early on the 21st a party of about twenty of the enemy attacked a post of the Wiltshires but were repulsed, losing an officer and several men killed.

Both the ridge commanding the River Harpies, and Haussy, were shelled heavily throughout the day, and Headquarters of the 57th Brigade had to move.

During the afternoon the G O.C., 57th Brigade, was warned that his Brigade would probably be required to continue the advance on the morning of the 23rd, in conjunction with an attack by the VI Corps on the right.

At night the 9th Welch relieved the 2nd Wilts., the latter moving back into reserve.

Under cover of an artillery and trench-mortar barrage the 8th Gloucesters at midnight attacked Ferme de Dieux with the object of establishing a bridge head east of the Harpies. The farm was found unoccupied, the enemy having cleared out as soon as the barrage fell: a post was then established just east of the river.

The 22nd was without incident and during the day final orders were received for the attack to take place on the 23rd. The 57th Brigade was to co-operate with the left of the 2nd Division (on the right of the 19th) on the high ground east of the River Harpies. The 57th Brigade was to capture Les Fourrieres and consolidate the high ground near St. Martin's Chapel.

The 8th Gloucesters were to carry out the attack.

"Zero" hour was 3.20 a.m.

Before "Zero," bridges had been placed across the river by the Sappers and Pioneers, and a number of troops were able to pass over before the barrage fell.

The enemy offered considerably more resistance than previously, and a small portion of the attack was held up by hostile machine-gun fire from a small copse. But this resistance was overcome and the advance continued, and by 4.30 a.m. all objectives had been gained. At about 6.30 a.m., however, machine-gun fire was suddenly opened from some sand pits south of Les Forrières. By means of rifle-grenade fire the Germans were forced into the open and driven into the Gloucesters' advanced posts, the whole party of thirty being either killed or wounded.

During this attack the 10th Warwicks pushed forward strong patrols and established posts. On the right of the 19th Division, the 2nd Division reported that, as so little opposition had been met with, the advance was being continued. Accordingly the G.O.C., 57th Brigade, was warned about 10 a.m. that his Brigade would advance in conformity with the 2nd Division. At 12 noon these orders were confirmed and the 8th Gloucesters were ordered to make good the line of the Capelle-St. Martin road, while the 10th Warwicks were instructed to push forward their right company to just west of the Ecaillon River.

The advance was carried out under a creeping barrage at 2.26 p.m., and the attack pushed home with great determination. The enemy was demoralised and the Gloucesters gained the St. Martin-Capelle road, while the right company of the Warwicks secured the Les Forrières-Vendegies road on their front. Patrols were then pushed forward through St. Martin to make good the bridge heads over the River Ecaillon, but little headway was possible owing to opposition from Bermerain.

The G.O's.C., 57th and 58th Brigades, then held a conference and arrangements were made for an advance by the left company of the 10th Warwicks of the former Brigade in conjunction with an advance by the 9th Welch and 9th Royal Welch Fusiliers of the 58th Brigade.

The barrage opened at 4 p.m. and the whole line advanced to the Vendegies-St. Martin road, thence along the railway to the Chausse Brunehaut. A few prisoners and several machine-guns were captured.

Patrols penetrated the outskirts of Sommaing and reconnoitred the line of the Ecaillon, but others who attempted to enter Vendegies were held up by heavy machine-gun fire from that village.

The 19th Division was relieved during the night of the 23rd/24th of October, the 61st Division having passed through the leading troops of the former. The Division then withdrew to billets in Avesnes-les-Aubert.

Captures during this period numbered 277 prisoners and 42 machine-guns. Many more machine-guns and trench-mortars were actually captured but could not be salved.

Casualties suffered by the Division were 111 officers and other ranks killed, 603 wounded, and 25 missing.

As usual, the operations of the infantry figure almost exclusively in the narratives, but at this period of the Final Advance battalions would never have been successful had it not been for the splendid support given by the Divisional Artillery, whose barrages were a marvel of accuracy and had a demoralising effect on the enemy. The strenuous work of moving the guns forward in rear of the rapidly-advancing front line was carried out without a grumble. Always on the move, always fighting, the gunners deserved (and received) the thanks of their comrades in the front line more closely engaged with the enemy. To the Royal Engineers and Pioneers the whole Division owed a very great deal of its success. The skill and gallantry with which they prepared and placed in position light pontoons across rivers in order to allow infantry to pass, and artillery bridges for the guns to move forward, was one of the marvels of the later stages of the War.

To the Army Medical Corps and Army Service Corps, who

tended the wounded and fed the troops on the move, respectively, too much praise cannot be given: to keep pace with the forward move in evacuating the wounded or making dumps for supplies was extraordinarily difficult.

In that great rush to Victory all units of a division were tested to the utmost, and the staff work was wonderful.

For a few days the 19th Division enjoyed a well-earned relief from the front line. There was a large influx of reinforcements after the above operations—mostly young soldiers without any previous experience of the War. Time was short in which to prepare them for the next battle, but training in open warfare began at once and it was surprising to see how quickly they grasped the principles; they were taught by instructors who were by now seasoned warriors.

THE BATTLE OF THE SAMBRE, 4TH-10TH NOVEMBER[1]
AND PASSAGE OF THE GRANDE HONELLE

By the end of October the enemy was in a desperate position. Staggering under the rain of heavy blows dealt by the British Armies he was very near total collapse. His *morale* had almost gone: in material his losses were irreplaceable, for he could not make good the enormous numbers of guns and machine-guns, and vast quantities of ammunition, which had fallen into our hands. Nor had he any reserves from which to replace the tens of thousands of prisoners taken from him. There were still, however, German troops who fought well and who did their best to hold up our advance.

The Battle of Valenciennes, fought on the 1st of November, gave us an almost south to north line from east of Le Cateau to east of Valenciennes. But the country over which the next advance was to take place was most difficult. On the south the Sambre River was in front of us: in the centre the great Forêt de Mormal, while north the fortified line of Le Quesnoy, an enclosed country of towns and villages and several small rivers, had to be crossed.

In the line of advance of the 19th Division there were no less than four of these small streams or rivers, numerous villages of fair size, railways, roads, hills and valleys—"hard going" both for infantry and gunners—while the Sappers and Pioneers were again kept ever busy with little or no rest.

[1]The 19th Division, though in reserve, is entitled to the "Battle of Valenciennes, 1st November," as one of its Battle Honours.

At a Corps Conference on the 31st of October plans for a further advance on the 4th of November were discussed, with the object of capturing the high ground east of the Petit Aunelle River. This was part of a great attack by the Fourth, Third and First Armies to be delivered on the 4th on a front of about thirty miles from the Sambre, north of Oisy, to Valenciennes.

During the evening of the 31st of October the G.O's.C., 56th and 58th Brigades, were informed that their Brigades were to carry out the attack of the 19th Division, the 24th and 11th Divisions attacking on the right and left simultaneously.

On the 2nd of November the 56th Brigade relieved the left brigade of the 61st Division from the road junction on the Villers Pol-Preseau road, about five hundred yards south-east of Fond des Vaux, thence to just west of the Ferme de Wult with picquets in the latter: the 1/4th King's Shropshire Light Infantry were on the right and the 9th Cheshires on the left; the 8th North Staffords were in reserve west of Maresches.

Detailed orders for the attack were also issued. The high ground just west of Jenlain was given as the first objective and the spur west of, and overlooking the villages of, Bry and Eth the second objective, with the latter, that part of Wargnies-le-Grand, north of the Bry-Villers Pol road, was to be captured.

The first objective was to be captured by the 56th Brigade, and the second by the 57th and 58th Brigades on the right and left respectively.

At 9 a.m. on the 3rd of November the G.O.C., 19th Division, assumed command of that portion of the front taken over by the 56th Brigade and established his Headquarters in Vendegies; the 58th Brigade also moved to Vendegies and the 57th to Montrecourt and Haussy.

Early morning patrols encountered the enemy near the cross-roads on the Villers Pol road and also near La Patte d'Oie, but at 10 a.m. the 11th Division reported that the patrols had failed to gain touch with the enemy; their front-line brigades had, therefore, been ordered to push forward and gain ground where possible.

The 56th Brigade was then ordered to send out patrols with the object of discovering the whereabouts of the enemy. These patrols were furnished by the Shropshires and Cheshires. The latter experienced no opposition until crossing the ridge just south-east of La Patte d'Oie, where heavy machine-gun fire was opened from the western outskirts of Jenlain and Chateau D'En Haut Ferme. The Shropshires came under similar fire from the high ground on the Villers Pol-Jenlain road; on the right the 24th Division was also under fire and could not advance. The front was, therefore, echeloned back from the left.

Under covering fire from the right company, the left company of the Shropshires was ordered forward. Simultaneously the left company of the Cheshires began to consolidate the ridge south-east of La Patte d'Oie and pushed forward strong patrols, who secured a footing on the high ground less than a thousand yards west of Jenlain: here they were in close touch with the enemy.

Between 1 p.m. and 4 p.m. a heavy hostile barrage fell on the whole area between Jenlain and Maresches. The Shropshire patrols had several stiff fights with the enemy's rear guards, but a platoon of the left company succeeded in pushing through the orchards north of the road running east from the gardens of the Château d'en Haut Ferme and got into the northern outskirts of Jenlain where they took a few prisoners. The effect of this very considerable advance by the Shropshires was to cause the enemy to withdraw in front of the Battalion, and the left company of the latter then pushed on through the northern edge of the village and established itself in a sunken road just north of the Halt on the railway running through Jenlain to Curgies, obtaining touch with the 11th Division. Meanwhile the right company of the Shropshires had also penetrated and passed through the western portion of Jenlain, and had made good the line of the railway south of the Halt.

But touch had not yet been obtained with the 24th Division and a defensive flank was therefore formed by the right company of the Cheshires, who moved to the sunken road running south-east from Jenlain.

By 4 p.m. the Cheshires had also driven the enemy from the high ground on their right flank and were established on the Blue Line, which had been fixed as the first objective for the attack on the 4th of November. This necessitated a considerable modification of the original plans.

The 58th Brigade was ordered to move its Headquarters forward, and the three battalions to their assembly positions north and north-west of Maresches: the 57th Brigade (then on the march to Vendegies) was ordered to continue the march to Sepmeries and billet there for the night.

The "jumping-off" line for the attack next morning was altered to the line of the main Le Quesnoy-Valenciennes road, the opening barrage to fall six hundred yards in front of the road. Forward posts and patrols were then withdrawn, as it was considered inadvisable to assemble for the attack east of Jenlain.

In intense darkness and heavy rain the 58th Brigade, moving up to their assembly positions on the left of the 56th Brigade, experienced great difficulty. But their difficulties must have been light compared with those experienced by the Divisional Artillery, which had to move forward over practically unknown ground and get their guns across country, for there were few roads or tracks in the line of their advance. Nevertheless all battalions were in position before "Zero" hour.

Divisional Headquarters were established in Sepmeries and Brigade Headquarters of the two attacking brigades in Ferme de Wult.

Dawn on the 4th broke under the worst possible conditions: the ground was wet and muddy from the heavy rain, and a heavy mist hung over the valleys which did not clear for several hours.

At 6 a.m. the barrage opened and the attack began. At first little opposition was encountered, but the enemy placed a heavy barrage on the western outskirts of Jenlain and on certain localities, especially Ferme de Wult. The Petit Aunelle River proved to be a more serious obstacle than was expected and some difficulty was experienced in crossing it. When the troops finally reached the opposite bank heavy machine-gun fire met them, but they were not to be denied and charged towards the enemy. The latter, therefore, abandoned their guns and fled before the attacking troops could get to close quarters. About one hundred prisoners were captured west of the river and the Cheshires took a field gun.

The heavy barrage on Jenlain had, however, delayed the 8th North Staffords (the supporting Battalion of the 58th Brigade) and they were late in passing through the leading troops on the Green Line.[1] They were, therefore, late for the barrage

---

[1]This Green Line was about half-way between the Bry-Eth road and the Petit Aunelle River.

Q

also, and came under considerable machine-gun fire from the high ground east of Wargnies-le-Grand. But our own machine-guns were at once brought forward, and under their fire a footing was obtained on the high ground north and north-east of Wargnies.

Hitherto the advance of the 19th Division had been in a north-easterly direction, but from the Green Line the direction of attack was now practically due east towards a Brown Line which, in this instance, was the Bavai-Bellignies road.

An attempt to push a platoon into Bry was frustrated by machine-gun fire.

At 8 a.m. the 57th Brigade was ordered to move to Maresches and Advanced Divisional Headquarters were opened at Ferme de Wult. But the 24th Division, on the right, had not yet reached the Green Line, and in order to protect the right flank of the 19th from enfilade fire from the southern portion of Wargnies-le-Grand, a company commander of the 9th Cheshires with his company "mopped up" the remainder of the village: he also attacked and captured a nest of machine-guns near the four cross-roads at Chapelle St. Roch. A considerable number of prisoners were taken in Wargnies. Posts were then established on the north-eastern outskirts of the village.

Heavy artillery and machine-gun fire, coming from Bry and Eth and the high ground east of these two places, met patrols from the 2nd Wiltshires and 9th Welch as they advanced in order to secure the crossing of L'Aunelle River. Although the crossing could not be secured (owing to this machine-gun fire) the Wiltshires, nevertheless, captured nine prisoners in the outskirts of Eth, but they suffered heavy casualties in trying to clear the village.

On the right the 24th Division had still not succeeded in gaining the whole of their objective. In order to assist that Division, and to gain ground along the line of the Wargnies-le-Grand and Bry-La Marlière road as far north as La Maison Blanche, the G.O.C. ordered an attack to take place at 4.30 p.m. in conjunction with attacks on the right and left by the 24th and 11th Divisions respectively. The 58th Brigade was ordered to throw back its left flank to gain touch with the 11th Division, whose objective was Hill 100.6 north of Eth. The 56th Brigade (on the right) gained its objective without opposition. On the left, owing to a miscarriage of orders, the attack by the 11th Division did not materialise, and the 58th Brigade met with severe opposition. The enemy's barrage was very heavy, and came down two minutes after the 19th Divisional barrage opened, the support and reserve companies of the 9th Welch and 2nd Wiltshires (right and left) suffering considerable casualties. In Eth the latter Brigade also suffered heavy losses from machine-gun fire from their left.

In spite of losses, however, the right company of the Welch gained, and established itself on, the Wargnies-le-Grand-La Marlière road. The left company swung back its left flank to join up with the Wiltshires, who had taken Eth with fifty prisoners and had established a line on the slopes east of the village, but were unable to gain the crest of the spur. The support company of Wiltshires formed a defensive flank facing north to protect the left and rear of the battalion.

The remainder of the evening and night passed quietly. The advance was continued at 6.20 a.m. on the 5th of November. With little opposition the 56th Brigade gained first the ridge west of Galotin, and later the eastern outskirts of La Flamengrie, but further advance was impossible owing to heavy fire from the high ground west of the Hogneau River. The 58th Brigade (on the left) reached the western slopes of the ridge west of Bettrochies, but all attempts to push on over the crest were stopped by heavy fire from a spur south-west of the village.

By this time darkness was falling, heavy rain all day had, in places, turned the country into a quagmire and the going was difficult. Added to these disadvantages, the men were thoroughly exhausted. For days and nights they had been on the go with but little rest, and the young soldiers especially found their powers of endurance strained to the utmost.

The G.O.C. Division, therefore, decided to wait until the next morning before continuing the advance. The objective for the 6th of November was the high ground immediately west of the Hogneau and the establishment of bridge heads over the River.

The gunners had moved forward and before dark had come into action near Eth and Bry.

The barrage fell at 6 a.m. on the 6th, and Bettrochies and the high ground west of the river were gained with very little opposition. But heavy machine-gun fire met all attempts to push patrols across the river. During the morning, however, a platoon of the 58th Brigade succeeded in establishing itself east of Bettrochies and close to the river. Machine-guns were sent forward and the Bois D'Ugi, Bois Dancade and slopes east of the river were kept under fire which materially assisted in keeping down the enemy's fire.

During the day the 57th Brigade, which had moved forward to Bry and Eth, relieved the 56th Brigade (less 9th Cheshires, who were ordered to remain under the orders of the 57th Brigade in support). The 56th Brigade then moved back to Bry and Eth in Divisional Reserve.

At 6 a.m. on the 7th, the 57th and 58th Brigades continued the advance. On the right the river was crossed and the 57th Brigade pushed right on across the Bavai-Bellignies road to a ridge and established a line roughly from the cross-roads just north of La Tonkin, thence southwards to east of the railway in the neighbourhood of Ferme du Petit Chène.

On the left the 58th Brigade also pushed across the river and occupied Bellignies and the Bellignies-Bavai road.

The Divisional front, however, at Houdain, had been considerably narrowed by the converging advance of the divisions on both flanks. The 57th Brigade, therefore, took over the whole of the 19th Divisional front, the 58th Brigade taking over the protection of the left flank of the Division, for which purpose the 9th Royal Welch Fusiliers occupied the high ground facing north and extending from Bellignies to the spur immediately north of Houdain.

Divisional Headquarters moved to the eastern outskirts of Flamengerie during the morning of the 7th, and gave orders that no further advance was to take place during the day owing to the exhaustion of the troops.

The advance had been extraordinarily difficult. The sodden state of the ground, and the enclosed country, presented considerable obstacles to troops, worn out and fatigued by continual fighting. The crossing of the Hogneau had again tried all ranks. The artillery had a hard task, and only by great perseverance was it possible to get the guns across the river and bring them into action near Breaugies and Ruisne.

At 7 p.m., however, Corps Headquarters sent a message saying that as Mezières had fallen the whole Corps was to advance "despite the fatigue of the troops and the exposed flank, as an advance on the part of the British would compromise the retreat of the German Armies from the south."

At 6 a.m. on the 8th of November, therefore, the 57th
Brigade, to whom the 9th Welch had been attached, advanced
without a creeping barrage. At 8.15 a.m. Tasnières was
reported clear of the enemy and Brigade Headquarters moved
to Château de Warnicamp, while Advanced Divisional Headquarters moved forward to Breaugies, the latter place being
heavily shelled during the day; one shell hitting a lorry containing the kit, mess equipment, etc., of Advanced Divisional
Headquarters, completely destroying it.

Again the artillery were met by dreadful difficulties in
getting their guns forward, but before dark they had come into
action north-east of Bavay.

By 8 a.m. the 57th Brigade had reached the eastern outskirts
of Malplaquet and had entered the Bois de la Lanière. Enemy
opposition now began to stiffen, and the 10th Royal Warwicks
(the left battalion) had sharp fighting with a hostile patrol in
the village, capturing one prisoner. In the neighbourhood of
the Cemetery, north of Malplaquet, two attempts to dislodge
a party of the enemy failed and the Warwicks sustained a
number of casualties.

Meanwhile, in order to secure the left flank of the Division,
the 9th Royal Welch Fusiliers of the 58th Brigade, by ex-
tending their right to Hon-Hergies, formed a defensive flank
facing northwards until the 11th Division came up into line.
Patrols were sent across the L'Hogneau River and reported
Hergies and Millot-Pollet clear of Germans. As the 11th
Division advanced into line with the 57th Brigade, the 58th
Brigade withdrew and moved to Houdain.

At 1.45 p.m. 57th Brigade Headquarters moved to Taisnières and Divisional Headquarters to Château de Warnicamp.

During the afternoon the right company of the 3rd Worcesters (right battalion of the 57th Brigade) advanced their
line about one thousand yards, coming into line with the 24th
Division, but were then held up by machine-gun and shell-fire.
The left company of the same battalion reached the railway in
spite of considerable fire from Bois de la Lanière: swinging
slightly to their right, however, they finally reached Les Bas
Vents just after dark, capturing *en route* one prisoner and
three machine-guns. Being some distance ahead of the flanks
they withdrew to the line of the railway.

At dusk the enemy in the Cemetery, north of Malplaquet,
retired, and the right company of the 10th Royal Warwicks

pushed forward as soon as it became dark, also to the line of the railway, taking two machine-guns in Bois de la Lanière. The remaining companies and Headquarters of the Battalion formed a defensive flank above the L'Erelle River.

The situation at midnight (8th/9th November) was as follows: The 57th Brigade held the line of the Maubeuge-Mons railway along the whole Divisional front with a defensive flank thrown back along the L'Erelle River: the 58th Brigade (less the 9th Welch) was concentrated in Houdain and Breaugies, and the 56th Brigade was in Taisnières.

Late at night orders for the advance to be continued on the 9th were received from Corps Headquarters: the 24th Division was to advance in a north-easterly direction to meet the 11th Division east of Bois de la Lanière: the 19th Division would then be squeezed out of the line.

At 7.30 a.m. on the 9th, meeting only with slight opposition on the eastern outskirts of Bois de la Lanière, the advance began. The 24th and 11th Divisions joined hands at 9.30 a.m., the 19th Division became Corps Reserve, and the troops were concentrated in the nearest villages.

Thus, north of Maubeuge and just west of the Maubeuge-Mons road, the 19th Division ended its fighting days.

On the 10th of November Divisional Headquarters moved to Wargnies-le-Petit. The 57th Brigade marched to the Flamengrie area and the 58th Brigade to Eth and Wargnies le Grand. Only the Divisional R.E. and the 5th South Wales Borderers (Pioneers) remained in the forward area under the C.E., XVII Corps: their services were so valuable that they could not be given a much-needed rest.

In the above positions the Division received news of the Armistice on the morning of the 11th of November.[1]

During the final advance the Division had lost 11 officers and 126 other ranks killed, 41 officers and 784 other ranks wounded, and 1 officer and 46 other ranks missing.[2] Captures included 212 prisoners, 2 field-guns, 45 machine-guns, and 9 trench-mortars. Many machine-guns captured were never collected, as there were no opportunities to salvage the area.

[1]During the first week of November Lieut.-Colonel P. E. Hodgson, the C.R.E, was promoted Brig.-General and C.E. of the XIV Corps in Italy. He was succeeded by Lieut.-Colonel A. N. Lawford.

[2]Between the 21st of March and the 9th of November, 1918, the total casualties suffered by the 19th Division were approximately 16,000 all ranks.

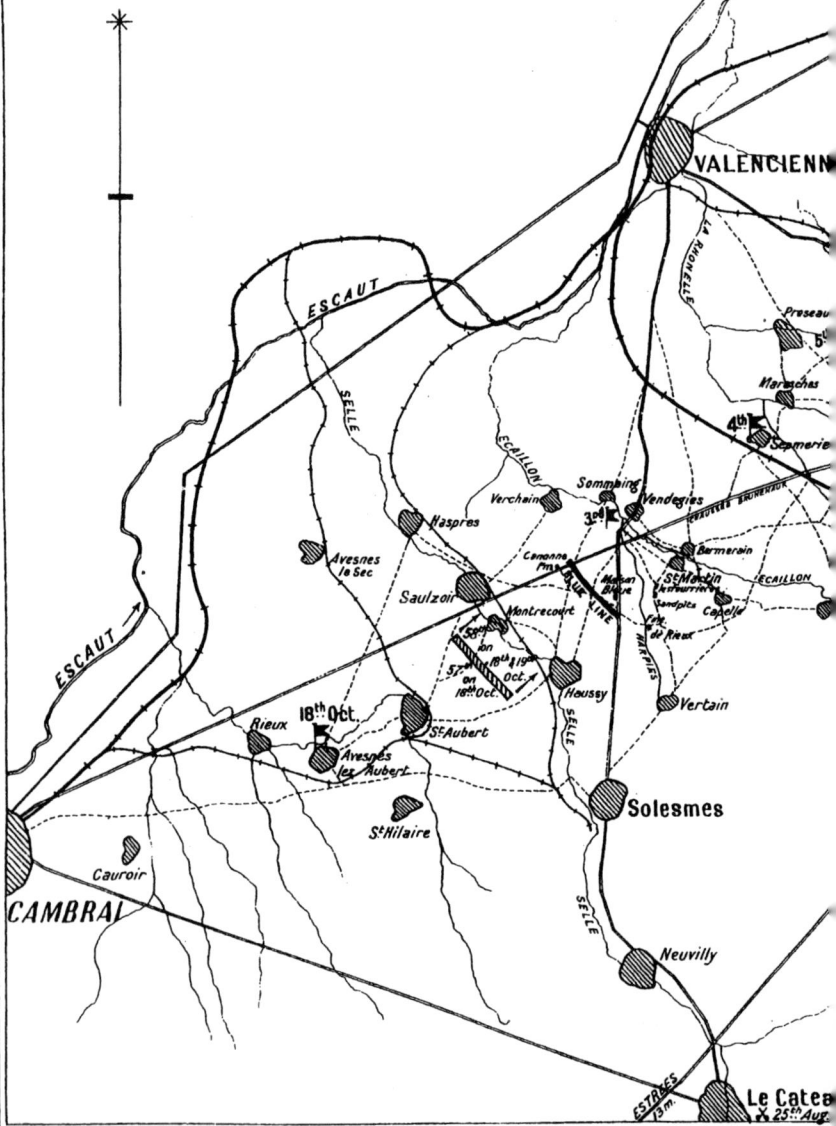

The Advance to Victory, 1918.

Operations of the 19th Division,

8th Oct. – 11th Nov.

Scale of miles.

Railways.... Single   Double

Divisional Headquarters..........

VALENCIENN

Preseau

Marsschas

4th

Sepmerie

Sommaing   Vendegies

Verchain   3rd

Haspres   Bermerain

Camonne St Martin

Avesnes le Sec   Maison Bleue   Capelle

ECAILLON

Saulzoir   Montrecourt

Spon 18th 19th on Oct.   Haussy   Vertain

18th Oct.   on 18th Oct.

Rieux   St Aubert

Avesnes les Aubert

Solesmes

St Hilaire

Cauroir   Neuvilly

CAMBRAI

ESTRES   Le Cateau
13m.   ✕ 25th Aug.

MONS — CONDÉ CANAL

MONS

Line at
Armistice
11-XI-18
about 4
miles East

Navay

HONNELLE

Bettignies

BROWN LINE

HILL
100·8

le Marlier

Eth

Bettrochies

Bellignies

Maison Blanche

Hon Hergies Taisnieres

Houdain

Malplaquet

FORET
DE
LANIERE

les Bas Vents

9th

Ancien
Pollet

Flamengrie

Bray

Colret

Ruines

Beaugies

St Waast

Bavai

Wargnies
le Gd

LINE

Wargnies
le Petit

GOMMEGNIES

MAUBEUGE

From
LANDRECIES

ROMAN ROAD

FOREST OF MORMAL

SAMBRE

Landrecies

CANAL

AVESNES

Foy

The fighting days of the 19th Division ended full of honour, and it is impossible to select one unit as having done more than another. The following letter from the Corps Commander (Lieut.-General Sir C. Fergusson), received by General Jeffreys on the 9th of November, pays tribute to the Division's fine qualities:

"I wish to express to you and the troops under your command my warmest congratulations on the success of the operations which have been completed to-day. An advance of nearly twenty miles, in spite of difficult country, continuous bad weather and the enemy's resistance, is a great week's work. It could only have been accomplished by the courage, tenacity and endurance displayed by all ranks, both in the firing line and behind it. This determination and soldierly spirit have overcome all obstacles and the record of the week is one of which all may be proud."

CONCLUSION

The 19th Division was not selected as part of the Army of Occupation in Germany, but on the 14th of November moved to the Rieux area, thence to Cambrai on the 25th, and later to the Candas-Canaples-Naours area. In December the demobilisation of all miners of the Division took place, and during January and February, 1919, the gradual demobilisation of the Division continued.

One incident during the last fighting days of the 19th Division had given extreme satisfaction to all ranks: the capture of Malplaquet where, in 1709, Marlborough had broken the power of France and had saved Europe from the domination of Louis XIV.

In his final despatch Sir Douglas Haig pays the following tribute to all troops under his command:

"In three months of epic fighting the British Armies in France have brought to a sudden and dramatic end the great wearing-out battle of the past four years. In our admiration for this outstanding achievement, the long years of patient and heroic struggles by which the strength and spirit of the enemy were gradually broken down, cannot be forgotten. The strain of those years was never-ceasing, the demand they made upon the best of the Empire's manhood are now known. Yet throughout all those years, and amid the hopes and disappointments they brought with them, the confidence of our troops in final victory never wavered. Their courage and resolution rose superior to every test, their cheerfulness never failing however terrible the conditions in which they lived and fought. By the long road they trod with so much faith and such devoted and self-sacrificing bravery we have arrived at victory."

In all these things the 19th Division took its full share.

SOME PERSONALITIES OF THE DIVISION

MAJOR-GENERAL (*now Lieut.-General Sir*) GEORGE D. JEFFREYS. General Jeffreys, both as a Brigade Commander and subsequently as Divisional Commander proved a veritable tower of strength to the Division. No man had a sterner sense of duty, and it was this outstanding characteristic which made him so deeply respected and esteemed. His passion and hero-worship was reserved, possibly, for his old regiment (the Grenadier Guards), which he has so greatly adorned. But perhaps in war days there was a tendency to under-rate his love for, and his pride in the 19th Division, which he commanded so successfully. Fearless in battle, but never unbending; an infinite capacity for taking pains; nothing was ever too much trouble if as a result the work thereby became more efficient. General Jeffreys was as fine a soldier as a professional army could hope to produce. Woe betide the slipshod man! woe betide the slovenly man! whether in habit, speech or thought. These received no mercy. In the dark days of March and April, 1918, he repeatedly rallied and reorganised the Division, so that it never failed to remain a fighting and organised unit. For his love of justice, his judgement, and sense of soldiership and orderliness, all ranks will ever remember his name with gratitude.

MAJOR-GENERAL (*now Lieut.-General Sir*) TOM B. BRIDGES was a Cavalryman, but before he joined the 4th Dragoon Guards he had previously served in the Royal Artillery. He was also a graduate of the Staff College, and had been Military Attaché in Brussels before the War. He had, therefore, an exceptionaly wide experience of soldiering in various forms, and he combined the dash of the cavalryman with a very sound and deep knowledge of his profession. Tall, dark, and good looking, his strong personality very soon impressed itself on the Division. He was intensely human and full of versatility and originality. Besides infusing his own spirit of enterprise into all ranks of the Division, he, in addition, was the means of bringing into the Division a number of very fine officers who, with him, were instrumental in making the Division the first-rate fighting organisation which it quickly became.

MAJOR-GENERAL C. G. FASKEN, C.B., the first Commander of the Division. After a distinguished career in the Indian Army he retired in 1914. On being re-called for service he was appointed to command the 19th Division, then in process of being raised. After surmounting many difficulties he took the Division to France in 1915 and commanded it during the Loos operations, and in the line during the early part of the winter of 1915, when he returned home.

BRIGADIER-GENERAL (*afterwards Major-General, and now Lieut.-General*) SIR T. A. CUBITT, C.B., C.M.G., D.S.O. A Staff College graduate, his regimental service was in the Royal Artillery. He combined in a remarkable degree knowledge and experience, and his strong personality quickly impressed itself on the 57th Infantry Brigade, which would have done anything for him. A fine leader and strong commander he was, withal, intensely human and always in sympathy with the feelings of those under him. His wealth and vigour of expression were only equalled by his kindness of heart and good fellowship, and his departure from the Division on promotion left a gap which was very difficult to fill.

BRIG.-GENERAL W. P. MONKHOUSE, C.B., C.M.G., C.R.A. of the Division 1916–1918, was a typical horse artilleryman, smart, dashing and a good horseman, yet none the less a sound and scientific gunner. He brought the artillery of the Division to a high level of efficiency and horse-mastership, and his invincible cheerfulness made him immensely popular with all arms and all ranks. He was one of the earliest amongst senior artillery officers to carry out reconnaissances from the air.

BRIG.-GENERAL A. E. GLASGOW, C.B., C.M.G., D.S.O. (commanding 58th Infantry Brigade, 1917–1919), was another most popular and capable Brigadier. Always imperturbable, nothing ever appeared to upset him, whilst his sound sense and genial personality gained for him the complete confidence of his Brigade.

BRIG.-GENERAL R. M. HEATH, C.M.G., D.S.O., commanded 10th Royal Warwicks 1916–1918, and 56th Infantry Brigade 1918–1919. A thoroughly sound and most popular officer, he made his Battalion one of the best in the Division, and made the 56th Infantry Brigade (recently re-formed of three previously unconnected battalions) into a happy and efficient unit.

He had served for a considerable period in the Egyptian
Army, and it was related of him that when advancing to the
attack with the Battalion he had a deck chair carried behind
him by an orderly, whilst a long cigar was seldom absent from
his mouth.

LIEUT.-COLONEL (*afterwards Brigadier-General*) P. WINSER,
C.M.G., D.S.O., 7th South Lancs. and 19th Battalion
Machine-Gun Corps. An able and determined battalion commander who, after long and good service in command of the
7th South Lancs., was selected to be the first commander
of the 19th Machine-Gun Battalion which, within a few weeks
of its formation, gave an excellent account of itself in the
desperate fighting of March–April 1918.

LIEUT.-COLONEL H. MONTGOMERY, D.S.O. (R.M.L.I.),
G.S.O.I., 1917–1919. A very capable Staff Officer, who was
always helpful both to his own and to subordinate commanders.
Though a deep thinker and full of ideas, he was none the less
eminently practical and his views were always sound and
sensible. A charming companion, he was as popular as he was
efficient and hard working.

LIEUT.-COLONEL G. HAWES, D.S.O. (*Royal Fusiliers*), A.A.
and Q.M.G., 1917–1919. A sound and tactful administrative
Staff Officer. Smart and débonnaire in appearance, he was
blessed with a sense of humour and an appreciation of the good
things of life. He did much to render the Division the happy
family that it always was.

LIEUT.-COLONEL P. E. HODGSON, D.S.O., C.R.E., 1917–
1919. A most capable and extraordinarily hard-working
C.R.E. No work was too hard nor too dangerous for him to
undertake, and he inspired his subordinates with his own
keenness and efficiency. Always imperturbable, nothing ever
appeared to rattle him, and he could be depended on for first-
rate work under any conditions. He had excellent field
company commanders, amongst whom MAJOR GODSELL, a
young and brilliant officer, was exceptionally notable.

The R.A. were fortunate in their Brigade Commanders,
amongst whom the most notable were: LIEUT.COLONEL
(*afterwards Brigadier-General*) E. J. R. PEEL, C.M.G.,
D.S.O., who succeeded Brig.-General Monkhouse as C.R.A.;

LIEUT.-COLONEL F. RAINSFORD HANNAY, D.S.O.; LIEUT.-COLONEL G. S. TOVEY, C.M.G., D.S.O.; and LIEUT.-COLONEL A. T. McGRATH, D.S.O., all first-rate gunners, whilst LIEUT.-COLONEL G. BRIDGES, C.M.G., D.S.O., and LIEUT.-COLONEL THE MARQUESS OF EXETER, C.M.G., were, in succession, efficient commanders of the D.A.C., in which, during the latter's command, the British drivers were replaced by natives of India.

LIEUT.-COLONEL G. W. SELBY, R.A., was a popular and excellent Brigade-Major, R.A.

LIEUT.-COLONEL LORD ALEXANDER THYNNE, D.S.O., M.P. (Royal Wilts. Yeomanry) commanded the 6th and 2nd Battalion Wiltshire Regt. He offered a splendid example of devotion to duty. Wounded in the Battles of the Somme, 1916, and again in the operations of March 1918, he each time returned to the Division as soon as he was well and refused to avail himself of the privilege that might have been his of staying at home as an M.P. Always a delightful companion, as well as a sound C.O., he was killed in command of the 2nd Wilts. within two months of the Armistice.

LIEUT.-COLONEL D. M. A. SOLE, D.S.O., commanding 10th Worcesters and 9th Royal Welch Fusiliers, was one of a number of Regular officers and ex-officers of the Worcestershire Regt. who joined the 10th Battalion of the Regiment on its formation in 1914. A stout-hearted and practical soldier and a determined commander, he brought the 10th Battalion to a high state of efficiency and infused into it the fine spirit of the Worcestershire Regt. On the 10th Battalion being absorbed into the 3rd Battalion, in June 1918, he took command of the 9th Battalion Royal Welch Fusiliers, and retained it till the Armistice.

Other officers of the Worcestershire Regt. who rendered splendid service in the 19th Division were: LIEUT.-COLONELS UMFREVILLE, D.S.O. (who commanded the 8th Gloucesters), W. A. BOWEN, D.S.O. (who commanded the 7th King's Own and 4th K.S.L.I.), and P. R. WHALLEY, D.S.O. (commanding 3rd Worcesters).

LIEUT.-COLONEL H. LL. JONES, D.S.O., was a cavalry officer of the best type who did excellent work in command successively of the 7th East Lancs. and 9th Welch, having in the latter case the advantage of being himself a Welshman.

Lieut.-Colonel H. W. Dakeyne, D.S.O., R. Warwick Regt., commanded the 8th North Staffs. from 1916-1919. Young, keen and active, he took over the Battalion as a mere remnant after the Ancre operations and made it into a thoroughly efficient unit.

Amongst the many other notable officers who served in the Division, the following may be mentioned:—
Brig.-Generals A. J. F. Eden, C.M.G., D.S.O., 57th Inf. Brigade, and F. G. Willan, C.M.G., D.S.O., 56th Inf. Brigade, both sound and capable Brigade Commanders.

Lieut.-Colonel (afterwards Brig.-General) R. A. Berners, D.S.O., R.W.F.; Lieut.-Colonel (afterwards Brig.-General) R. B. Worgan, D.S.O. (Indian Army), 9th Cheshires, both first-rate battalion commanders.

Lieut.-Colonel A. S. Fitzgerald, D.S.O., 10th R. Warwicks, a sound and steady C.O.

Lieut.-Colonel L. F. Smeathman, D.S.O. (Hertfordshire Regt.), who most efficiently commanded the 9th R. W. Fusiliers.

Major R. G. S. Cox, M.C., R. Inniskilling Fusiliers, who, after serving from its formation in command of 57th Company, Machine-Gun Corps, succeeded Lieut.-Colonel Winser in command of 19th Battalion M.G.C.

Lieut.-Colonel W. Parkes, D.S.O., M.C., who, after long service as Adjutant of the 8th Gloucesters, eventually took command of the Battalion.

Majors Lord Howard de Walden and H. Ll. Williams, D.S.O., M.C., both of the 9th R.W.F.

Lieut.-Colonel C. F. King, D.S.O., 9th Cheshires and 9th Welch, and Major J. G. Martin, M.C., 8th North Staffs, both of whom were civilians at the outbreak of war, and proved most gallant and efficient officers.

Majors Sewell, D.S.O. (Staff Capt. and Brigade Major, 56th Inf. Brigade), and Brindley, D.S.O., 10th R. Warwicks, both did long and good service with the Division, as did the following (amongst many other) officers promoted from the ranks:—

MAJOR J. J. TYNAN, D.S.O. (6th Wilts. and 9th R.W.F.), ex-R.S.M. of the Inniskilling Dragoons, whose sound military knowledge, combined with his gallantry, enterprise and ready wit, proved of the greatest value to the units with which he served.

MAJOR F. SNOOK, M.C. (8th North Staffs.) ex-C.S.M., Grenadier Guards, who did excellent work as Adjutant of his battalion and subsequently as Commandant of the Divisional School of Instruction, did yeoman service for the Division.

CAPT. RUDGE, M.C. (Adjutant 10th Worcesters and 9th R.W.F.), ex-Sergt. Grenadier Guards and ex-whipper-in of the Bicester Hounds who, besides being an excellent officer and instructor, considerably surprised some of his superior officers (who did not know his past history) by his riding, and "hunting noises," when hare hunting in the devastated area.

COLONEL HINGE, C.M.G., and COLONEL HARTIGAN, D.S.O., were two of the most notable of the various officers who held the appointment of A.D.M.S. of the 19th Division.

Among the officers brought into the Division by General Bridges were:—

LIEUT.-COLONEL (*afterwards Brig.-General*) W. LONG, Royal Scots Greys. Lieut.-Colonel Long, affectionately known almost throughout the army as "Toby Long," came to the infantry at a time when many of the best cavalry officers were doing the same. The oldest son of the well-known statesman, the Rt. Hon. Walter Long, his name was one to conjure with in Wiltshire, and no more appropriate appointment could have been made than that of Lieut.-Colonel Long to command the 6th Battalion of the Wiltshire Regt. His popularity was only equalled by his keenness and ability as a soldier, and he quickly made the 6th Battalion of his County Regiment into one of the most reliable and efficient units in the Division. "Toby Long" was always in good spirits, no matter how depressing the circumstances, and his infectious laugh is not likely to be forgotten by anybody who knew him. His untimely death when commanding the 56th Brigade was one of the greatest losses among its younger members which was sustained by the British Army during the War.

Another very distinguished officer introduced into the 19th
Division in the early months of 1916 by General Bridges was
his brother-officer in the 4th Dragoon Guards, LIEUT.-COLONEL
A. CARTON DE WIART. This officer had already lost a hand in
the second battle of Ypres and an eye when fighting in
Somaliland; but nothing, neither wounds nor hardships nor
dangers, deterred him from coming back to the fighting
line, not merely when he was fit, but usually before he was fit.
A description is given in this volume of his winning the V.C.
when in command of the 8th Gloucesters, but throughout the
War he constantly displayed the utmost bravery combined
with the most conspicuous ability. He had a quiet, soft voice,
and his manner was not in the least of the kind sometimes
associated with spectacular bravery. His one remaining eye
was as keen as a hawk's, and his opinion on any military
question was invariably sound. His influence over his Battalion was, as can be imagined, immense, and there is no
doubt that his men would have followed him anywhere. It was,
perhaps, characteristic of him that when wound stripes were
first introduced into the army, he did not at first wear them,
though he had at that time been wounded four or five times.
Some one asked him why he did not wear the wound stripe,
and his reply was: "Well, any damn fool can see that I have
been wounded."

LIEUT.-COLONEL C. V. TROWER.   One more officer should
be mentioned and that one is COLONEL C. V. TROWER.
Colonel Trower, when the war broke out, was already
nearly sixty years of age, and had completed his term
in command of a battalion of his regiment—the South Wales
Borderers. He, however, raised the 5th Pioneer Battalion
of the South Wales Borderers and commanded it until, in
September 1918, he had completed a further four years' term
in command of a battalion of his regiment. He was a sound and
experienced soldier, whose geniality was only equalled by his
ability and determination. He soon became recognised as the
"Father" of the Division, and was beloved, not only by all
ranks of his own battalion, but by all with whom he came in
contact throughout the 19th Division. In spite of his age, he
went through all the hardships of the winters in the line which
he shared with the younger men of his battalion, much of the
efficiency of which was due to his careful training.

19th DIVISION

Landed in France July 17th-20th, 1915.

G.O.C.

Major-General C. G. M. FASKEN, till 13/12/1915, replaced by
Major-General Tom B. BRIDGES, till 16/4/1917, replaced by
Major-General A. R. MONTAGU-STUART-WORTLEY, till
    24/5/1917, replaced by
Major-General C. D. SHUTE, till 19/6/1917, replaced by
Major-General G. T. M. BRIDGES, wounded 20/9/1917,
    replaced by
Major-General G. D. JEFFREYS.

B.G.R.A.

Brig.-General C. E. LAWRIE, till 26/12/1915, replaced by
Brig.-General R. FITZMAURICE, till 14/7/1916, replaced by
Brig.-General W. P. MONKHOUSE, till 12/9/1918, replaced by
Brig.-General E. J. R. PEEL.

B.G. 56TH BRIGADE

Brig.-General B. G. LEWIS, till 22/12/1915, replaced by
Brig.-General C. H. C. VAN-STRAUBENZEE, till 14/6/1916,
    replaced by
Brig.-General F. G. M. ROWLEY, till 20/11/1916, replaced by
Brig.-General W. LONG, killed 28/1/1917, replaced by
Brig.-General E. CRAIG-BROWN, till 5/9/1917, replaced by
Brig.-General F. G. WILLAN, till 10/4/1918, replaced by
Brig.-General R. M. HEATH.

B.G. 57TH BRIGADE

Brig.-General L. T. C. TWYFORD, till 16/6/1916, replaced by
Brig.-General C. C. ONSLOW, till 22/7/1916, replaced by
Brig.-General G. D. JEFFREYS, till 30/12/1916, replaced by
Brig.-General C. R. BALLARD, till 6/4/1917, replaced by
Brig.-General T. A. CUBITT, till 21/5/1918, replaced by
Brig.-General A. J. F. EDEN, wounded 10/8/1918, replaced
    temporarily by
Lieut.-Colonel WHALLEY, till 30/8/1918, return of Brig.-
    Gen. A. J. F. EDEN.

B.G. 58TH BRIGADE

Brig.-General G. T. BECKER, replaced by
Brig.-General D. M. STUART, till 19/1/1916, replaced by
Brig.-General G. D. JEFFREYS, wounded 14/4/1916, replaced
on 29/4/1916 by
Brig.-General A. J. W. DOWELL, till 10/1/1917, replaced by
Brig.-General A. E. GLASGOW.

R

DIVISIONAL TROOPS

CAVALRY
"C" Squadron, Yorkshire Dragoons, transferred to II Corps Cavalry, 9/5/1916.

CYCLISTS
19th Cyclist Company, to III Corps, 21/5/1916.

ROYAL ENGINEERS
81st, 82nd, and 94th Field Companies.

PIONEERS
5th Battalion South Wales Borderers.

MACHINE-GUN COMPANIES
56th Machine-Gun Company formed provisionally in October, 1915, till February 1916.
56th, 57th, 58th Companies, joined from United Kingdom, 14/2/1916.
246th Machine-Gun Company, joined from United Kingdom 19/7/1917.
19th Battalion Machine-Gun Corps formed 22/2/1918.

Note.—The 22nd Battalion Durham Light Infantry (Pioneers), arrived from United Kingdom 17/6/1916, and were attached till 2/7/1916; were then transferred to 8th Division.

ROYAL ARTILLERY

86TH BRIGADE, R.F.A.

"A," "B," "C" and "D" (each four 18-pounders).
Reorganised 25/5/1916, into three 4-gun 18-pounders, and one 4-gun 4·5 in. (Howitzer).
"D" (18-pounder) to 89th Brigade: "A" 89 (Howitzer) joined and designated "D"86.
Reorganised 9/9/1916 into three 6-gun 18-pounders and one 4-gun 4·5 in. (Howitzer). "C" broken up, half to "A," half to "B."
A new 4·5 in. (Howitzer) Battery joined from United Kingdom, 11/11/1916, and was designated "C," was broken up 28/1/1917, half to "D"87, half to "D"88.
Brigade was reorganised in February, 1917, into three 6-gun 18-pounders and one 6-gun 4·5 in. (Howitzer).
"B" 260 (6 18-pounders) joined from 51st Division, 11/2/1917, and was designated "C." One section (2 4·5 in. Howitzers) joined "D" from 61st Division, 11/2/1917.
Brigade became A.F.A. Brigade, February, 1917.

87TH BRIGADE, R.F.A.

"A," "B," "C," "D" (each four 18-pounders).
Reorganised 25/5/1916 into three 4-gun 18-pounders, and one 4-gun 4·5 in. (Howitzer). "D" (18-pounder) to 89th Brigade. "C"89 (Howitzer) joined and designated "D"87.
Reorganised 9/9/1916 into three 6-gun 18-pounders, and one 4-gun 4·5 in. (Howitzer), "B"89 complete, and half "A"89 joined and were posted, one section to each "A," "B" and "C."
"D" made up to 6 Howitzers, 28/1/1917, one section joining from "C"86.

88TH BRIGADE, R.F.A.

"A," "B," "C," "D" (each four 18-pounders).
Reorganised 25/5/1916 into three 4-gun 18-pounders and one 4-gun 4·5 in. (Howitzer). "D" to 89th Brigade; "D"89 (Howitzer) joined and designated "D"88.

Reorganised 9/9/1916 into three 6-gun 18-pounders and one 4-gun 4·5 in. (Howitzer). One section of "A" posted to "B." "C"89 (4 18-pounders) complete joined remaining section of "A" and was designated "A"88, one section of "A"89 joined "C."
"D" made up to 6 Howitzers 28/1/1917, one section joining from "C"86.

89TH BRIGADE, R.F.A. (HOWITZERS)

"A," "B," "C," "D" (each four 4·5 in. Howitzers).
"B" transferred to Second Army (31st Brigade, 28th Division) 7/8/1915.
Reorganised 25/5/1916, into three 4-gun 18-pounders.
"A" to 86th Brigade, "D"86 joined and designated "A"89.
"C" to 87th Brigade, "D"87 joined and designated "B"89.
"D" to 88th Brigade, "D"88 joined and designated "C."
Brigade ceased to exist as from 9/9/1916: Half of "A" to 87th Brigade, and half to 88th Brigade.
"B" complete to 87th Brigade.
"C" complete to 88th Brigade.

56TH INFANTRY BRIGADE

7TH KING'S OWN LANCASTERS	7TH EAST LANCASHIRES	7TH SOUTH LANCASHIRES	7TH LOYAL NORTH LANCASHIRES
Disbanded 22/2/1918 replaced by 9TH CHESHIRES	Disbanded 6/2/18 replaced by 4TH SHROPSHIRE LIGHT INFANTRY	Disbanded 14/2/1918 replaced by 8TH NORTH STAFFORDS	Disbanded 6/2/1918

4th King's. Attached 3/12/1915 to 18/12/1915, then to 58th Brigade.

57TH INFANTRY BRIGADE

10TH WORCESTERS	8TH NORTH STAFFORDS	10TH ROYAL WARWICKS	8TH GLOUCESTERS
Reduced to T.C. and transferred to 25th Division remainder absorbed and replaced by 3RD WORCESTERS	Transferred to 56th Brigade 4/2/1918		

58TH INFANTRY BRIGADE

9TH CHESHIRES	6TH WILTSHIRES	9TH ROYAL WELCH FUSILIERS	9TH WELCH REGIMENT
Transferred to 56th Brigade 4/2/1918	Redesignated on 20/9/1917 as 6TH WILTSHIRE YEOMANRY BN. Reduced to T.C. and transferred to 30th Division 13/5/1918, remainder absorbed and replaced by 2ND WILTSHIRES		

4th King's, joined 18/12/1915, transferred to 33rd Division, 25/2/1916.

AWARDS OF THE VICTORIA CROSS
TO THE 19TH DIVISION

CAPT. (*temp. Lieut.-Colonel*) ADRIAN CARTON DE WIART, D.S.O., Dragoon Guards (La Boisselle, France, July 2nd, 1916).

For most conspicuous bravery, coolness and determination during severe operations of a prolonged nature. It was owing, in a great measure, to his dauntless courage and inspiring example that a serious reverse was averted.

He displayed the utmost energy and courage in forcing our attack home. After three other battalion commanders had become casualties, he controlled their commands, and ensured that the ground won was maintained at all costs.

He frequently exposed himself in the organisation of positions and of supplies, passing unflinchingly through fire barrage of the most intense nature.

His gallantry was inspiring to all.

(*London Gazette* No. 29740, dated September 9th, 1916.)

No. 20572. PTE. THOMAS GEORGE TURRALL, 10th Worcs. Regt. (La Boisselle, France, July 3rd, 1916).

For most conspicuous bravery and devotion to duty. During a bombing attack by a small party against the enemy the officer in charge was badly wounded, and the party having penetrated the position to a great depth was compelled eventually to retire.

Private Turrall remained with the wounded officer for three hours, under continuous and very heavy fire from machine guns and bombs, and, notwithstanding that both himself and the officer were at one time completely cut off from our troops, he held to his ground with determination, and finally carried the officer into our lines after our counter-attacks had made this possible.

(*London Gazette* No. 29740, dated September 9th, 1916.)

Temp.-Lieut. Thomas Orde Lawder Wilkinson, 7th L. N. Lancs. Regt. (La Boisselle, France, July 5th, 1916).

For most conspicuous bravery. During an attack, when a party of another unit was retiring without their machine-gun, Lieutenant Wilkinson rushed forward and, with two of his men, got the gun into action, and held up the enemy till they were relieved.

Later, when the advance was checked during a bombing attack, he forced his way forward and found four or five men of different units stopped by a solid block of earth, over which the enemy was throwing bombs.

With great pluck and promptness he mounted a machine-gun on the top of the parapet and dispersed the enemy bombers. Subsequently he made two most gallant attempts to bring in a wounded man, but at the second attempt he was shot through the heart just before reaching the man.

Throughout the day he set a magnificent example of courage and self-sacrifice.

(*London Gazette*, dated September 26th, 1916.)

No. 12639, Pte. James Miller, late R. Lancs. Regt. (Bazentin-le-Petit, France, July 30th-31st, 1916).

For most conspicuous bravery. His battalion was consolidating a position after its capture by assault. Private Miller was ordered to take an important message under heavy shell and rifle fire and to bring back a reply at all costs.

He was compelled to cross the open, and on leaving the trench was shot almost immediately in the back, the bullet coming out through his abdomen. In spite of this, with heroic courage and self-sacrifice, he compressed with his hand the gaping wound in his abdomen, delivered his message, staggered back with the answer, and fell at the feet of the officer to whom he delivered it.

He gave his life with a supreme devotion to duty.

(*London Gazette* No. 29740, dated September 9th, 1916.)

SECOND-LIEUT. HUGH COLVIN, attd. 9th Cheshire Regt. (E. of Ypres, Belgium, September 20th, 1917).

For most conspicuous bravery in attack.

When all the officers of his company except himself—and all but one in the leading company—had become casualties and losses were heavy, he assumed command of both companies and led them forward under heavy machine-gun fire with great dash and success. He saw the battalion on his right held up by machine-gun fire, and led a platoon to their assistance.

Second-Lieut. Colvin then went on with only two men to a dug-out. Leaving the men on top, he entered it alone and brought up fourteen prisoners.

He then proceeded with his two men to another dug-out which had been holding up the attack by rifle and machine-gun fire and bombs. This he reached and, killing or making prisoners of the crew, captured the machine-gun. Being then attacked from another dug-out by fifteen of the enemy under an officer, one of his men was killed and the other wounded. Seizing a rifle he shot five of the enemy and, using another as a shield, he forced most of the survivors to surrender. This officer cleared several other dug-outs alone or with one man, taking about fifty prisoners in all.

Later he consolidated his position with great skill, and personally wired his front under heavy close range sniping in broad daylight, when all others had failed to do so.

The complete success of the attack in this part of the line was mainly due to Second-Lieut. Colvin's leadership and courage.

(*London Gazette*, No. 30372, dated November 8th, 1917.)

TEMP.-CAPT. MANLEY ANGELL JAMES, M.C., 8th (S.) Glouc. Regt. (Nr. Velu Wood, France, March 21st, 1918).

For most conspicuous bravery and devotion to duty in attack. Capt. James led his company forward with magnificent determination and courage, inflicting severe losses on the enemy and capturing twenty-seven prisoners and two machine-guns.

He was wounded, but refused to leave his company, and repulsed three hostile onslaughts the next day.

Two days later, although the enemy had broken through on his right flank, he refused to withdraw and made a most determined stand, inflicting very heavy losses on the enemy and gaining valuable time for the withdrawal of guns. He was ordered by the senior officer on the spot to hold on "to the last" in order to enable the brigade to be extricated. He then led his company forward in a local counter-attack on his own initiative, and was again wounded. He was last seen working a machine-gun single-handed, after having been wounded a third time.

No praise can be too high for the gallant stand made by this company, and Capt. James, by his dauntless courage and magnificent example, undoubtedly enabled the battalion to be withdrawn before being completely cut off.

(*London Gazette* No. 30770, dated June 28th, 1918.)

LIEUT. (*Temp.-Capt.*) JULIAN ROYDS GRIBBLE, 10th (S.) R. Warwick Regt. (Beaumetz, Hermies Ridge, France, March 23rd, 1918).

For most conspicuous bravery and devotion to duty. Capt. Gribble was in command of the right company of the battalion when the enemy attacked, and his orders were to "hold on to the last." His company was eventually entirely isolated, though he could easily have withdrawn them at one period when the rest of the battalion on his left were driven back to a secondary position. His right flank was "in the air" owing to the withdrawal of all troops of a neighbouring division. By means of a runner to the company on his left rear he intimated his determination to hold on until other orders were received from battalion headquarters—and this he inspired his command to accomplish. His company was eventually surrounded by the enemy at close range, and he was seen fighting to the last. His subsequent fate is unknown.

By his splendid example of grit Capt. Gribble was materially instrumental in preventing for some hours the enemy obtaining a complete mastery of the crest of the ridge, and by his magnificent self-sacrifice he enabled the remainder of his own brigade to be withdrawn, as well as another garrison and three batteries of field artillery.

(*London Gazette* No. 30770, dated June 28th, 1918.)

LIEUT. (*Act.-Capt.*) ERIC STUART DOUGALL, M.C., attd. "A" Battery, 88th Brigade, R.F.A. (Messines, Belgium, April 10th, 1918).

For most conspicuous bravery and skilful leadership in the field when in command of his battery.

Captain Dougall maintained his guns in action from early morning throughout a heavy concentration of gas and high-explosive shell. Finding that he could not clear the crest owing to the withdrawal of our line, Captain Dougall ran his guns to the top of the ridge to fire over open sights. By this time our infantry had been pressed back in line with the guns. Captain Dougall at once assumed command of the situation, rallied and organised the infantry, supplied them with Lewis-guns, and armed as many gunners as he could spare with rifles. With these he formed a line in front of his battery which, during this period, was harassing the advancing enemy with a rapid rate of fire. Although exposed to both rifle and machine-gun fire, this officer fearlessly walked about as though on parade, calmly giving orders and encouraging everybody. He inspired the infantry with his assurance that "So long as you stick to your trenches I will keep my guns here." This line was maintained throughout the day, thereby delaying the enemy's advance for over twelve hours. In the evening, having expended all ammunition, the battery received orders to withdraw. This was done by man-handling the guns over a distance of about 800 yards of shell-cratered country, an almost impossible feat considering the ground and the intense machine-gun fire.

Owing to Captain Dougall's personality and skilful leadership throughout this trying day there is no doubt that a serious breach in our line was averted.

This gallant officer was killed four days later whilst directing the fire of his battery.

(*London Gazette* No. 30726, dated June 4th, 1918.)

INDEX

Lightning Source UK Ltd.
Milton Keynes UK
UKOW05f1923120114

224431UK00001B/33/A

9 781843 422082